Lands Never Trodden

The Franciscans and the California Missions

LANDS NEVER TRODDEN

The Franciscans and the California Missions

John J. O'Hagan

CAXTON PRESS
Caldwell, Idaho
2013

ISBN 978-087004-563-9

Library of Congress Cataloging-in-Publication Data

O'Hagan, John J.
  Lands never trodden : the Franciscans and the California missions / John J. O'Hagan.
      pages cm
  ISBN 978-0-87004-563-9
  1. Missions, Spanish--California--History. 2. Franciscans--Missions--California--History. 3. California--History--To 1846. 4. Indians of North America--Missions--California--History. 5. Spanish mission buildings--California--History. I. Title.

  F864.O36 2013
  979.4'01--dc23

                        2012051630

Lithographed and bound in the United States of America

CAXTON PRESS
Caldwell, Idaho
184121

TABLE OF CONTENTS

Mosqueda Portrait: Junipero Serra.
Reprinted with the permission of the Santa Barbara Mission Archive Library.

Acknowledgements

This book is dedicated to Rick Chivaroli. Your thoughtfulness and generosity were the genesis of this work. With our Thanks—John and Letitia

"Not that it is worth anybody's attention, but it may help to a knowledge of these lands that had never before been trodden by a Christian foot."— *from a letter written by Junipero Serra, July 3, 1769, as he began founding the California missions.*

Chapter 1

INTRODUCTION

In 1769, a year before some nervous British soldiers fired on an unruly crowd on the edge of Boston Harbor, at the extreme other end of the American continent on the edge of San Diego Harbor, a group of Franciscan missionaries laid the beginnings of Mission San Diego de Alcala. Before the United States would declare its independence from Great Britain in 1776, five more such missions had been founded. When the Treaty of Paris formally concluded the Revolutionary War, and recognized the United States of America as a new world power, the number of missions on the still virtually unknown west coast of the continent had grown to nine. The missions continued to grow until in 1823, forty years before the beginning of our Civil War, they comprised a chain of twenty-one thriving enterprises, covering 600 miles from San Diego to Sonoma.

The missions as an institution didn't last a hundred years, but the missions as monuments to faith, dedication, and perseverance are with us today. Virtually all of the missions—or some part of each of them—continue in existence today, more than two hundred years later. A thoughtful examination of these complexes, their history, and particularly of the lives invested in them can provide us with significant insight into a way of life that brought to our soil a religious zeal and dedication of singular purpose seen nowhere else in the United States. Further, in studying these institutions we will gain significant insight into some highly important events, largely ignored in the standard histories.

In Europe in the eighteenth-century, nameless serfs were perfecting towering churches, at the urging and with the financing of kings, cardinals and city-states. In that same century, in what was then Spain's Alta California, nameless serfs were constructing towering churches, urged only by driven priests and using whatever material could be sweated from the land around them. Bernard Duhaut-Cilly, who was traveling along the California coast on a trading expedition in 1827, made a particularly astute observation about Mission Santa Barbara that could apply to all the missions. Duhaut-Cilly commented at length on the difficulties faced by Father Ripoll in building Santa Barbara, noting that the natives, previously unschooled in any sort of building techniques and taught by equally-unschooled priests, had erected what he unhesitatingly referred to as "edifices." It was not just the finished buildings that drew his admiration. He commented on the difficulty of first wresting the raw materials from the land, then transporting them over prodigious distances, only then commencing to build. Unlike in Europe, there was no system to arrange for supplies and craftsmen to complete the project. First the timber had to be felled, the stone quarried, and both transported over roads that likely had not existed but had been built for the sole purpose of bringing the material to the site. Consciously or not, the process of building the missions had to be something along the line of, *We are to build a mission. First we must find material, next we must get the material to the site, next we must build roads from there to here, next we must train the natives, next we must begin building and always we must constantly supervise and oversee.* Despite this excruciating process, as Duhaut-Cilly noted ". . . [Father Ripoll] took little more time to complete the building than would have been needed in Spain."

Duhaut-Cilly was describing Mission Santa Barbara and the work done by Padre Antonio Ripoll. All of his points, in describing the difficulties and challenges in building that mission, would be equally valid with regard to every one of the missions. In fact, the argument can be made that Father Ripoll, in completing the building Duhaut-Cilly so much admired, had a relatively easy task. Ripoll was actually working on the fourth church at Santa Barbara almost forty years after work began on the first church. And Father Ripoll had a much more structured support system in place than had Fathers Antonio Paterna and Cristobal Oramas, who founded Santa Barbara in 1786.

The work so admired by Duhaut-Cilly almost two hundred years ago still survives, marking a culture older than our history as a country. History is written by the victors and the California missions have had not just one but two victors to muddy the record. Neither the Mexican government after independence from Spain, nor the American government after the Mexican-American War, had any interest in enhancing the status nor recognizing the accomplishments of the culture they had just displaced.

Because that culture ended up being the "losing" culture in our history, and because it is located on the extreme edge of our westward expansion, it has never garnered the attention of popular historians, and has only minimally been considered by serious historians. *A Religious History of the American People*, written in 1974, devotes only two pages of more than eleven hundred to the California missions, while it gives an entire chapter to "Roman Catholicism in the American Colonies." Even the four-volume *History of the Catholic Church in the United States*, while it does have a chapter entitled "The Catholic Church in the Spanish Colonies," turns out to be discussing Florida, Carolina and Virginia, where ironically there is hardly any trace of those endeavors. It completely ignores California.

Every fourth grade student in California completes a study of the California missions, but throughout the rest of the country, they are virtually unknown. They remain unknown until, often by happenstance, on a visit to one of the Golden State's more famous attractions, a starkly beautiful whitewashed building appears in a valley or even more incongruously on a major city street. Then there might be a quick visit, a tour and a brief history. The story of each of these buildings and the story of the entire endeavor is so much more than can be learned in a quick tour of an empty, silent church.

The Franciscan friars who founded the California missions were a unique blend of faith, fanaticism, devotion to duty, and unremitting labor. They gave up life as privileged persons, resident in a great world power, in order to labor in grueling toil in the New World. Junipero Serra himself had been offered a professorship even before completing his seminary studies. He rejected that position of security and prestige to argue, at first unsuccessfully, for a chance to become a missionary. He persisted until he was allowed to go to New Spain—what is now Mexico. One of Serra's confreres, Father Antonio Jayme, had been appointed to a professorship in philosophy as a young man of barely twenty-five. He left that post for the California missions five years later, and was martyred in San Diego five years after that.

3

For a period of time it was fashionable to cast the Franciscans as fanatics, who embarked on a systematic program of genocide and the deliberate elimination of the Indian culture. Recent scholarship has begun to move away from that posture. There is no denying that as a result of introduced diseases and enforced control of the living conditions of the Indians, the mortality of the Native Americans skyrocketed after the establishment of the mission system. Inadvertent exposure to disease cannot by any fair standard be considered a genocidal act. Thirty years after the founding of Mission San Diego the Royal Society of Medicine refused to publish Edward Jenner's paper on smallpox. Almost another one hundred years would pass before Pasteur's paper on germ theory would be published. Acquired immunity was something the Spaniards had, without knowing they had it. Undoubtedly every one of them had survived measles as a child and most of them had probably been exposed to smallpox. They had no idea they were carrying to "neophytes" and "gentile"* alike diseases that would devastate them. It is true that virtually all of what are sometimes referred to as the "crowd diseases" (measles, mumps, chicken pox, influenza, etc.) were bought to the Americas and to the unfortunate natives by the conquering Spaniards. The charge of genocide, however, is one completely unsupported by any medical or historical evidence. It stretches the imagination to attempt to charge the Franciscans or indeed any of the Spaniards with anything other than ignorance. In truth, every facet of the Spanish plan for conquest—and in particular the mission model—depended heavily on the work and labor of the native peoples. Two Franciscans per mission certainly could have no hope of building a mission if in the process they killed off all of the native workers. As well, the Franciscan's major task was to bring souls to God, a task that patently could not be accomplished if the owners of those souls perished before being instructed and baptized in the new faith. The Spanish, unlike other conquerors of the New World, never sought the elimination of the native peoples as part of the plan of conquest. The Spanish plan of *"reduccióne"* specifically contemplated that the conquered people become subjects of the realm and that they, rather than imported colonists, would secure the territory for the king, pay taxes to support him and become loyal subjects.

---

* The Franciscans referred to recently converted natives as neophytes. Those who had not accepted Catholicism were called gentiles.

Each mission has its stories of sacrifice, suffering, defeat and triumph. There are also stories of romance, mystery, political intrigue, violence and death. Those stories will be visited in some detail in these pages. The primary emphasis of this book is on the people who faced and met the daunting challenges of creating civilization from an untamed land. The story is an amazing one of commitment, sacrifice, bravery and cruelty. It is a story of not just an idealistic group of missionaries, but of courageous men and women of all stripes: Spaniards, Mexicans, Native Americans, Russians, Yankees, and many who probably were never sure just how they would describe themselves.

There are certainly documented cases of the Franciscans imposing harsh standards on the natives under their control, and even harsher punishments when those standards were not met. Those punishments, as distasteful as we may find them today, were largely in accord with the then-existing views and moral standards. "Largely," though, is a very important word in this context. More than once in the chapters that follow, we will come across incidents that can only be characterized as cruelty. Of the 146 Franciscans who served in the California missions, most were men of dedication, understanding and love. Clearly, though, there were some who never should have been honored with ordination and who certainly never should have been trusted to serve in extreme circumstances without effective oversight. An excellent, or perhaps not-so-excellent, example of the standard of the day can be found in this description of a schoolroom at the *presidio* in Monterey. The following describes punishment meted out to the children of the officers of the *presidio*, and being administered by a soldier serving as a classroom teacher:

> At a certain hour the copies were examined and the ferule was in constant motion at that hour. "Here is a blot you young rascal." "Pardon master, I will do better tomorrow." "Hold out your hand." Thus ran the usual preliminary conversation. A more terrible implement of torture than the ferule, however, lay on the master's table: a hempen scourge of many iron-pointed lashes held in reserve for serious offences, such as laughing out loud, running in the street, playing truant, spilling ink or, worst of all, failing to know the Christian doctrine. The guilty child was

stripped of his shirt, often his only garment, and stretched on a bench with a handkerchief stuffed in his mouth, to receive the dread infliction."[1]

An interesting incident occurred in 1826 when mountain man Jedediah Smith was visiting Mission San Gabriel. One of the events Mr. Smith noted during his stay was that he had had to give one of his men "a little flogging" because of "impertinence." This incident reminds us of the fact that well into the nineteenth century employers had no compunctions about flogging employees who they felt were "impertinent." In fact, it wasn't until 1874 that corporal punishment was banned in the United States military. Corporal punishment is still legal in public schools in twenty states.

In the minds of the Franciscans, and more importantly in the Spanish law, Indians in the mission system were considered to be the children of the missionaries. The Franciscans were seen as serving *in loco parentis* for the Indians under their care. The missionaries were convinced that they were absolutely responsible for the salvation of their neophytes, and a failure of one of those neophytes was a failure on the part of the missionary. In addition to the instances of corporal punishment being used on the natives, there are documented cases of the Franciscans intervening aggressively, on behalf of those same natives. Finally, during the entire mission era and in fact for thirty years after it ended, slavery was a perfectly acceptable institution in all of the United States.

The Spanish policy of reducing the natives to workers in the mission system, whatever its negative consequences, had one overlooked, but very positive and unique outcome in the history of the conquest of North America. It is the only instance in that long, sad history when the conquerors consciously worked to train the natives in skills important to the new way of life. The Spanish plan in the mission system called for the establishment of large building complexes. The Spanish plan also called for only two missionaries at each mission. Obviously those two priests could not hope to construct such buildings by themselves. Use of a native workforce was the only way they could accomplish their objectives. Junipero Serra very early recognized the contributions that the natives, once properly trained, could make to the Spanish empire. In his very detailed report prepared when he returned to Mexico City in 1773, Serra asks that carpenters and blacksmiths be sent to the missions so that "we would be able to have some of the newly converted youths learn the trade."[2] The governor agreed, the skilled labor was sent, and thus began the transformation of at least some of the natives from laborers to artisans. Many of the California missions are still graced with the work of native Californians from the eighteenth-century.

There is no other instance in the history of North America where displaced natives were taught any skills by their conquerors, let alone any of the fine arts. The most common pattern was that they would be exterminated, or shuttled off to reservations. The indigenous people of North America were hardly seen as human by most of their conquerors. Junipero Serra, on the other hand, made a point of objecting to the term "*gente de razon*" (people of reason) for the non-Indians, in his words "just as if the Indians did not have the use of reason too." [3]

It is this, the transmission to a Stone Age culture of eighteenth-century skills that is one of the most overlooked and one of the most enduring accomplishments of the Franciscans of the California mission system. The difficulties for both sides, the Franciscans as directors, the Indians as workers, must have been overwhelming. The Franciscans had to teach a people with no written language to read plans in a language not their own; and to transform an abstract concept from paper to reality. The natives had to master the concept of scale and perspective. Not to be forgotten is the fact that at each location, at least initially, neither of the parties spoke the language of the other. Despite such difficulties they succeeded quite well.

The Franciscans worked tirelessly to bring what they sincerely believed to be the benefits of Christianity to what was, in their view, a doomed society. There was very much an "end times" mindset to Junipero Serra's essentially medieval education. Serra, in a letter to Father Juan Andre at the college of San Fernando, refers to the hope that "in these last centuries, the gentiles will be converted."[4] This belief, that time was running out to save the heathen, gave Serra and his contemporaries not only justification for their activities; it imparted a particular urgency to their activities. "Driven" is a word often used to describe Junipero Serra, considering with what he saw as the impending end of the world, driven he undoubtedly was. There is no disagreement that by today's standards, their methods and the results would not be acceptable. They certainly were operating from a per-spective of cultural superiority, but it was the only perspective avail-able in the eighteenth-century. The Franciscans brought temperance and an attempt at justice to a violent land in a violent era. Absent the Franciscans, the Spanish conquest of California and its people could have mirrored the far more bloody conquests of Peru and Mexico which had taken place 150 years earlier.

History is not well served by interpreting past acts by contempo-rary standards. Junipero Serra and his missions were the agents of what has been called "the inevitability of history." Cultures wax and wane and come into conflict with each other, and always there is a winner and a loser. There is clear anthropological evidence that the Kumeyaay-Shoshone (Diegueno) people who greeted the Spaniards in 1769 were relatively late arrivals to the area, who had themselves dis-placed the Hokans only a thousand years earlier. The Spanish-Indian experience was a huge clash of cultures, and in that clash, the Indians lost. They lost their freedom, their land, and their culture. The objec-tive of this book is not to examine in great detail that clash. Where particular clashes impact on the overall story—the founding of the missions—they will be treated openly and honestly.

Consider the accomplishments of the missionaries in these terms. In the sixty-five years of the California mission experience, 146 Fran-ciscan priests served in the California missions.* From the founding of the first mission up to the last, there were never more than twenty or thirty priests in California at any one time, and never more than two or three at any one mission. Somehow this dedicated band built and maintained twenty-one missions covering more than six hundred miles of wild, essentially untamed territory. Most of these priests had left Spain as young men and died years later, still serving in California. At least two were martyred; two others were likely murdered; and the majority died in what can only be described as grim and dire circum-stances. In that same period of time, the entire Spanish military and indeed the entire Spanish bureaucracy managed to construct only four presidios: at San Diego, Monterey, Santa Barbara, and San Francisco.

---

*   Although the Franciscan order, then as now, consisted of both priests *and* brothers, all who served in these missions were priests. Confusion arises because they often referred to them selves as "fray" or "brother," but in this they were referring to themselves as brothers in the order.

When secularization came and the decline of the missions began, " . . . the Indians at the twenty-one missions herded 396,000 cattle, 62,000 horses and 321,000 hogs, sheep and goats, and harvested 123,000 bushels of grain. Sixty-five years before, there had not been a single cow, horse, hog, sheep, goat or grain of wheat in the entire province of Alta California."[5] It was those vast agricultural and ranching concerns that made California so important, first to the Spanish Crown, then to the Mexican Republic, and finally to the ever-expanding American empire. In the expansion of the United States west from the Mississippi, California is the only case of acquiring an already-settled land. When the United States took possession of California in 1846, it took possession of established cities, a system of roads, military posts, agricultural, livestock and industrial complexes. The United States has the Franciscans and the California mission system to thank for that.

Endnotes

1   Bancroft, Hubert Howe. *History of California Vol. II, 1801-1824*. San Francisco:The History Company Publishers, 1886.

2   Tibesar, Antonine. O.F. M. *Writings of Junipero Serra, Vol. I*. Washington, D.C. Academy of American Franciscan History, 1955.

3   Ibid, *Vol. IV*. p. 169.

4   Ibid, *Vol. I* p.137.

5   Krell, Dorothy, ed. *The California Missions: A Complete Pictorial History and Visitor's Guide*. Menlo Park: Sunset Books, 1979.

Chapter 2

WHY THE MISSIONS

C ontrary to popular belief, the missions, that today extend in an orderly line along California's Highway 101 and Highway 1, were not built "a day's journey apart for travelers." There were no travelers along these routes in the eighteenth-century, and very few in the nineteenth. Junipero Serra himself, in discussing plans for missions in the future, refers to the fact that a principal aim was for the missionaries who come to serve in California to be able to travel "by land and they would sleep at least every third day in a mission."[1] He suggests "a chain of missions twenty-five leagues distant one from the other."[2] A Spanish league in the eighteenth-century was approximately 2.6 miles. Thus Serra was proposing missions sixty-five miles apart: not a day's walk for anyone, and only accomplished on horseback by the most experienced equestrian, riding very hard under ideal conditions. Original plans for many of the missions are still in existence, and in very few of them are found guest quarters, nor do they include any sort of dedicated accommodations for travelers. The missions were large and spacious complexes, and there is no doubt that many travelers, and in fact many well-known travelers, stayed at them. Hospitality and a Christian welcome to strangers are essential tenets of the Franciscan creed. Their plans, though, were never to be a chain of hostels along the California coast. As late as 1830, at the very height of the mission project, Juan Bandini, a customs official with the Mexican government, was asked to prepare a report suggesting some uses for the mission property when the planned secularization came to fruition. His description of a typical mission property is illuminating. Bandini describes dwellings for the priests, dwelling for the neophytes, storerooms, granaries, shops and manufacturing areas, even corrals and patios. Nowhere does he talk about guest quarters or hostels.

Nor were the missions built in a chronological line from south to north. If one wanted to visit the missions in the order they were built, one would have to start at San Diego, travel north over 400 miles to Monterey, then south again eighty miles to Jolon, further south 250 miles to San Gabriel, north once again to San Luis Obispo, further north to San Francisco, then south again to San Juan Capistrano, north once more to Santa Clara, and so on in a meandering trek through all of California's coastal valleys; a daunting journey even in the twenty-first century, but amazingly, one accomplished over and over again in the eighteenth. The missions were a key element in the plans of political and military authorities who saw them as strategic outposts at key harbors and passes. While they were built and staffed by men of God, they were planned and sited by military men and bureaucracrats.

The military and political objective of the missions was to solidify Spain's claim to Alta California. Russian efforts to migrate and colonize from the north downward and the increasing frequency of British ships along the Pacific coast brought a certain urgency to the rulers in Madrid and Mexico City. They had largely ignored the northern reaches of their New World empire for two hundred years and decided they could no longer do so.

Had the Spanish not responded aggressively to the Russian encroachment, by implementing the missions project, the history of California and of the United States may have taken an altogether different course. Had the Russians and not the Spanish colonized California—had Monterey been a port staffed by an ascending imperialist Russia rather than a fledgling Mexican republic—Commander Sloat would not have had such an easy task proclaiming in 1846 that "henceforth California will be a portion of the United States." Further, it is unlikely that forty years later Russia would have been so keen to divest itself of Alaska, if she and not Spain had established a chain of twenty-one outposts in California.

The mission outposts were not just churches, but agricultural and industrial complexes. It was in large measure because of the development of the cattle and grain industries, which had their conception and birth with the missions, that Alta California became important first to Spain and then Mexico, and then to the United States. From the outset and up until the dismantling of the missions, the missionaries found themselves in a delicate balancing act between church and state. There was virtually no separation between those two institutions in eighteenth-century Spain. The Franciscans in California may have considered themselves as servants of God but they were also agents of the king. In the history of the missions, we will find frequent instances of Franciscans interfering in affairs of state, and politicians interfering in matters of the church. Most startling of all is the number of times the efforts of each were successful.

The objective of the missionaries was the salvation of the souls of the native populations. The natives, of course, were not consulted on this, but in the minds of the Franciscans, it was an imperative moral duty to convert these unfortunates. They truly believed that they were charged with a moral obligation to bring their "ignorant" brethren in the New World to Christ. The theology of the day held that all unbaptized persons were damned to an eternity of suffering in hell. In order to save the native peoples from this horrible fate, the Franciscans were willing to endure deprivation, danger and great personal suffering. Fame, wealth or security were nowhere in their plans, and whatever criticism might now be brought to a study of their endeavors, greed or personal enrichment has never been suggested. All of these men avidly sought the rigors of the ends of the earth and a future of hardship, poverty and suffering for what they truly believed was the greater glory of God. California in 1769 was indeed the ends of the earth. The men who chose to serve there were from a privileged class in one of the world's great powers. They were all volunteers and without exception they were highly educated and cultivated men. One of the worst things they faced in their new assignments was loneliness. Ideally there were two priests assigned to each mission so they at least had a companion of like education and background to discuss matters with. Circumstances did not always allow such staffing, and when in 1782 it was proposed that the missions could operate with just one missionary Father Fermin de Lasuen recoiled in horror:

> Loneliness in this work is for me a savage and cruel enemy which has afflicted me greatly. I fled from it, thanks be to God, in face of evident risk of dying at its hands, and now as I see it raise its ugly head, even from afar,

I tremble at the inconceivable danger in returning to the battle. May this latter serve as an excuse because it means so much to me. I am not unaware that the missions close to the presidios, like the one in my charge, are cared for in a very different manner. But the supply of missionaries in proportion to the missions is so restricted, and the replacement of those who die or fall sick is so tardy, impeded and difficult that the misfortune which I fear worse than death could easily become my lot.[3]

Lasuen went on to make it clear in no uncertain terms that he would ask for a return to the College of San Fernando if such a proposal was ever enacted.

Unfortunately, given the dual role the Franciscans tried to fill, there was almost immediate and constant conflict between their duties. God's greater glory was generally not at all the objective of the government these priests represented. Visitor General Jose de Galvez, who had arrived in Baja California in 1768, was the man charged with the overall responsibility for settling Alta California. He had specific, if impractical, ideas for doing this.

Until the Jesuits ran afoul of the Spanish crown in 1767, they and not the Franciscans had handled mission affairs in the New World. Galvez did not like what he viewed as the Jesuits' benign approach to Christianizing Baja California. In his view, the natives attached to Jesuit missions in Baja California were allowed to wander about at will, pretty much living life as they had, and they were not likely to become productive members of Spanish society any time soon.

Thus, when the Franciscans were tasked with establishing a new set of missions in Alta California, Galvez gave them specific rules and objectives, ones he felt would ensure that the errors of the Jesuits would not be repeated. Galvez decreed that the Indians were to wear clothes, to be given land to work in agriculture, and to feed themselves from what they produced. Perhaps his most destructive order, and the one which to this day comes under most criticism in a discussion of the California mission system, was that all of the natives within a mission's domain would be made to live in permanent residence on mission property.

In this last, Galvez was just reinforcing what had long been the official Spanish policy. The Spanish government, in its earlier conquest of the Philippines and Central America, employed a policy known as *reducción*. Simply put, this was a policy that stated that all inhabitants of a conquered land would be "reduced" to living in the towns and missions the Spanish constructed. All had to live within the sound of the church bells, so that they might be summoned to work, prayer, meals, and all of the daily activities. *Reducción* by force, though, was not seen as an acceptable method. In fact, it was specifically forbidden by Spanish law: "No governor, lieutenant or *alcade ordinario* can or may send armed parties against the Indians with the purpose of reducing them into the missions . . . (T)he penalty for violation of this law is loss of office and payment of two thousand pesos."[4]

This regulation, and two thousand pesos was a very significant amount in 1769, goes a long way toward addressing the accusation that the native Californians were forcibly transported to mission settlements. There is no historical evidence that any of the California natives were ever rounded up and herded in to the missions as a means to establish the missions. There is no dearth of evidence that many times, natives who had joined the missions later recanted, tried to leave and were aggressively pursued and returned to the missions against their will. The Spanish approach to establishing the mission system in California in 1769 was not much different than the approach of our own volunteer military today to filling its ranks. That is, you do not have to join the army, but if you decide to join the army, you are not thereafter free to wander about at your own volition. The commitment of the natives to the mission system, whether they knew it or not—and likely it was not made terribly clear to them—was for life.

Initially the Franciscans swayed the natives to align themselves with the missions with promises of a better life. The Franciscans were undoubtedly very convincing salesmen, and the natives were unfortunately not very sophisticated buyers. It is likely that the blandishments the newcomers offered were attractive to the natives: food, clothing, shelter, protection. Probably little was said about the unremitting labor which would be required and certainly no emphasis was given to the fact that this was a lifetime commitment. There was no going back. Once that pattern became clear to the native Californians, circumstances in the Spanish territory had changed to the extent that in many cases there was no real choice left. As Spanish control over California spread, and as the mission works and herds caused increasing changes to the environment, the natives, as matter of survival, had little choice but to relocate to mission property. Mission herds and mission agricultural development destroyed the natural topography which had been the mainstay of their lives for generations. It was effectively a matter of aligning one's self with a mission, or die of starvation. Alignment that comes about in reluctant and negative circumstances is not likely to be a permanent and committed alignment. Repeatedly in the history of the missions, issues were brought to a violent head by the attempts of the Indians to return to their old lifestyle, and the efforts of the Franciscans and the soldiers to recall them. The Franciscans frequently found their work of years undone with one brutal punitive expedition, often initiated by themselves, to return the natives to their life as converts and mission-dwellers.

The intent of founding the missions depended on the perspective of the person being asked. To the Spanish bureaucracy, the intent was to solidify claims to lands and revenues for the crown. To the Spanish military, the intent was to provide a system of support for far-flung troops, and to pacify indigenous people. To the Franciscans, the intent was for the greater glory and honor of God, and to bring souls to heaven. These conflicting views permeate the history of the missions and they all ultimately played one against the other on the question of secularization.

Secularization—the process of transferring something from religious or ecclesiastical use to lay or civil use or ownership—is a very important term in the history of the California missions. Other than their founding, there is no event as significant as secularization. No story of the missions is complete without a discussion of this process, a process that ended the history of the missions as an institution and very nearly ended the history of the missions for all time. As has been mentioned, the missions were just one leg of the three-legged stool that was the Spanish model for colonization. The "*presidio*/priests/ *pueblo*" concept envisioned that each would replace its predecessor. That is, once the military had conquered a land and pacified it, the priests would establish a church and convert the natives, and once the natives had been converted to Catholicism and the Spanish way of life, the mission complex would give way to a town, governed by appointed and selected laymen. The model of secularization as decreed by the Spanish *cortes** meant that the mission and its holdings would be removed from the authority of the "ordered" priests who had founded it, in the case of California always the Franciscans, and put under the control of a local bishop.† In fact, the decree specifically contemplated that the friars would be appointed as curates of their former missions. So these missions were never intended to be part of the Franciscan domain forever. According to the original plan, they would, after ten years, become the responsibility of a diocese, under the authority of its bishop, and run by his priests.

As is too often the case, the ideal of secularization and the practicalities of secularization were far apart. The Franciscans resisted having their California missions secularized, always finding one excuse or another, generally that the natives were not yet ready to handle their own affairs. In their defense it must be pointed out that California never had a bishop until 1840, so there was in fact no one they could have turned control of their property over to. They feared, and subsequent events would show their fears to be well founded, that if the missions were secularized, with no bishop to oversee the process, the lands, buildings and indeed the people would be exploited and destroyed.

Time and a change in government made secularization inevitable. Ultimately though, it was a Mexican government, and not a Spanish one, to which the missions would be ceded. With Mexican independence, what had been a model of colonization for an empire an ocean and a continent away became one of the first orders of business for the new republic. It had become very obvious to the new government in Mexico City and more importantly to its governor in California that the missions comprised not just huge tracts of land but vast economic holdings in cattle, sheep and agriculture. On January 6, 1831, the then-governor Jose Maria Echeandia ordered immediate seculariza-

---

*　　The *cortes* is the term for the national legislative assembly of Spain. The term is used in much the same way as the United States Senate and the United States House of Representatives are referred to as "Congress." The *cortes* has power not just to enact laws, but to amend the constitution.

†　　Even today, the priesthood of the Catholic church is generally comprised of "ordered" priests, i.e. Franciscans, Jesuits, Dominican etc. and "diocesan" priests, i.e. priests not committed to a particular order but serving the bishop of a diocese.

tion of all the missions. Even then, it would be a year and a half before the process began to take hold, and several more years before it was completed. In 1834, Governor Figueroa issued the "Official Decree of Confiscation" for all of the missions, and the last of the twenty-one missions was actually secularized in 1837.

Whatever the view of the Mexican government towards secularization, those charged with implementing it saw it as an opportunity to enrich a select few. When the Franciscans finally accepted the inevitability of the end of their control over the missions, their reactions were varied: Father Jose Sanchez at San Gabriel wished that it might happen "tomorrow" so that he wouldn't waste any more time on "these miserable wretches." His superior, Father Narcisco Duran's, reaction was decidedly more charitable but no less pessimistic. Father Duran saw the government's plan as a scheme to convert the mission properties to the advantage of a few well-placed persons. He had doubts that any of the natives would ever see any benefit from secularization. Father Duran's view was to prove all too accurate. The success of the missions was to be their undoing. When new settlers moved to California after the Mexican Revolution, making that land available for private development became an imperative. The missions and their attendant lands, livestock and crops were viewed with envy by a new generation of *Californios*. Fervor and agitation for secularization—now, the term contemplated returning not to another ecclesiastical authority but to the public realm—became overwhelming. Usually the clamor for secularization was couched in terms of returning the land to the natives, to whom it rightfully belonged.

In fact, these were the terms of the final secularization order in 1833. The mission lands were to be converted to *pueblos*, the Indians were to be entitled to half of the lands, and other properties were to be distributed to other interests. Both local authorities and the Franciscans objected to the plan. Although secularization had been accomplished in Baja California with fair success, they were sure that their charges in Alta California were too naïve and gullible to handle the entire concept of private property, which was totally foreign to their culture and traditions. They were afraid the natives would be exploited and left in a far worse condition than they ever had been under what was admittedly a system of enforced serfdom. These objections fell on deaf ears, and the worst fears of the friars came to pass. There was some initial distribution made to the Indians, but nothing to compare with what was given to others, and the fortunate few natives who did acquire land found it next to impossible to hold on to it. They were completely unsophisticated with regard to the nuances of Spanish law, and within a few short years, essentially all of the land turned over to the Indians had been taken from them by means foul and fair. When in 1846 the territory passed from Mexican to American rule, the process of divesting the Indians of their holdings accelerated. Secularization, which should have been an exercise in political education and empowerment for the natives, quickly degenerated into an unseemly scramble for mission land and property. By the very terms of the secularization decree, the Indians were obliged to assist in common labor in the vineyards, orchards and fields. They were not allowed to sell or encumber land they were given to work. They were not allowed to sell any livestock. The interests of the natives were completely subsumed to naked greed and cupidity on the part of California's early governors.

Not only did secularization bring out the worst in the civil authorities, it led to another of the charges and counter-charges regarding the Franciscan's handling of the process. *Matanzas*—large-scale slaughter of cattle—took place at many of the missions in the months leading up to the actual secularization. Of this fact there is not much dispute; what is disputed is the scale of the killings and the motivations behind them. For years the common theory was that the Franciscans engaged in a slaughter of the herds under their control, for the sole purpose of denying the secular authorities the fruits of their labor. Thousands of carcasses were left to rot in the field, with only the hides being harvested. One writer claims that at Mission San Gabriel, one hundred thousand head of cattle were slain.* In fact, cattle hides were virtually the only part of the cow that had any real value in the mid-1800s. The meat from the slaughter of a large number of cattle could not be used beyond the very local population, and could not be preserved for ultimate distribution to any mass market. Cattle hides, on the other hand, when dried and tanned, could be and were shipped all over the world, and were virtually the "coin of the realm" in Mexican California. The Franciscans, it is clear, saw the end of their reign looming and did engage in a concerted effort to liquidate their assets (i.e., cattle). In

---

* The Franciscans, meticulous record-keepers that they were, can prove that there were never more than 26,300 cattle at San Gabriel.

doing so they hoped to use the money acquired from the sale of cattle hides, to buy clothes for the neophytes who very soon would not have the missions as a source of clothing.

Governor Alvarado used the missions and their livestock as his personal checkbook. Businessmen or others who were owed money by the government were given a warrant for so many cattle, or so much wheat, which they collected from the missions. Governor Vallejo decided that the Indians of San Rafael and San Francisco de Solano were too unsophisticated to work the mission lands they had inherited, so he gathered them onto his own holdings where they then worked for their "room and board." Governor Chico leased San Luis Rey for $580 a year. Perhaps most infamous in his disposal of the secularized missions was Governor Pio Pico. Pico could read the handwriting on the wall and could see that the Mexican American War then being waged was not going in favor of the Mexican government. In direct contravention of an order from his government, which he must have figured would very shortly have no authority in California, he transferred title to all of the missions except San Francisco, San Carlos, Santa Cruz, San Antonio and San Francisco de Solano. He gave San Miguel away in payment of a debt, sold San Luis Obispo, which had been valued at $70,000, for $510, and gave Santa Inés to his niece for a wedding present. In the days immediately prior to the American acquisition of California, Pico engaged in a "fire sale" of mission property with no regard for legalities or titles. The United States government, when it acquired the missions as part of the conquest of California, began to examine carefully the legal basis for the taking of these properties. Between 1848 and 1865, sometimes by judicial order and sometimes by executive order, title to every one of the missions was returned to the Catholic Church.

By the time of secularization, the missions were no longer the center of life in the communities which had grown up around them. Most of the missions by then had been abandoned and vandalized. Statues at San Carlos Borromeo were actually used for target practice by wandering bands of cowboys. Ironically, the mission roof tiles, which fifty years earlier had been the salvation of the missions, now hastened their decline. The roof tiles of the empty missions were nearly indestructible, and very attractive to the settlers beginning to establish communities around the abandoned buildings, who took the tiles for use on their own dwellings. Without the protective roofs over the adobe walls, the rains soon reduced them to crumbling ruins.

From the final act of secularization in 1836 until the late 1800s and early 1900s, the once-imposing buildings were left to the ravages of nature and the despoilment of men. They were used as everything from private residences to hog farms, from saloons to barns and stables. Some fared slightly better than others, but none fared well.

Had it not been for a group of farsighted Californian citizens in the late 1800s and early 1900s, secularization would have been the end of the missions, and we would not have the monuments we have today to marvel over. In 1895 Charles Lummis founded the Landmarks Club, lamenting that unless something was done, there would shortly be nothing left of the missions but heaps of adobe. Ten years later, Senator Joseph Knowland joined the fray, ranting that no other country in the world would allow such treasures to be so ignored. The Landmarks Club was an organization of prominent citizens, most of them not Catholic*, who recognized the beauty and historical significance of the missions and who set out to save them from total ruination. Through the efforts of men such as this, and of groups such as the Native Sons of California, the Hearst Foundation, The California Missions Foundation and the California Mission Studies Association, the missions have been preserved and/or restored, and the efforts to maintain them for future generations continue.

Endnotes

1   Tibesar, Antonine. *Writings of Junipero Serra, Vol I.* Washington, D.C.: Academy of American Franciscan History, 1955

2   Ibid., Vol. III, 19.

3   Kinneally, Finbar. *Writings of Lasuen, Vol. I.* Washington, D.C.: Academy of American Franciscan History, 1965

4   Archivo General de Indies Recopilacion de Leyes de los Reinos de las Indias, Vol. X, Titula IV, Libro III. Seville.

---

*   In fact Senator Knowland was a 33rd degree Mason.

Chapter 3

THE BEGINNINGS 1521-1770

Spain had ruled Mexico, which then included Alta California, since 1521, when Hernandan Cortez combined treachery and bravery to defeat Montezuma and the Aztecs. But it wasn't until the mid-1700s, when Russian, British and American traders began to show up in increasing numbers along the California coast, that much thought was given to "upper" California.

Originally, Spain used primarily the Jesuit and the Dominican orders of to build its churches in the New World. For still unfathomable reasons, in 1766 King Carlos III banned the Jesuits from Spain and from its overseas empires. On January 24, 1767, the Viceroy of Mexico received a secret order from Madrid. All Jesuits in Mexico were to be arrested and exiled to Europe. No exceptions were allowed, not for age, infirmity nor illness. The order was carried out ruthlessly and efficiently, and in many cases in the middle of the night. Over two thousand Jesuit priests, many of them ill, frail and elderly, were shipped to Spain despite the fact that most of them were natives of Mexico. In Spain, they were interred in cloistered monasteries and then transferred to the Papal States or other countries in Europe. None ever returned to Mexico. There was never any explanation by Carlos III for the expulsion, other than what he referred at that time to as "matters within my breast." There were vague allusions to a plot by the Jesuits against His Majesty and the state of Spain. There is no historical evidence that such a plot existed anywhere, except perhaps in the minds of other members of Carlos'court.

While Carlos III was planning this still-inexplicable act, his representatives in New Spain were planning what their course of action should be against an increasingly bold series of incursions by the Russians on their northern territories. Reports of parties comprised of as many as three hundred Russians landing on the northern California coast were being circulated. Although these reports were later found to have absolutely no basis in fact, they certainly brought a sense of urgency to Spanish plans for Alta California. The decision was made in Mexico City, and seconded in Madrid, to establish a seat of government at Monterey Bay and begin the colonization of Alta California. The Spanish model of colonization generally followed a three-pronged approach of military, religious and civilian progression, or "*presidio*, priests and *pueblo*." The military (*presidio*) was responsible for conquest and pacification, and the priests would establish a permanent place of worship, industry and education that would be the center of a civilian population eventually developing into a town (*pueblo*). The establishment, governance and maintenance of the *presidio* and the *pueblo* required an intensive effort and commitment of resources of the secular authorities. The priests, on the other hand, offered dedicated, disciplined men with their own internal rules of order and obedience, generally with self-imposed standards much higher than any which could be imposed by secular authority. All they needed were some tools, some seeds and a minimal military guard and they would build a self-supporting enterprise.

When the decision was made to colonize Alta California, what would have been the most logical source of manpower—the Jesuits—no longer existed in any Spanish territory. The Dominicans had assumed the duties of the former Jesuit missions in Baja California, and so the Franciscans were tapped to establish missions in Alta California. Junipero Serra, fifty-six years old at the time, was chosen to lead the effort.

The man who would be referred as the "Father of California" was born Miguel Joseph Serra on November 24, 1713, on the island of Majorca, a district of Spain. His parents were apparently singularly devout peasant laborers, spending much time at the local rectory. Young Miguel learned Latin from the local priests, along with his native Majorcan dialect and Spanish. Because of his obvious intelligence and promise, his parents enrolled him in school in Palma, the capital of Majorca. His education there, as with all of his education, was directed by priests, and along with his secular subjects he was taught liturgical practices and the Divine Office of the Catholic Church. He was enraptured with the lives of the saints, and in particular with those of martyrs. He openly expressed his own desire to earn the crown of martyrdom. To no one's surprise, at the age of sixteen he became a novice of the Order of St. Francis. When he took his final vows, he took the name Junipero, after one of the early companions of St. Francis, the founder of Junipero's new order.

Serra was obviously not just a devout person, but a person of intellect and intelligence. He was specially selected for courses in philosophy and theology, and even before he was ordained, he was appointed as a Professor of Sacred Theology at the University of Raymond Lull in Majorca. While fulfilling these duties, he managed to acquire for himself a doctorate in theology. This is telling background on a man who would give up this life of privilege and comfort and depart for the ends of civilization to bring the word of God to the wilds of California. Serra had a faith and a level of dedication unfathomable in today's world. An earnest desire to save fellow men from a terrible eternity was the prime motivator of Serra and all of his *confreres*. They were prepared to give up all, and sacrifice all, in the hopes of saving what they truly believed to be doomed souls.

Exactly when Serra felt the call to serve as a missionary to the new world is not clear, but as his biographer and early companion put it, the call was virtually a personal revelation and voice from God, that told Serra he should devote his energies to saving his "lost brethren" in the Americas. He and a friend, Father Francisco Palou, together petitioned to be sent to the Americas. Their initial petition was rebuffed, apparently because plans had already been made for a group of missionaries to embark soon. However, several of the friars originally slated to leave for the New World recanted, citing their fear of the sea. Fathers Palou and Serra were chosen to go.

They left Spain for the New World on August 28, 1749, when Serra was thirty-six years old. Intriguing insight into the man who was singularly most responsible for the California missions can be found in his farewell to the Old World. On August 20, 1749, Junipero Serra wrote a letter to Father Fransech Serra, a distant cousin and also a Franciscan priest*, giving his thoughts on embarking on this adven-

---

* There were three Serras in Mallorca who were members of the Franciscan order in the eighteenth-century. Junipero Serra, the subject of this book, his cousin Fransech in Petra, and yet another Fransech in La Puebla, who was a well known poet.

ture. In that letter he talks hardly at all of himself or his new venture. In paragraph after paragraph he urges his friend to console his relatives, his sister, his brother-in-law, but most of all his parents. He wishes to assure them that despite their sorrow and sadness he is convinced that he is embarking on God's work: ". . . do me the favor of consoling my parents who, I know are going through a great sorrow… I wish I could give them some of the happiness that is mine …Tell them how badly I feel, at not being able to stay longer …father, rest assured that I keep your words always before me, just as if I hear them from your mouth…Good by father mine! Good by, mother mine! Good by Juana my sister! Good by my brother Miquel!"[1] The letter is not a "farewell until we meet again." The letter is a forever goodbye from a man who knows that his entire future life lies with the venture he is embarking on. He was never to return to the land of his birth. He would die thirty-five years later near Monterey, California.

The voyage to Mexico took 128 days and had all of the dire elements one might expect of an eighteenth-century trans-Atlantic voyage. A captain so villainous that the padres took turns staying awake for fear he would murder them; cramped unsanitary quarters; a shortage of water; and a storm "…so terrible that on the second night we gave ourselves up for lost and thought there was nothing else to do but to prepare for death."[3]

Having arrived in Vera Cruz, their travails were hardly at an end. They now commenced walking to Mexico City, a distance of more than three hundred miles. The trip as recounted by Palou was full of hardships and even miraculous interventions in fording rivers, surviving ice storms and barely escaping starvation. According to Palou's account, no less than St. Joseph himself appeared and assisted them in their journey.

It was on this trip that Serra suffered an injury to his leg that plagued him for the rest of his life. Despite the eventually long-term nature of the damage, Serra himself could never remember exactly how he suffered this wound. He could not recall being bitten by a snake, or pierced by a cactus spine or anything else, so whatever the cause, it was apparently not traumatic enough to be memorable; current medical consensus is that it may have been caused by an insect or spider bite. Nonetheless, the wound and its effect on his body was so severe that twenty years later during the initial journey to California, Gaspar de Portola himself urged Serra to abandon his mission.*

On arriving in Mexico City, Father Serra was attached to the College of San Fernando. The college had as one of its duties the maintenance of several missions in upper Mexico. To his delight, within six months of his arrival Father Serra was assigned to missionary work in the Sierra Gorda. He worked in five missions Jalpan, Landa, Tlaco, Tancoyoi and Conca for the next nine years. This work was the first of Serra's successes, for he managed after several years to have a church constructed and to have the native population engaged in farming, building and artistic work.

In 1758 Father Serra was recalled from the Sierra Gorda with plans to send him north of the Rio Grande. He was designated to go to the San Sabas River, located in present-day Texas. His departure for Texas was halted when Fathers Alonso Terreros and Joseph Estevan were killed at their mission by marauding Comanches. The Spanish Army would allow no travel to that obviously very dangerous area. Instead of returning to the Sierra Gorda, Father Serra remained at the College of San Fernando for the next nine years. He taught at the college, and preached missions to the local populace.

A recounting of one of Serra's sermons brings some perspective to the culture and religious practices of his time, and to the charges of cruelty and mistreatment of the native population that would later be leveled against all of the Franciscans. The author is describing one of Father Serra's sermons:

> In one of these, in imitation of his patron, San Francisco Solano, he took out a chain, and having let fall his habit so that his shoulders were bared, and after having exhorted them all to penitence he began to lash himself so cruelly that the whole audience broke out in sobs, till finally, one man rising up hurried into the pulpit, took the chain away from the penitent Father, came down with it, stood up on the platforms of the presbytery, and then imitating the example of the Venerable preacher, he stripped himself

---

*   We are told that he had one of the mule drivers give him a poultice which was used on the mules when they injured their legs

to the waist and began to make public penance, saying with tears and sobs: "I am the ungrateful sinner before God who should do penance, and not the Father who is a Saint." So unstinted and without compassion were the blows that he gave himself that he soon fell down before all the people who judged that he was dead. But having received Extreme Unction and Holy Communion he died a little later.[3]

So much for the idea of judging Junipero Serra's activities by contemporary standards.

When not exhorting his congregation to gory acts of penance, Father Serra apparently used his time in Mexico City to cultivate political connections which would serve him in good stead in the California missions. Repeatedly in his work in California he found himself in conflict with military and civilian authorities, and repeatedly his petitions to Mexico City were granted. This was likely due to relationships he established and the respect he had earned with the Spanish governors in Mexico City.

In 1767, Spain decided the time had come to solidify its hold on Alta California. The Franciscans were given the task of establishing a chain of missions there, and Father Junipero Serra was appointed president of those missionaries. As he had left a life of comfort and privilege in Spain eighteen years ago, on May 15, 1769, he once more left his life in the capitol of New Spain for the uncharted territory known as Alta California. He was to personally found nine missions over the next seventeen years. On his death the work he began continued until there was a total of twenty-one missions in Alta California.

Serra would labor prodigiously in California for the next fifteen years. When he died on August 28, 1784, there were nine missions extending over five hundred miles of previously uncharted California. Each of these missions was the busy center of a thriving, growing community. There were not just churches but homes, schools, businesses, farms and ranches. To put his accomplishment into perspective, we need only look to the other side of the continent. The year Junipero Serra died, 1784, was the same year that Daniel Boone began his explorations of the Appalachian and Ozark mountains.

For his travels and explorations and for the settlements he founded, Junipero Serra is rightly called the founder of California. He is one of two persons from California featured in the statuary hall of the United States senate. There, each state has been given the opportunity to have featured statues of two of their most important historical figures. Junipero Serra shares the honors from California with Ronald Reagan, the fortieth president of the United States. Interestingly, until 2006 both of California's statutes were of religious figures: until that date, Thomas Starr King, a Unitarian Minister from San Francisco, shared the honor with Junipero Serra. The Rev. Mr. King was an ardent human rights spokesman. He was credited by President Lincoln with dissuading the people of California from seceding and forming their own republic during the Civil War. However, two years after the death of Ronald Reagan, the California legislature voted to replace the Rev. Mr. King, whom hardly anyone had any knowledge of, with President Reagan.*

Endnotes

1   Tibesar, Antonine. *Writings of Junipero Serra, Vol. I.* Washington, D.C.: Academy of American Franciscan History, 1955.

2   Palou, Francisco. *Relación Histórica de la Vida del Ven. P. Fr. Junipero Serra.* Translated by C. Scott Williams. Pasadena: George Wharton James, 1913.

3   Ibid. pp. 42-43

---

*   One of the arguments put forward to remove Mr. King was that "he wasn't a native of California." In fact neither was Ronald Reagan, who was born in Illinois, nor Junipero Serra, who wasn't even born in the United States.

LANDS NEVER TRODDEN

Chapter 4

MISSION SAN DIEGO

*M*ision de San Diego de Alcala (The Mission of Saint Didacus of Alcala), was founded on July 16th, 1769. It was named after a Franciscan Brother, not a priest, of the fifteenth century. His feast day is November 12.

San Diego was to be only the "base camp" for the first important *presidio* which would be built at Monterey.

The expedition sent to settle San Diego was actually several separate groups. In overall command was Don Gaspar de Portola. Portola was the governor of both Baja, and Alta California. He decided to take personal charge of this important change from what had been a policy of benign neglect of the northern territories. He had a contingent of soldiers, and native bearers consisting of about three hundred, in several different parties.

There was also a group of four Franciscan priests,* under the authority of Junipero Serra. Technically Portola was overall commander of both military and clerical groups. As a practical matter, though, there was no reason for him to ever exercise any authority over the priests.

Logistically, the expedition was even further fractured. Two ships, the San Antonio and the San Carlos, left La Paz a month apart, on January 10 and February 15, 1769. A third ship, the San Jose, was being built at San Blas and it would follow later with additional supplies and soldiers. Overland expeditions also left in two separate groups. Father Juan Crespi was with the first group, leaving about the same

---

* Fathers Fernando Parron, Juan Vizcaino, Francisco Gomez, Juan Crespi, in addition to Father Serra.

31

time as the San Antonio, and Father Junipero Serra with the second, leaving May 15.

The rigors of any of the journeys cannot be overstated. By land, hunger and thirst and an unforgiving landscape took their toll, and by sea the ravages of scurvy reduced the ships' crews to useless and dying skeletons. Father Serra, upon arriving in San Diego around July 1, 1769, noted in a letter to a friend, "Here are also the two vessels the San Carlos and the San Antonio, the former, however without sailors, all having died of the scurvy except one who with the cook survives."[1] Approximately three hundred men had formed the total of the four expeditions, and less than half of them made it to San Diego. The San Jose was never seen again after leaving the Sea of Cortez. It had to be clear at the very outset, even before the founding of even one mission, that the challenges to this undertaking would be formidable. The difficulties of the task would have dissuaded lesser men.

Once arrived in their new home, the missionaries found themselves occupied in endeavors they had not anticipated when they left Baja California. The first and most time-consuming task was to care for the gruesomely sick sailors from the two ships. The second was to dig graves and bury the dead. Despite this inauspicious start, Junipero Serra forged ahead.

Gaspar Portola did not tarry in San Diego. Before the mission was even founded, on July 14 he took the bulk of his military force and two priests, Fathers Juan Crespi and Francisco Gomez, and moved north in search of Monterey. Sebastian Vizcaino had described Monterey as " . . . a harbor protected from all winds. . ." Vizcaino had named it Monterey to honor his patron, the then-viceroy of Mexico, who included in his honorifics the title Conte de Monte Re. Monterey, was seen as the capitol of the new territory from the time plans to settle California had first been drawn up. Portola's orders from Mexico had been to establish *presidios* at San Diego and Monterey and halfway between the two, so finding the harbor at Monterey was essential to his task.

Father Serra remained in San Diego with fathers Fernando Parron and Francisco Gomez, and approximately forty-five others: soldiers, a few sailors, a carpenter, a blacksmith, servants and Indians from Mexico. On July 16 they constructed a rude shelter of tree branches and fronds for the celebration of Mass and the dedication of Mission

San Diego. They immediately began construction of more permanent huts, one of which ultimately became the church.

Relations with the Indians at San Diego got off to a very rocky start and were never, in the entire history of the mission, ideal. Less than a month after Portola and his soldiers left, the mission was attacked by the natives. Although vastly outnumbered, the Spaniards had fire-arms against the Indians' bows and arrows, and the attackers retreated, suffering several killed. Within a few days they reappeared, this time with their wounded, seeking medical treatment. They were treated and apparently the only retributive action taken was that a compound was built to surround the mission works, and the Indians were not allowed to bring their weapons into the compound.

Portola's search for the harbor of Monterey was a fruitless and by all accounts grim one. He undoubtedly passed the harbor that Vizcaino had described one hundred and seventy years earlier, not once but twice—once going north, and then again returning south—but didn't recognize it. Portola's inability to recognize Monterey Bay on this journey has puzzled historians ever since. "It is," says historian Hubert Howe Bancroft, "and must ever remain more or less inexplicable that the Spaniards should have failed at this time to identify Monterey. All that was known of that port had resulted from Vizcaino's visit, and this knowledge was in the hands of the explorer in the works of Venegas and Cabrerea Bueno. The description of landmarks was tolerably clear."[2] What was not tolerably clear was the one absolute that navigators of the sixteenth and seventeenth century had at their disposal: latitude.

Cabrero Bueno, who was Vizcaino's navigator had recorded the latitude of Monterey as 37 degrees in 1602. *The latitude of Monterey Bay is in fact 36°36'.* If Portola's men were seeking the bay at 37° they would have been twenty-four miles off. Lieutenant Fages with the Portola expedition recorded their latitude as 36°44' when they were trying to figure out where Monterey Bay was. Portola's party was undoubtedly looking down at Monterey Bay but Vizcaino's description and Bueno's errant measurement threw them off.

Vizcaino's overblown description of the port was likely the most difficult problem. Considering the almost completely sheltered San Diego and San Francisco bays, which the explorers were familiar with, it is hard to imagine the shallow arc that is Monterey Bay as "sheltered from all winds," which in fact it is not. Sergeant Don Jose de Ortega accompanying Portola expresses this very doubt. "On October 5ᵗʰ or 6ᵗʰ we reached Pt. Pinos and according to the indications of Captain Vizcaino and piloto Cabrera Bueno, and our latitude as well we should have thought ourselves already at Monterey; but not finding the shelter and protection ascribed by them to the port caused us to doubt, since we saw a bight over twelve leagues across with no shelter except for small craft at the point, although he said the bight is large enough to hold thousands of vessels, but with little protection from some winds."[3] The party continued north until they came to San Francisco Bay and the impassable barrier it presented to a party without boats.

On November 12 they gave up the search and turned south to return to San Diego. For some reason on his return journey and during his second stop at the unrecognized Monterey Bay, Portola had not one, but two crosses erected at different sides of the bay. One of these crosses was the guiding landmark when the harbor was "discovered" nine months later. There is no evidence that Portola, at any other site in his stumbling journey up and down the California coast, erected any monuments. If he saw no particular significance in this shallow bay, why did he have the two monuments erected there? It has been speculated that Portola did in fact recognize the harbor and was totally unimpressed with it, particularly after the grueling ordeal that had brought him to it. Rather than try to argue with his distinguished predecessor, he began circulating the story that tides and sands had shifted in the seventy years since Vizcaino's voyage, and the harbor no longer existed. Juan Crespi, who accompanied Portola on the trek gave some credence to this explanation, as did Junipero Serra later in San Diego.

Eight months after he left, Portola and his party stumbled back in to San Diego. They had been reduced to killing and eating their mules. When Portola returned to San Diego and reported that Monterey Bay seemed not to exist, Serra could not resist taunting him with the jibe that his failure was akin to going to Rome without seeing the pope.

Portola, upon struggling back into San Diego, was clearly fed up with the whole venture. He was first of all the governor of Baja California and an explorer only by happenstance. He began plans to abandon San Diego and move everybody back to Baja California.

Here we have perhaps the first of several historic interventions by Serra. He argued with Portola. He was not prepared to abandon his first fledgling mission. In all actuality, he had no more success in his endeavors than had Portola. In fact, of the forty-nine people who had been left with Serra, only twenty were still alive when Portola returned. Serra had only one convert and just the foundations of permanent buildings to show for almost a year's worth of sacrifice and hardship. In Serra's mind, though, return was not an option. The cross he had planted at that crude first mission was to take root and spread throughout Alta California. Of this he was convinced. God had sent them on this trek with success in mind, and he was committed to being God's hand in seeing that it took place. On February 10, 1770 Serra wrote a letter to Francisco Palou, then serving as the president of the California missions, in which he lamented the talk of abandoning the project. He asks Palou to exercise whatever influence he may have to quash such thoughts. He complains not at all of the harsh conditions they are living under; in fact he states, "although our physical necessities are not a few, yet while we have left a tortilla and some herbs from the field, what more do we need?...being here without news and without being able to go on and being in doubt as to whether we will have to abandon what has already been obtained is what afflicts me…"[4] As has been noted "what has already been obtained" was virtually nothing, yet Serra remained committed. As Portola planned to leave, and Serra insisted on staying, one can only imagine the impassioned arguments between these two men, professional soldier and priest.

Surely in this debate Portola had not just the full weight of logic, but the will of the majority on his side. No one in this pathetic band other than Serra and his close friend Father Crespi could have been in favor of staying. When Portola initially agreed to stay just a little longer the sailors almost rose up in mutiny. Sickness, deprivation, starvation and death had been their lot for almost two years. The Indians had remained not just aloof, but unfriendly. The primary priestly duty the Franciscans performed was to bury the dead. Serra himself was suffering from a suppurating wound on his leg and was just recovering from scurvy. The harbor of Monterey, which had been one of their primary objectives, did not seem to exist. Nothing supported Serra's argument for staying, and everything seemed to militate toward Portola's plan to leave. And yet, Serra prevailed.

His success was largely due to the fact that Juniper Serra, among his many attributes, possessed those of a very capable politician. During his time in Mexico City he had developed a close relationship with Jose de Galvez. As the *visitador*, or king's representative in the New World, Galvez was a rising star in the Spanish bureaucracy and it was he who put Portola in charge of the military expedition to the north, and he who had chosen Serra for the ecclesiastical arm of it. While his choice of Portola was simply that of finding a person on the ground who could undertake the mission, his choice of Serra was more that of a friend giving to a friend a desired assignment.

So Serra won out and Portola agreed to a short wait. There is no record of this momentous discussion which would determine the future of California, between Portola and Serra. It is probable that Serra's trump card, which bought a least a temporary stay from Portola, was his personal relationship with Portola's boss Galvez. Serra and Crespi had determined that they would stay no matter what Portola did. It seems likely that they would not have survived had this been the case.

It was agreed then, that if by March 20 relief and additional supplies had not arrived from Mexico, Portola and the military contingent would abandon San Diego, forget about finding Monterey Bay, and return to Baja California. Serra and Crespi, if they so chose, could fend for themselves. Portola and his soldiers sat down to wait. Serra and his priests knelt to pray. They began a novena, nine days of prayer devoted to a petition for a particular favor from God. It is likely that the novena began on March 10, since the expedition's patron saint was St. Joseph, and the novena was offered through the particular intercession of St. Joseph whose feast is March 19. On the afternoon of the nineteenth, a sail was sighted on the horizon! Hope flared only to disappear with the sail, which continued north. It returned, though, four days later. The *San Antonio*, full of provisions, sailed into San Diego Bay. The expedition was saved. The Spanish presence in California would continue for almost two hundred more years, and the Franciscan presence remains to this day.

The *San Antonio,* under the command of Captain Juan Perez, had left San Blas, headed not for San Diego but for Monterey. Based on reports that were sent back to Mexico City over the past many months, it was assumed that Portola was on the way to Monterey or perhaps had already established a base there. Perez's primary orders were to support and re-supply this putative new settlement. This was the reason he did not stop in San Diego initially. Short of Monterey, the *San Antonio* found itself low on water, and it was decided to go ashore in the Santa Barbara channel for fresh water. While loading the water, the crew of the *San Antonio* was told by the natives that their countrymen had passed there twice, once on the way north, and again on the return trip south. The natives were actually able to give Captain Perez the names of some of the soldiers who had traveled through. This put Perez into a bit of a quandary. If the expedition or any large portion of it had gone back south, was there any point in his continuing north? As is often the case, uncontrollable circumstances decided the matter for him. He lost one of his anchors while getting under way in the Santa Barbara Channel. Now he had no choice. He could not anchor in Monterey, nor anywhere else on the California coastline, with only one anchor. He decided to return to San Diego to hopefully avail himself of a spare anchor from the *San Carlos*. Arriving in San Diego, he found the *San Carlos,* the disheartened Monterey expedition, the Franciscans—and a savior's welcome. San Diego was re-supplied, the morale of all was improved and the decision was made for yet another effort at finding elusive Monterey Bay.

A month later on April 16, 1770, the *San Antonio* sailed again, but this time to the north. Destination: Monterey Bay. Captain Perez and Junipero Serra were on the *San Antonio.* Portola and Crespi led a party by land, full of new hope, buttressed with fresh supplies and soldiers and determined to not fail in what had been one of the primary objectives all along: the establishment of a *presidio* and settlement at Monterey.

The land expedition arrived at Monterey after forty days of travel, and this time had no trouble at all recognizing it. Supposedly Portola, Crespi, Fages, Serra and Perez, five different men in two different parties, almost immediately recognized Vizcaino's bay as soon as they saw it on the second journey. "As Portola, Crespi, and Fages walked along the beach that afternoon, returning from a visit to the cross, they looked out over the placid bay, when the truth suddenly dawned upon their minds and they in one accord exclaimed: 'This is the port of Monterey which we seek; it is just as Vizcaino and Cabrera Bueno described it.' "[5]

When Father Serra started north with Perez on the *San Antonio*, Fathers Fernando Parron and Francisco Gomez were left in charge of finishing Mission San Diego. That departure must have been a wrenching moment for all concerned. Serra surely had concerns about the future of this still-struggling enterprise in which he had invested so much of his own energies. Gomez and Parron must have questioned the winds of fate that had thrown to them such an overwhelming task. The mission at San Diego must be completed and must succeed. If Serra left any final instructions surely this would have been one of them: The mission at San Diego must be completed. Serra's absolute certitude in this objective was clear. He had made it clear a month earlier, saying even if everyone else returned to Mexico, he would not abandon the project. Now this task fell to these two men. It was their job to make that happen. At forty-two and forty-one years of age, Parron and Gomez were mature but inexperienced men in a foreign and hostile land. They had both survived an attack by the natives in which one of their party was killed and several others wounded. They had no means of logistical support, no specific set of instructions, no particular expertise in building, architecture or engineering and certainly no resources to draw upon. A major undertaking of their church and their country rested squarely on their shoulders.

If there were doubts about the future of San Diego when Serra left, they must have been magnified a hundredfold when within the year, both Gomez and Parron gave up the task and returned to Mexico because of ill health. Now, before any of the original building was even complete, Mission San Diego was handed off to a third administrative team. Placed in charge upon the departure of Fathers Gomez and Parron were Fathers Luis Jayme and Francisco Dumetz. Dumetz himself shortly returned to Mexico because of ill health. This left, for a time, a young Father Luis Jayme as solely responsible for the success of the "Mother of All the Missions."

Father Jayme was twenty-nine years old. He had been born Melchor Jayme in San Juan, Mallorca in 1740. At the age of fifteen, he was enrolled in the convent school of San Bernardino, in Petra, the capital of Mallorca, the same school Junipero Serra had attended years before. He took the name Luis on his ordination. He was obviously an intelligent and gifted young man, because on completion of his studies he was appointed a "Lector of Philosophy." He held this post for almost five years. In 1770 he gave up what had to have been a very comfortable position of priest-academician in one of Europe's most prestigious seminaries to volunteer for the missions in New Spain.

This pattern of privileged men of class choosing a life of hardship and rigor is repeated throughout the missions' history. It is very likely one of the prime reasons for the success of the missions. The missionairies were not just the best and the brightest of their generation, but they were guided by the highest of all principles: a love of God and a heartfelt concern for their fellow men.

Father Jayme would ultimately prove himself not just a man committed to his task, but a man willing to die for it. He remained undaunted by the obstacles which arose. From time to time other priests were sent to assist him, but generally the young priest had sole responsibility for the completion and success of this first mission. In October of 1772 Jayme wrote a letter to Father Raphael Verger, the Guardian of the College of San Fernando in Mexico City. He complained in gruesome detail about the abuses the soldiers were visiting on the Indians, particularly the women. An extensive excerpt from his letter will demonstrate the problems he, or more correctly the Indians had to deal with:

> As for the example to be set by the soldiers, no doubt some of them are good exemplars and deserve to be treated accordingly, but very many of them deserve to hanged on account of the continuous outrages which they are committing in seizing and raping the women. . . . At one of these Indian villages near this mission of San Diego. . . the gentiles therein many times have been on the point of coming here to kill us all, and the reason for this is that some soldiers went there and raped their women. . . . On the 11th day of September of the present year there went to the Indian village called "El Corral" the soldiers Castelo, Juan Maria Ruiz, Bravo, and another . . . and a sailor named Ignacio Marques. . . . Soldier Castelo carried a gentile woman into a corral . . . and inside the corral the said soldier had sexual intercourse with the woman and sinned with her. ... After this they released the woman and went to the Indian village, and the soldier whose

name is not known seized another woman violently and carried her into the same corral and sinned with her there. He came out, and soldier Bravo entered and sinned with her. He came out and the soldier Juan Maria Ruiz entered and did the same. He came out and the soldier Castelo entered and did the same. . . . In order that these outrages should not become known, solders Castelo and Bravo told Jose Antonio, the Indian, . . . that if he told the father they would punish him. . . . On the afternoon of the same day the two women came to tell me about what had happened. They came into the mission weeping . . . Diego Ribera serving as my interpreter for greater clarity, he being the one whom I use to teach the Christian Doctrine.

I was informed of this case twice by the said two women, and three times by Jose Antonio, the said Indian, and they always agreed on everything. . . . this same Indian who had told me about this case was placed in stocks without my being notified, and I took him out in defiance of the corporal of the guard, for I judged, and rightly so, that they were going to punish him so that he would not confess the truth concerning the said case.[6]

In 1773, a new group of seven priests arrived from Mexico, and Father Vincente Fuster became Father Jayme's permanent assistant, while the others were assigned to the other five missions that by that time had been founded. Jayme and Fuster continued work on the San Diego complex. In early 1774, four thousand adobe blocks had been manufactured and the foundation of a church ninety feet long was completed.

Unbelievably, though, after a four-year struggle of trying to develop the original mission that Serra had founded, Jayme arrived at the decision to move it. Not to abandon it, but to start all over again. The affinity of the mission and its neophytes with the *presidio* and its soldiers was intolerable. Accordingly, in August of 1774, the mission was moved from its original site to the site we today know as Mission San Diego. The four thousand adobe blocks were left behind.

Time and again the story of the missions is one of just such a leap of faith, a decision that, "all that has been done so far has been for naught, and so we must do more." The Franciscans were never deterred from stretching their meager resources yet further. Within a year, a church, dwellings for the missionaries, a storehouse and a smithy were all well underway at the new site. Still, Mission San Diego struggled mightily to survive. The location, while it may have been more conducive to converting the natives, was not at all conducive to agriculture. Six years after its founding the mission produced less than fifty bushels of wheat and had only ninety-seven converts. Father Crespi, in Monterey with Serra, despaired in a letter that he had heard that San Diego was to be abandoned. San Diego, though, was not abandoned, with the most meager of supplies arriving: some flour from, of all places, the second mission, San Carlos.

Father Jayme's efforts at San Diego, and Father Jayme himself, were to come to a brutal end on November 4, 1775. That night, a group of natives (by some accounts as many as eight hundred) surrounded the mission, burned most of the buildings to the ground, and killed Father Jayme. Apparently in an excess of zeal and trust in the Indians, Jayme had walked out to them as the attack was in progress and, with arms extended, exhorted them to love God. He was engulfed in a mob of the attackers and beaten to death. Besides Father Jayme, a blacksmith and a carpenter were killed, and the mission almost totally destroyed by fire.

Father Luis Jayme became the first, but not the last of the Franciscans in California to give his life to the task they had undertaken. Jayme was a former student of Serra's and a friend. Nonetheless, when Serra heard of his death, in the strange mindset of service to God and ultimate sacrifice, Serra exulted. "Thanks be to God; that land is watered; now will follow the conversion of the San Diego Indians." [7] A mindset such as this can hardly be envisioned in our world today. To Junipero Serra and the Franciscans, revenge and retribution, if any, was in the hands of God. In the hands of men was only work for the salvation of souls.

Father Serra, aside from being encouraged at the death of his friend, was concerned about the reaction of the Spanish military to this event. He wrote Viceroy Bucareli in Mexico City and implored him that retribution be avoided. In his view, harsh punishment of the Indians would only cause problems in the effort to win them over. The Viceroy apparently accepted his arguments, writing back that, "In view of the prudent and Christian reflections expressed in your letter inclining to soften the rebels by kindness rather than subdue them by punishment, I have written *Commandante* Rivera so to act, thinking it the best method of pacifying and winning them."[8] Unfortunately this letter was written April 3, 1776; in December of 1775, a volatile Captain Fernando Rivera y Moncada had already departed Monterey, on a mission to exact punishment upon the guilty Indians. This would be the first, but certainly not the last, appearance of Captain Rivera in the history of the missions. He traveled south, on a campaign of flogging and intimidation, while Captain Juan De Anza, recently arrived in California from Arizona, was ordered to turn south at San Gabriel to join him.

In March of 1776, Captains Rivera and de Anza and their troops arrived at San Diego. They were there to bring those responsible for the burning of the mission and the death of Father Jayme to justice. One of those responsible happened at the time to be confessing his part in the massacre to Father Fuster, in the temporary chapel that had been established in one of the warehouses of the *presidio*. Rivera appeared on the scene and demanded his surrender. Father Fuster refused to turn the penitent over to the captain, and claimed that the Indian enjoyed the sanctuary of the church, and could not be taken by the military. Spanish civil law clearly recognized the law of sanctuary—and also allowed for its abrogation, but only upon a sworn statement. This was explained to Captain Rivera. Rivera's response was that the building was not a church, but a warehouse being temporarily used as a church, so the law of sanctuary did not apply. The priests remained obdurate: the Indian was under their protection. With sword drawn, Rivera entered the chapel and had his soldiers drag the Indian—who we are told was named Octavio—away.

Father Fuster, who had witnessed the murder of his friend Father Jayme, perhaps at the hand of this very prisoner, was outraged at this violation of church sanctuary. He immediately "excommunicated" the soldiers.* This small event, an argument over who exercised ultimate authority over an Indian peasant, was to have far-reaching and long-

---

*   As a matter of canon law, only a bishop can actually excommunicate a Catholic, and Fuster undoubtedly knew that. Perhaps he thought that if soldiers could skirt civil law, priests could skirt canon law.

standing results. It would be the catalyst for a simmering antagonism between the head of the Franciscans and the head of the military/civilian government of California. It would affect the relationship between these two instruments of Spanish colonial expansion in California for the next seventy years. The fact that Fuster took such an extreme step against Rivera, correctly or otherwise, is particularly enlightening of the mindset the early Franciscans had towards the natives. All of the evidence is that Fuster was emotionally destroyed by Father Jayme's death. He exhibited all of the classic signs of survivor's guilt. "Fuster had expressed in his reports and in his conversations with Font a feeling of remorse that he had lived and Jayme had died."[9] Despite this trauma, he was prepared to defend the natives, whether it was from the Devil or the military.

Not only Fuster, but also but Father Lasuen felt that their duty to the Indians outweighed Rivera's wish to enforce civil law and military rule. The next day, as Father Lasuen began Mass, he noticed that in the congregation were some of the soldiers who Fuster had excommunicated. He ordered them from the church and would not continue the Mass until they had departed.

Father Serra himself arrived back in San Diego eight months after the mission's destruction and the murder of Jayme. He found relations between the priests and the soldiers abysmal. Never good, it had not been helped by the priests' challenge of Rivera's authority in the matter of the rebelling Indians. Because of this deadlock between the two groups, little had been done to rebuild the destroyed mission. Serra and Rivera met to discuss the situation. The discussions did not go well. Serra and Rivera had been at odds from the outset of Rivera's appointment, and the tensions caused by the Indian uprising did not help them at all.

This on-again, off-again, success/failure mode of operation was characteristic of most of the missions, and another reason for us to admire them. San Diego, the first of the missions, was one of the most unlucky and seemingly unsuccessful of all of the missions, at least through its early history. Destruction by fire, a surly and uncooperative military, inadequate water for its agricultural endeavors, an Indian population that was at least indifferent and at times overtly hostile—if Mission San Diego had been established in the twentieth century as the prototype for a chain of franchises all along the California coast, the corporate structure that had envisioned the project would have quickly abandoned it. Ten years after its beginning, the mission was still struggling: four separate buildings had been begun and all of them, for one reason or another, had been abandoned. Were it not for infusions of food from the second and third missions, famine would have ended all of its miseries.

However, the missions were not a corporate structure, nor even a political one. They were, in the minds of the Franciscans, the work of God. Whatever cultural firestorm such an endeavor might ignite today, the necessity of the conversion of the natives was a sincere belief on the part of the priests. They were the salvation of the Indians. The theology of the time was clear: the native Californians were their brothers, and those brothers were doomed for all eternity. The Franciscans were prepared to sacrifice themselves to save these unfortunates.

This, then, was the atmosphere when the head of the Franciscans asked the head of the military for help in rebuilding Mission San Diego. Matters were certainly not helped by the fact that Rivera was, by all accounts, almost totally unhinged by his excommunication. To be excommunicated, even in a somewhat irregular fashion, was no small thing to a Spanish officer in the eighteenth-century. There is evidence that Rivera was physically sick and not emotionally himself over the idea of being cut off from his church. He made a personal appeal to Serra to have the interdict lifted. Serra refused to intervene and let stand the excommunication. As it happens, Rivera's concerns and his petition to Serra were both ill-founded. He was never actually excommunicated, despite Fuster's pronouncement. On the other hand, if he had been excommunicated there was nothing Serra could do since, as only a bishop can excommunicate, it takes a bishop to reverse the order.

With Serra's intransigence on this matter went perhaps the last hope of real cooperation between these two powerful representatives of Spain in California. As time went on, the paths of the two men continued to cross and as each held a towering sense of honor the rift only grew. Rivera once delivered to Serra letters from Mexico that Serra suspected had been opened and read. Serra once demanded immediate delivery of some mules that had been sent to the missionaries but that the military had found necessary to use. With regard to the rebuilding of the burned mission, Rivera showed his own intransigence. Not only would he provide no assistance in the rebuilding of the mission: he tried to stop it.

Rivera informed Serra and some of the sailors from the *Principe,* who were assisting in the rebuilding, that rumors of another attack were rife. He ordered the sailors and marines to return to their ship. There was a discussion and some resistance, but Rivera was the senior officer and his orders were followed. Captain Choquet of the *Principe* expressed his distaste for the move, observing that it was a shame for the Spanish army to suspend work at the mere rumor of hostilities, and he did not stop there. He notified the viceroy of Mexico of these developments. Although it is not entirely clear that there was a causal nexus between Choquet's letter and what happened next, in March of 1777 Viceroy Antonio Bucarelli ordered Rivera back to Loreto, Mexico, and asked Governor Felipe de Neve to take up residence at Monterey. The move was a promotion for Rivera, because at that time there was only one governor for the two Californias—Baja and Alta—and that post was located in Loreto in Baja California. The person serving in Baja California was the governor of both Californias, and the person serving in Monterey was a "sub-governor" for Alta California who, while he had wide latitude in conducting the affairs of the territory, was required to submit reports to Loreto. In today's terms, Rivera was "kicked upstairs," and Serra was left to proceed with his plans with no interference

In his letter to Serra, the viceroy was clear as to how he viewed the matter: " The suspension of the work on the destroyed mission of San Diego must have caused severe pain to your Reverence. It has greatly displeased me as well, the more so as I became aware through Don Diego Choquet of the frivolous motives that brought it about. I presume that, with the twenty-five soldiers sent to reinforce the *presidio*, Don Fernando Rivera will devote himself to the erection of the mission of San Juan Capistrano; but if he does not, the governor of the province who has orders to reside at Monterey will do so. I have ordered the governor to have San Diego reestablished, and not to punish the ringleaders of the late outbreak, hoping that they will themselves learn to regret their misdeeds."[10]

This missive, clearly critical of Captain Rivera's actions, must have galled him to no end. It certainly could not have helped his view of the Franciscans when one of the last official acts he was asked to perform before he left California was to order the release of the Indians he had imprisoned in that heated exchange with Father Fuster.

In his biography of Junipero Serra, Father Francisco Palou gives an interesting sidebar to this incident. According to Palou, one of the Indians who had been imprisoned after the 1775 attack had been a participant in the first attack, right after the mission was founded in 1769. He alone of the original attackers had remained unrepentant and hostile, and had joyfully been part of the second attack. Father Serra visited him in prison and begged him to repent and be forgiven. He remained obdurate. Shortly after Serra's visit, he committed suicide by hanging himself, on August 15, 1776, seven years to the day after the first attack and two weeks before Rivera was ordered to free him.* The new church was dedicated by Junipero Serra in 1777, and then assigned to Father Fermin Francesco de Lasuen. Father Lasuen would complete the building, serve at San Diego until 1785, and in California until his death in 1803.

While Mission San Diego itself had no further troubles of particular note from the Indians, the area generally remained unstable and violent; not just at San Diego but also at San Gabriel and San Juan Capistrano, where the natives, while protesting some injustice—often the abuse of their women—were cruelly treated by the soldiers. Raids to capture supposedly outlaw Indians often ended in the deaths of the first Indians the soldiers came upon. "In carrying out his orders the sergeant surprised the foe at Pamo, killed two of the number, and burned a few who refused to come out of the hut in which they had taken refuge."[11] The casual, dismissive language of "burned a few" illustrates too well the attitude of the Spanish military towards the natives.

This violent approach to settling issues was institutionalized at San Diego with California's first-ever sentence of capital punishment on April 11, 1778. Four Indian chiefs had been captured in the raid on Pamo described above. In command of the San Diego *presidio* at that time was Lieutenant Jose Francisco Ortega. Although he was totally without such authority, he condemned the prisoners to die by firing squad. He summoned Fathers Lasuen and Figuer from San Diego Mis-

---

*   There does seem to be some question as to whether his death was a murder or a suicide. Perhaps the volatile Captain Rivera was not going to let some silly order prompted by the overly-sympathetic priests frustrate his personal sense of justice.

sion to prepare the Indians for death. "You will cooperate," Ortega ordered, "for the good of their souls in the understanding that, if they do not accept the salutary water of holy baptism, they die on Saturday morning; and if they do, they will die all the same."[12] Although the threat and the orders were clearly issued, the sentence was apparently never carried out, for in a letter written on April 22, Serra writes Father Lasuen and mentions the fact that he does not believe the sentence of these poor unfortunates will be executed. Over a year later he again writes Lasuen, "It gives me great joy to hear that the men who had been sentenced to death are not only persevering in a better way of life, but are even becoming apostles, converting others and bringing them to the fold of our Holy Mother Church"[13]

The new church at San Diego was finally completed in 1780, and in 1785, Father Lasuen reported that in addition to the church there was a granary, a storehouse, residences for the natives and for the priests, and outside facilities for livestock and tanning. Still, Mission San Diego lived a precarious existence. Converts were few and the natives remained resistant to the changes being forced on them. The Franciscans were meticulous record keepers, and one thing evident in these records is that the death rate of the neophytes at San Diego was at times a frightening fifty percent. Whatever spiritual blessings the missionaries believed they brought, it is clear that the temporal benefits were more like a curse.

In 1811, Father Pedro Panto was taken violently ill. His cook, a native named Nazario, was arrested, and admitted to putting poison in the padre's soup. His motivation was to "escape the father's intolerable floggings, having received in succession fifty, twenty-five, twenty-four and twenty-five lashes in the twenty-four hours preceding his attempted revenge."[14] The number and frequency of the floggings is much in question. Zephyrin Englehardt asserts that no missionary would have dared to ignore a prohibition against more than twenty-five lashes allowed only once. Whatever the number, Father Panto was clearly an unpopular disciplinarian, and his actions drove Nazario to a desperate attempt at revenge. The conflicting role of the Franciscans in these matters is illustrated by the fact that when a trial was first proposed for Nazario, Father Panto did not want to prosecute, and actually refused to testify. The prosecutor had to write the then-president of the missions, Father Narcisco Duran, to ask that Panto be ordered to testify. The order was given but only with the proviso that if Nazario was found guilty, he must not receive capital punishment. Both Father Panto and Nazario survived the immediate incident. Nazario was sentenced to eight months of labor at the *presidio* and Father Panto died, interestingly about the same time as Nazario was completing his sentence. The priest who buried Father Panto felt compelled to note on the death register that, "He died from poisoning by the cook." One must ask, eight months later?

When not dealing with the daunting issues that accompany the subjugation of an unwilling population, the missionaries continued in their work of building. In 1803, the church was damaged by an earthquake but apparently not extensively, because a replacement was not begun until 1808. That church was finished in 1813, and it is this building which is the existing Mission San Diego. All of the California missions were almost permanent works in progress. There was always some improvement to be made, and the general response to a failure of design or location was to build more.

Water for the crops at San Diego was always critical, so in the first few years of the nineteenth century the padres began an extensive irrigation project. That project culminated in 1813 with a dam, 245 feet long, ten feet high, thirteen feet wide, six miles upstream from the mission. The site for the dam was recommended by the native Kumeyaay tribe, and the dam itself was built with their labors. The Franciscans planned and supervised it, but the Indians certainly built it as they did virtually everything in the entire history of the missions. Kilns were fired up onsite, a mortar of lime and seashells was compounded, and large rocks from the surrounding land used as the building blocks. Next, an aqueduct was constructed to carry the water to the mission crops, six miles away. Already the Franciscans had brought agriculture, even today California's largest industry, to the state, and when it was clear that the success of agriculture was dependent on irrigation, they brought irrigation to the state. Having proved their worth as architects, engineers and construction managers, they became hydraulic engineers. The efforts in constructing the irrigation works were apparently well worth it, because San Diego was soon sending to market olives for oil, hemp and wheat, and in 1821, reported 21,000 bushels of wheat, barley and corn. This might have been the apogee of San Diego's story.

Even before official secularization, the military and civilian authorities had begun encroaching on the mission holdings. In 1823, mission lands were taken and given to military officers in return for service. In 1827, when the fathers objected to supplying the military with provisions without compensation, the governor ordered that they be requisitioned by force.

The conversion of mission buildings and lands from ecclesiastical to secular authorities created tremendous challenges with regard to the preservation of the artwork and treasures in the missions. The Franciscans made conscientious efforts to preserve the artifacts, moving them from mission to mission, often just ahead of civilian interlopers. Many of the faithful from the decaying missions preserved and protected the treasures in their homes, often through more than one generation, until they could be returned to the restored church. Even today, many of the missions have artwork that originally was located at another facility. Much of San Diego's artwork is still located at Mission San Luis Rey in Oceanside. While much of the original artwork has been recovered, much remains missing.

After the United States took control of California in 1846, the United States Army appropriated Mission San Diego as a military post. Ironically, the first unit to be stationed at Fort Stockton, as the San Diego Mission had been named, was Company B of the "Mormon Battalion." The idea of a religion that at the time was firmly committed to polygyny occupying an institution built by a religion that would not even recognize divorce is almost too ironic to contemplate. The United States Army occupied the mission buildings until 1858 and apparently left it no worse, and perhaps slightly better than they found it, covering it with a shingle roof to replace the original thatched roof. When the army left, the mission's deterioration was inevitable and rapid. It was soon reduced to an almost unrecognizable group of crumbling walls and ruins.

In 1893, fifty years after Mission San Diego was secularized, one observer noted, "Of the once proud church but a few crumbling walls remain, and the day is almost at hand, when even these will have passed away. The spot will then be marked only by the gravestones of its founders."[15] Fortunately, the author of that statement did not reckon with the foresight of Charles Fletcher Lummis, William Knowland, William Randolph Hearst, the Landmarks Club and thousands of Californians whose appreciation of the treasures in their midst gave us the monuments we have today.

Mission San Diego today:

Mission San Diego is located at: 10818 Mission Road, San Diego, CA, 92108; (619) 281-8449.
http://missionsandiego.com

The mission church is actually the fifth structure built as a mission in San Diego and the fourth one built on this site. The first one was built in 1769 on Presidio Hill above what is now "Old Town" San Diego. In 1774, Father Jayme moved the mission from that location to this site and built a new church. That church was burned in the 1775 uprising that cost Father Jayme his life. A church to replace that one was finished in 1780. That church was destroyed in an earthquake in 1803, and a new, larger church to replace that one was finished in 1813. That church was reduced to a complete ruin after secularization, and the church we see today was reconstructed from that ruin. Restoration efforts actually began as early as the 1890s, but the church was not rededicated until 1931.

Even before entering the church, San Diego's most arresting attraction—its *campanario,* or bell tower—strikes the visitor. This tower is perhaps the most common feature the comes to mind when people think of the California missions. The mission's five bell *campanario* is an artistic, architectural and photographically breathtaking tower. It is often used as *the* iconic symbol of the California missions. Only one of the five bells in the *campanario* is from the original mission. It is the large "royal" bell denoted by its crown top, which signifies that it was cast at the order of the king of Spain. When the mission found itself subject to the looting and pillaging that were the worst ravages of secularization, many of its artifacts and furnishings were appropriated by the local gentry. One of the bells had found its way to St. Joseph's church in Old Town. Two more were in the adobe house known as "Ramona's Marriage Place," the historic adobe associated with the novel Ramona. One was retrieved from the mess hall of the United States military barracks in San Diego. The largest of all of the bells—the "*Mater Dolorosa*"—was cast from the remains of five bells that had been sent to the mission from the viceroy of Mexico in 1796.

In the churchyard is a cemetery containing the remains of scores of Indians, virtually all of them victims of diseases their "saviors" brought, and virtually all in unmarked graves. Unfortunately, at San Diego as at all of the missions, one of the first things the Spanish brought to the natives was death.

Inside the church there are several items of note. First is the long, narrow shape of the church. Almost all of the early missions were constructed in this fashion, primarily because of mechanical and architectural necessity. The Franciscans did not have any practical way of stringing longitudinal supports together, and so their churches were limited in width by the size of trees available to support the roofs. A similar problem did not exist with regard to length, because the walls served as supports. Even the walls, though, were dictated in their design by architectural limitations. This is the reason the windows in most of the missions are designed to be very high up on the walls. The windows were not, as is commonly believed, high and narrow as a security means. Their placement was simply a recognition that the lower and wider the windows were, the more weight their horizontal frames would be required to bear.

The interior of the church is almost totally redone, with some work being completed as late as the 1970s. The *reredos* (ornate backdrop to the altar) was part of this restoration. There were no records and no pictures of the original workings, but these were reconstructed using surviving exemplars in other missions. While much of what we look at is reconstruction, or new construction in an old fashion, this should not diminish the grandeur of the building, nor the ancient artifacts it houses.

The tiles on the mission floor are of two distinct colors, the darker ones being tiles salvaged from the old church. The missions as constructed and used originally did not have pews in them. The congregation stood or kneeled on the floor as the service dictated. At the time the missions were constructed, the congregants were separated by gender, men on one side, women on the other. In some of the missions, although not San Diego, there is actually a row of contrasting tiles running down the center of the church, denoting the line of separation.

Immediately inside the door of the vestibule in the church itself, there on the walls behind you are portraits of Mary, Mother of Sorrows, and Joseph, Jesus' foster father. The large painting of the Mother of Sorrows is from the original mission that was burned in 1775. It was saved from the fire and from the subsequent deterioration of secularization to be placed in the current church. Just past these portraits is a large wooden crucifix that was carved in Mexico. In the baptistery is the oldest wood carving in the mission, an image of Saint Anne, the mother of Mary and the patroness of mothers. The baptismal font itself is a replica of the one in the church in Mallorca where Junipero Serra was baptized. All of the stations of the cross lining the church's walls are hand-carved and were brought from Spain for the mission.

One of the most striking—some would say startling—fixtures in Mission San Diego is the armless *corpus* of Christ on the cross. It is not a less-than-intact survivor of the mission's travails. The *corpus* is older than the church, and possibly older than the Franciscan presence in California. It was carved in Italy in the 1700s but is a fairly recent addition to Mission San Diego. It was purchased for the church by the pastor in the 1930s. He found it on trip to Rome at a bargain price because of the missing arms. He had every intention of having the arms restored before using it in his church. At the time, a group of the Sisters of Nazareth were in residence at Mission San Diego and conducting a school there. One of the nuns, when she saw the statue and was told of the plans to restore it, had a better idea. She reminded the pastor that St. Teresa of Avila had once commented that "the people must be the arms of Christ." Obviously that resonated with the priest, because the crucifix was installed as is.

To the left of the altar is a small polychrome statue of Saint Gabriel the Archangel, and to the right, one of Junipero Serra. The Serra statute comes from Mallorca, Junipero Serra's birthplace. The statues exhibit a uniquely Hispanic touch, seen in several of the missions: Many of them are clothed. Miniature robes, veils and sandals have been made for the statues, and they are often changed as the liturgical seasons dictate.

Buried beneath the sanctuary are Father Luis Jayme, California's first martyr; Father Juan Figuer, who died in 1784; Father Juan Mariner, who died in 1800; Father Jose Panto, who died in 1812 (supposedly poisoned by a disgruntled neophyte); and Father Fernando Martin, the last Franciscan to serve at San Diego, who died in 1838.

In 1976, more than 200 years after Junipero Serra erected a thatch-roofed church of mud bricks in San Diego, Mission San Diego de Alcala was designated a minor basilica by Pope Paul VI. Originally the term *basilica* referred to a specific architectural style of church, the primary element of which was its cruciform structure. Over time and in current usage, the term means a church that is imposing, beautiful and historically significant. San Diego de Alcala is certainly all of that; imposing in its stark, almost sere, whitewashed exterior, beautiful in the restoration of its interior and artwork, and important as the "Mother Church" of all of the California missions.

Mission San Diego - armless Corpus.

Mission San Diego - bell tower.

53

Endnotes

1   Englehardt, Zephyrin. *The Franciscans in California.* Harbor Springs: Holy Childhood Indian School, 1897.

2   Bancroft, Hubert Howe. *History of California, Vol. I.* San Francisco: The History Company Publishers, 1886.

3   Ibid.,152-153

4   Palou, Francisco. *Relación Histórica de la Vida del Ven. P. Fr. Junipero Serra.* Translated by C. Scott Williams. Pasadena: George Wharton James, 1913.

5   Englehardt, Zephyrin. *The Franciscans in California.* Harbor Springs: Holy Childhood Indian School, 1897.

6   Geiger, Maynard, trans. *Letter of Luis Jayme, O.F. M. San Diego, October 17, 1772.* Los Angeles: Dawson's Book Shop, 1970.

7   Englehardt, Zephyrin. *The Franciscans in California, 226.*

8   Ibid., 226

9   Sandos, James A. *Converting California: Indians and Franciscans in the Missions.* New Haven : Yale University Press, 2004.

10   Englehardt, *The Franciscans in California.* 230.

11   Bancroft , *History of California, Vol. I* , 316.

12   Ibid. 316

13   Tibesar, Antonine. *Writings of Junipero Serra, Vol. III.* Washington, D.C: Academy of American Franciscan History, 1956.

14   Geiger, Maynard. *Franciscan Missionaries in Hispanic California – 1764-1848; A Biographical Dictionary.* San Marino: Huntington Library, 1969.

15   Powers, Laura Bride. *The Story of the Old Missions of California – Their Establishment, Progress and Decay.* San Francisco: Wm. Doxey, 1893.

Chapter 5

SAN CARLOS BORROMEO

*L*a Mision de San Carlos Borromeo del Rio Carmelo (The Mission of Saint Charles Borromeo of the Carmel River), the second mission, was founded on June 3, 1770, less than a year after founding San Diego and well before that first mission was anything approaching a sure thing. This mission is named after Saint Charles Borromeo, a sixteenth-century Italian nobleman, archbishop and cardinal of Milan. "De Carmelo" simply means "of Carmel," and was added to distinguish it, by the name of the nearby Carmel River, from another church with the same name founded at the *presidio* in Monterey. In December of 1771, Junipero Serra moved the mission to the present location in the Carmel valley. Thus, what all refer to as the mission at Monterey is not in fact in Monterey, but in the Carmel valley six miles away. Today it is almost always referred to as Mission Carmel. St. Charles's feast day is celebrated by the Catholic Church on November 4.

Again, Portola's failure to find Monterey Bay on his earlier trip is perplexing. Captain Perez of the *San Antonio* had no trouble recognizing it. Perhaps the different perspectives (Vizcaino and Perez both approached by sea and Portola was traveling on the land) made the difference. At any rate, on this journey it seems as if everyone knew Monterey as soon as they saw it.

The news of the "rediscovery" of Monterey Bay and the founding of the mission there was joyously received in New Spain and in Mexico City. Plans were made to proceed full bore with the mission project. Serra's request for more priests was willingly met. The plan for the missions called for two priests at each mission: One to conduct the spiritual affairs of the mission and the other to see to the temporalities, and each to provide company for the other cultured and educated man laboring in the wilderness. In early 1771, ten more priests were dispatched to Monterey, and Serra was ready with plans to distribute them to San Diego, San Buenaventura, San Gabriel, San Antonio and San Luis Obispo. With the exception of San Buenaventura, which would not be begun until 1782, Serra did have all of the other missions underway within two years of the arrival of this new blood. When Serra left San Diego with Portola to locate the elusive Monterey Bay and found the second of the missions there, he was taking more than just the next step in a vague plan formulated years earlier in Mexico City. This was the first real test of the realities of that plan. Would it work, to found a mission and then, before it was even finished, go on to found a second? And before that one was established, to found a third and so on until the chain was completed? Initially the plans called for missions and *presidios* at San Diego and Monterey and halfway between those two ports. It soon became obvious, though, that the tremendous distances involved in settling Alta California would necessitate more missions. Serra's zeal for souls was such that he often got out in front of the military commanders of California, to the distress of all concerned. Since the original plans called for a minimum of two priests at each mission, as soon as they had two extra priests, both Junipero Serra and his immediate successor Fermin de Lasuen, took that as all the justification they needed to found another mission.

The Spanish government had always planned to make Monterey the capitol of Alta California. Mission San Carlos, initially founded at the *presidio* in Monterey, very quickly and for a long period of time became the "capitol" of the California missions. It was here that Junipero Serra established his headquarters, and San Carlos remained the headquarters of the California missions until 1815. Because of its proximity to both the Spanish and Mexican capitols of California, Mission San Carlos was very much involved in the political machinations of early California.

It was from Mission San Carlos that Father Serra directed the establishment of seven more missions over the next thirteen years. Besides being Serra's headquarters, San Carlos was the mission he was most personally attached to. In fact, in his very first letter to Inspector General Galvez, written the day before he even dedicated San Carlos, he commented that he planned to stay in Monterey until God decided otherwise.*

The founding of this second mission, as with the founding of San Diego, was tempered by the realities of the harsh life they all faced. On the same day that Mission San Carlos was founded, a burial was performed for a member of the *San Antonio's* crew, one Alejo Nino who died of unspecified causes, likely scurvy. While Serra forged ahead with his ambitious plans for more missions, an obviously relieved Portola lost no time in returning to Mexico City. He turned the governorship of California over to Pedro Fages and a month later sailed for Mexico never to return to California. Portola's departure was a loss to the mission efforts. Portola and Serra had a deep mutual respect for each other and seemed to be able to appropriately share the duties each was charged with. With Portola's departure, the next many years would see fractious disputes over authority between the religious and secular leaders of California.

Mission San Carlos was initially founded on the site of the *presidio* in Monterey. That church, the oldest continually used church in California, is generally referred to as the Royal Presidio Chapel, and is located on Church Street in downtown Monterey. The two churches— the one at the *presidio* and the one on Carmel valley—have a very similar design. The same architect designed both.

Unlike the situation in San Diego, where the proximity of soldiers and natives was a problem, it seems that at Monterey, the problem was more likely the proximity of soldiers and priests. This strained relationship was the reason behind the relocation of the church. Serra claims that soldiers assigned to work at the mission were told to take their rations at the mission, but to work for the *presidio*. Pedro Fages, the new governor (Military Commandant of Alta California was his actual title), complained that the construction of the mission compromised the security of the *presidio*. There were complaints regarding the placement of the cemetery, the cross in the cemetery and the burial place of a soldier. Whatever the facts, the picture in retrospect is one of two grown men, Serra and Fages, feuding in a most unseemly manner.

The strained relationship between Governor Fages and Serra was not only due to the location of buildings. Together, Serra and Portola

---

* Serra did in fact stay at San Carlos Borromeo until he died fifteen years later.

had undergone the rigors of establishing a foothold in Alta California and the horrors of establishing a Spanish presence in the new land. Serra undoubtedly viewed himself with some justification as the seasoned veteran in the colonial efforts. Fages became the "new kid on the block." He was an ambitious career soldier. He saw in his position in California an opportunity to enhance his reputation and further his career. He was apparently an imperious and rigid man, and Junipero Serra was equally so. Within a month of taking command, Fages found himself the subject of a letter of complaint Junipero Serra wrote to his old friend, Visitador General Don Joseph de Galvez. Serra complains that Fages misappropriated some lanterns intended for the missions. This insignificant event was probably little more than an opportunity for Serra to offer a complaint about Fages.

The real source of conflict was that Serra wanted to forge ahead immediately and found missions to both the north and south of Monterey. Fages was cautious about spreading his troops too thin, and would not allow missions to be built if he could not provide what he felt was adequate security for them. But Serra, having left mission number one at San Diego in charge of two of his priests, and having just started mission number two at Monterey, was already thinking of mission number three. "I earnestly entreat you," he writes Father Palou in Baja California, "to send two more missionaries who with the four here, will enable us to establish the mission of San Buenaventura, in the channel of Santa Barbara that land being much adapted for the purpose than San Diego, Monterey, or any other yet discovered." [1] As will be seen, although Mission San Buenaventura was to be a long time coming, Serra would not be deterred from his grand scheme of a chain of missions.

As with all of the missions, San Carlos started as crude adobe chapel. Early on, Serra envisioned this mission as a "noble stone church." The adobe building, though, was to serve until long after Serra's death. With the adobe still drying on Mission San Carlos, Serra traipsed off to found San Antonio, forty miles to the south, on July 14, 1771. He does not abandon San Carlos at Carmel, nor San Diego. He is the father president of all of the missions; throughout the founding of all the missions, Serra never diminished in his efforts toward any one of them. If God had given him the days he no doubt would have begun building missions in the Central valley.

58

Despite the removal of the mission from the immediate precincts of the *presidio*, conflicts between soldiers and priests continued. Correspondence between Serra and Fages and the viceroy of Mexico continued and was unremittingly sniping. Because the Franciscans were better than the military at documenting events, the record we have is primarily Serra's, and leaves the impression that Fages was unyielding and unrealistic. Without a doubt Serra was equally so. Serra, as has been noted, was well regarded in political inner circles in Mexico City. He apparently tired of the endless "he said-he said" cycle of correspondence and decided to tell his side of the story without the many months' delay attendant to correspondence between Monterey and Mexico City. In October 1772, Serra left for Mexico to present his case in person. In March of 1773, he appeared before Viceroy Antonio Bucareli in Mexico City.

Serra presented a petition with thirty-two recommendations. Bucareli accepted most of them. One of those recommendations was the removal of Lieutenant Fages as military commander of Alta California. Serra prevailed in this recommendation, another indication of the tremendous political capital he had. He would have been wise to take the victory he had gained and move ahead. Unfortunately, he went two steps further: he made a specific recommendation that Jose Francisco Ortega, serving as the commandant at San Diego, be given the job. Then Serra, a man of some discretion and political acumen, made what may have been the most serious political mistake of his career. He specifically recommended that Don Francisco de Rivera y Moncado not be given the job. This was to prove a most unwise overreaching on Serra's part, and one that would trouble him, and the California missions, for the next seventy years. The Viceroy rejected Serra's recommendations regarding a successor to Fages and did in fact appoint the maligned Rivera to the post.

The Spanish court in Mexico City was a small and jealous group, and the machinations surrounding political appointments were at least as toxic as those we see in our process today. There was jostling and maneuvering and attempts to affect the outcome of pending appointments. Although Rivera and his supporters won in this case, and while he was pleased and honored at the appointment, he was furious when he found out that Junipero Serra had recommended someone else, and he found particularly disturbing the fact that Serra had made negative comments about his qualifications for the job. From then on, relations between Junipero Serra and Don Fernando Rivera were unremittingly contentious, and Fernando Rivera arrived in Monterey in March of 1774 to take up his new duties as governor of Alta California already at odds with the most influential man in that region. Considering the relationship between Serra and Rivera at arm's length, it does not take a terribly vivid imagination to arrive at the conclusion that the problems between them arose simply from the fact that Rivera was as devoted to his king as Serra was to his God. This gulf between king and God is intractably woven into the entire history of the mission project.

Regardless of this resentment, everything known about Fernando de Rivera suggests that he would have done his duty as he saw it, and would not let personal feelings interfere with that duty. Rivera had served in the Spanish army since he was seventeen, first as a common soldier, but soon rising to officer ranks. In 1751, he was called from the ranks and installed as the captain of the *presidio* at Loreto in Baja California. Such a jump in rank was virtually unheard-of in the Spanish army. Rivera must have demonstrated truly impressive capabilities to merit it. He was an officer who, from all records, put his duty first, his soldiers' welfare next and himself last of all. He served admirably in a variety of posts, not just in California but all over the southwest. He was in the first expedition to arrive in San Diego in 1769, a full month before Portola and Serra. He had accompanied Portola on the ill-fated hunt for Monterey. He served as sub-governor of Alta California for four years, and then as governor of Baja California when Viceroy Bucareli restructured the posts. He would die in a battle with the Yuma Indians near the Colorado River in 1781. Particularly telling with regard to Rivera's value system is the fact that he apparently served the last seven years of his life without pay, and at his death in the service of his country, his wife and children received no compensation, being saved from absolute poverty only by the generosity and charity of his brother.

Rivera and Serra, two strong and complex men, were each being asked to pacify and settle a huge expanse of wild territory with the barest minimum of resources. Rivera, who was charged with maintaining peace and order throughout all of upper California, never had more than sixty soldiers, generally drafted from the lowest ranks of Spanish society. Serra was asked to build a mission every six months and never given anything more than two priests per mission to maintain them. When not building missions, overseeing missions, supervising priests over an area of approximately seven thousand square miles or meddling in politics, he didn't hesitate to lament his own failings. "Nevertheless I do not regret to have founded the missions. Through our efforts some souls have gone to heaven from Monterey, San Antonio and San Diego…If not all have yet become Christians here it is because of our ignorance of their language. I often imagine that my sins make me unworthy of the gift to converse with them in their language."[2]

Serra and Rivera were able to hold their personal differences in check until external forces bought things to a head. As has already been detailed, in Rivera's mind the revolt in San Diego and the death of Father Jayme called for swift and punishing retribution. In the minds of Father Serra and the rest of the Franciscans, the prudent course of action called for "turning the other cheek." The end result was a direct and uncomfortable confrontation between the priests and the *presidio*. With the taking of the Indian prisoner from the temporary church in San Diego, Rivera had exercised his political and military power to achieve an immediate victory. Father Fuster's "excommunication" of him for the act, though, caused him great personal and emotional suffering. By several accounts, he lost his effectiveness as governor because of it. Viceroy Bucarelli once more was forced to intervene. He restructured the chain of command of the two Californias, instructed Governor Felipe de Neve to take up residence in Monterey, and had Rivera return to Loreto, in Baja. In February 1777, Rivera left Monterey. The score was apparently now Serra, two; governors, zero.

Felipe de Neve replaced Rivera with a new title of governor of the Californias in February of 1777, and almost immediately he, too, became embroiled in a controversy with Junipero Serra. However, the issue between de Neve and Serra was not church interference in government affairs, but rather government interference in church affairs.

A little bit of Catholic doctrine is needed as background. Of the seven sacraments of the Roman Catholic church, four of them— baptism, reconciliation, Eucharist, and anointing of the sick or last rites—would ordinarily be effected by priests. Two others, confirmation and holy orders, would ordinarily be effected by bishops; and one, the sacrament of matrimony, is actually effected by the two parties to the marriage themselves. The term "ordinarily" is one loved by lawyers and liturgists, almost as much as its inevitable companion "exceptional." Canon law allows that in "exceptional" circumstances, the rite of confirmation may be delegated by a bishop to an ordained priest. Certainly if there were exceptional circumstances existing for a bishop to exercise this delegation, they existed in California in the seventeenth century. The nearest bishop was 600 very difficult miles away in Sonora, Mexico; California did not have a bishop until 1835.

Given the inaccessibility of a bishop and the importance of the sacrament of confirmation,* Serra petitioned Rome for authority to perform this rite. The petition was granted, but because of the sharing of power between church and state in New Spain, it had to be approved by royal authority as well. This approval was obtained and Serra was notified of the permission in mid-June of 1778, with the condition that his authority to confirm would expire in 1784. He wasted no time in exercising this new prerogative: before the end of August he had confirmed 180 persons at San Carlos, and immediately left on a trip to San Diego, performing confirmations at each mission on the way there and back. By the end of 1779, he had confirmed more than 2,000 Indians, and a smaller number of Spanish military personnel and colonists.

If Antonio Bucareli had not died in 1779 and if the Spanish government had not been prone to periodic restructuring of its bureaucracy in Mexico City, the question of authority to confirm might never have been called into question. Unfortunately, when Bucareli died, California was removed from the direct authority of the viceroy and placed under a "captain general" in Sonora. The governor of California now reported to the captain general, and it was this new captain general who then reported to the viceroy. Appointed as captain general was one Don Teodoro de la Croix.

Shortly after his appointment, de la Croix, for some unexplained reason, demanded through Governor de Neve that he obtain proof of Serra's authority to administer the sacrament of confirmation. Why de la Croix saw this as important has never been made clear, but this seemingly simple inquiry would absolutely consume the life of priests, bishop and politicians for the next two years.

---

* At confirmation, Catholics are deemed to have accepted, on their own, the responsibilities as a Catholic which were accepted for them by their godparents at baptism.

Serra's somewhat injudicious reply to de Neve's demand for proof of his authority to confirm was that if did not have authority to confirm, why had it never been questioned by Viceroy Bucareli? That sort of defiant non-response was not what de la Croix was looking for. His rejoinder was that it mattered not to him what the viceroy may have done in the past: California was no longer under the direct control of any viceroy, least of all a dead one, and he, the captain general, exercised authority in these matters, and would the papers please be forwarded? Now Serra's response was that he did not actually have the papers. He had received them, reviewed them and when he was sure they granted him the authority he was seeking, had returned them to the College of San Fernando in Mexico City. Perhaps the captain general could obtain them from that institution directly? In April of 1780, a demand for the papers was repeated, along with an order that no more confirmations be performed. Serra stepped back, promised he would not confirm any more people until the matter was resolved, and pushed the matter up to his superiors at the College of San Fernando in Mexico City. Concomitantly, de Neve punted back to de La Croix and de La Croix, despite his earlier assertion of ultimate authority, had to accede to the instructions of the viceroy, now one Don Martin de Mayorga. Removed from the immediate battle lines drawn in California, the viceroy and the father guardian in Mexico City reviewed the issues and the documents so important to any question of protocol in the Spanish court. They determined that Serra had been properly granted the authority to administer confirmation, and that all was in order. The viceroy sent a letter to Governor de Neve, at least mildly remonstrating with him for interfering with Serra's work and ordering him to cooperate in assisting Serra. In September 1781, a year and a half after he had ceased confirming at the order of Captain General De La Croix, Serra—now with the blessing of Viceroy Don Martin de Mayorga—recommenced administering the sacrament. A year later, Governor de Neve was recalled to Mexico, and in September of 1782 Pedro Fages, the first governor Serra had issues with, was re-appointed to the post. Serra three, governors zero.

Serra and Fages got along no better on Fages' second go-round than they had on his first. The former issues between Serra and Fages, those of logistics and staffing for new missions, were no longer of concern. In the ten years since Fages had left, Junipero Serra had founded seven more missions. The questions of new missions or locations of missions was now a moot one; Junipero Serra had demonstrated to the civil authorities the value of the missions as important to the settlement and stability of Alta California, and the decisions regarding new missions or not had effectively been taken away from the governor of California. Now, the primary conflicts between the two men revolved around administrative issues concerning the established missions and the growing population of California. There had been a long-simmering dispute between the citizens of the town of San Jose and the Franciscans at Mission Santa Clara. Serra claims that Fages made only a pretense of examining the facts of the controversy but then "went right ahead with what he had in mind." There was a persistent problem of requiring the Franciscans to pay postage on reports they sent regarding the administration of the missions, and a complaint that there was literally not enough paper in California to prepare all the required reports. Fages stops providing wine for the Masses said at the *presidio,* and Serra stops sending the priests from the missions to say Mass at the *presidio*. Serra's most serious complaint about Fages concerns his treatment of the natives when they are accused of stealing livestock. He asks if the viceroy has directed the men under him, and Fages would be one of those men, "to castrate the gentiles, hang the gentiles, disembowel the gentiles and butcher the gentiles indiscriminately for having eaten a mare or two which had strayed in their home many leagues away. All of these sad instances have taken place under Señor Fages' administration and other instances besides of cruelty in their treatment of Christians."[3]

In their long and tumultuous history, Don Pedro Fages and Junipero Serra would always find something about the other to complain about. Personalities seemed to be an overriding catalyst that caused ongoing conflict between the two. Junipero Serra was growing old and was not well, but he continued to run "his" missions, and indeed much of California, very much with a hands-on approach.

While San Carlos more than any other mission, was Serra's mission and his home base, he did not spend his time there in calm reflection. His vision of what could be accomplished now went well beyond the original plans for missions in San Diego, Monterey and halfway between. He traveled not just to the other missions as they were founded, but even back to Mexico when the demands of his missions required it. He continued to handle a dizzying array of logistical and personnel matters. In one letter written during his time at San Carlos, he discusses at length and in excruciating detail the disposition of ten new missionaries recently arrived; cases of supplies received by ship; plans for the celebration of the Feast of Corpus Christi; the training of some Indian boys as acolytes; plans for missions in San Francisco, Santa Clara, San Buenaventura, and San Antonio; the care of several of the missionaries who were ill; money and provisions that must be properly distributed; packing cases full of tools that had arrived; whether or not it would be wise to remove some natives from the Santa Barbara Islands; the need for more troops to defend the missions; the distribution of some bells that had arrived for the missions; the necessity of making sure each ship that came to Monterey had a store of meat for the friars; the number of natives baptized; and concern about some livestock that had not been received. He appends to another letter a five-page memorandum detailing supplies ranging from plows, axes and spades to "four *tercios* of flour, one *tercio* of rice, and one *tercio* of red beans."

He also continued to be a thorn in the side of the Spanish military and civilian authorities, particularly with regard to responsibility for the native population. A careful reading of the correspondence on this issue reveals that it was not simply a power struggle for control of the Indians, as Serra's detractors would have it. He refers to the natives he is trying to protect as "gentiles" which tells us they are not converts or mission subjects, who would be called neophytes, but rather non-converted Indians struggling to maintain their old ways in the face of increasing Spanish dominance and control over their land. Although the gentiles were not Serra's nor any Franciscan's responsibility, he did not hesitate to speak up forcefully for them.

Carmel remained under Serra's control until his death in 1784. Appointed to succeed him in February 1785 was Father Fermin de Lasuen.

The problems of Governor Don Pedro Fages did not at all end with Serra's death. To the contrary, Don Pedro Fages soon found himself embroiled in a battle with his own wife that would make his issues with Serra seem minor irritants. The domestic dispute between Eulalia Callis Fages and Don Pedro might, in today's media, be reported as

"The Prisoner of Mission San Carlos." The story was a sensational one of love, sex, betrayal and outrage.

Eulalia Callis was twenty-two when she married fifty-year-old Pedro Fages, then a captain of long experience in the Spanish army and in Alta California. Eulalia was by all accounts a woman of high fashion, but with an open and giving heart. Initially, she was not thrilled with the prospect of moving to California, but on being assured that Monterey was not an outpost of barbarism, she agreed. On the trip from San Diego to Monterey, she was so stricken by the impoverished and naked lifestyle of the Indians that she began giving away her own clothes, until one of her servants reminded her that if she continued, she herself would be naked by the time they got to Monterey. When they arrived in Monterey the couple already had one son. Eulalia had miscarried of another child on the trip from Mexico to California, and in August of 1784 she delivered a third child, a girl. Shortly after the birth of her daughter, she returned to her earlier opinion: Alta California was no place for a woman of breeding, and she expressed her wish that her husband would resign his position and return with his family to Mexico. This, Don Pedro was disinclined to do. Things went from bad to worse, and Señor and Señora Fages took to separate bedrooms.

The arrangement was not as discomfiting to Don Pedro as Eulalia might have hoped, and one day in early 1785, she discovered him *in flagrante delicto* with a young Indian girl. One can only imagine the scene which ensued: a wronged Catalonian wife, an imperious Catalonian officer, a fumbling of clothes in disarray and a cowed servant girl, certainly more victim than temptress. Doña Eulalia flew from the house, voicing her outrage to all who would hear. A frantic Don Pedro went to the mission and asked the Franciscans to intervene, which they did, to no avail. Eulalia was not cowed by the clerics, proclaiming to them that "the devil might carry her off before she would live again with her husband." [4] Husband and wife took up separate quarters, and Eulalia instituted divorce proceedings. This was not an acceptable situation for the representative of the royal court in Alta California, especially not since he had been asked to return to Mexico to help lead an expedition to seek another land route between Mexico and Alta California. It would not do to have the governor gone while his estranged wife regaled any and all with her story of her husband's perfidy. Perhaps particularly troubling to Don Fages was that his wife's accusation were causing not a little discontent among the soldiers he commanded. Fages was considered an extreme disciplinarian by the rank and file, particularly in matters of sexual behavior. He had issued an order that soldiers who behaved "scandalously" must be severely punished, sometimes to the extent of imprisonment at hard labor. In a community as insular as Spanish Monterey, Doña Fages' tale of woe was undoubtedly the topic of many barrack-room conversations. Once more, Fages asked the Franciscans to intervene, requesting that Father Matias Noriega at San Carlos remove his wife from her quarters at the *presidio* and ensconce her at the mission. Noriega sent a subaltern to Doña Eulalia with an order to vacate her quarters and remove herself to the mission. If not intimidated by the governor of California, Señora Fages was not about to be intimidated by a junior officer with an order from a priest. She barricaded herself in her quarters with her son. Finally, her husband broke down the door, tied his unrepentant wife up, and carted her off to the mission. He placed his son in the care of relatives while he returned to Mexico.

Doña Fages was apparently held in "durance vile" at Mission San Carlos for at least two months. During those two months while she was effectively prevented from bandying her tale of woe about the *presidio* and the streets of Monterey, she was not at all deterred from telling her story. She fired off letters to the bishop in Sonora and to the assistant inspector of the *presidios*, Nicolas Soler. Her letter to Soler, written April 12, 1784, will give some idea of the type of woman Eulalia Fages was, of the depth of her feelings and of the likely justice of her cause:

> It is the case that I found my husband physically on top of one of his servants, a very young Yuma Indian girl. Well-founded suspicions and the girl's easily obtained confession put me in the position of being the sentinel who discovered the incident. Even though prudence should have prevailed (this is my crime) I was overcome by passion, which fueled the flames of my rage, which caused me to cry out publicly against this infamy. Your Honor, what person would not acknowledge the wrong that has been done to them even though the pain has passed. A few hours later this guilty party was besieged with an on-

slaught of advice and words of persuasion for her to return to her husband. It was all very well meaning. However the wound was still fresh and since the medicine was applied at the wrong time, it had no effect. Thus, dramatic measures were taken. It is from the pain of these measures that I seek Your Honor's magnanimous mercy.

Reverend Father Fray Matias Antonio de Noriega, the priest at the nearby mission, ordered that the offended party be locked in a room guarded by soldiers from the troop. Placed there incommunicado she began to prepare her case. The most important piece of evidence in this case was the girl's statement. Kneeling before the judge, the girl uttered what she could, constrained by the fear of the punishment she faced. This testimony was followed by cries to restore her (Callis's) husband's reputation (as if he had lost it with just that one woman). The judge forgot to obtain statements from everyone at the presidio who had evidence, according to the girl. In cases such as this, the law requires that the testimony be from credible witnesses, such as midwives or others who have knowledge of the situation. The proceedings of this case have been drawn up as best as can be expected under the circumstances and they have been sent to the Illustrious Bishop of Sonora. We await news of his decision with regard to the offended party. Was it not important for Your Honor to allow this woman of sound mind to be heard? Apparently not. Perhaps one fears what she will say in her defense.

There is further evidence: on Ash Wednesday in the presidio church, the priest who celebrated Mass also was the judge on the case. After reading from the Gospel and preaching the sermon, he ended by vilifying me and had the soldiers throw me out of the church. This is what he said. "Detain that woman so that I can put a gag over her mouth." He made it known that he would excommunicate anybody who spoke to me or who spoke about the matter. The error of these peoples' ways is due to their ignorance with regard to the matter. On my saints day they tied me up and transferred me to Mission San Carlos. The cloister was rigorous. There were few candles. They stood watch over me and forced me to eat even though I was sick. I conclude this wretched tale of suffering with the threats of the aforementioned Father, who said he would have me flogged and placed in shackles.

I shall consider the first insult to my person as my cross to bear. I am told that the crimes committed against me were not that serious and my desires for satisfaction are merely earthly and transitory. Hence, I am told that I should forgive my husband and return to him, a surrender that would force the most innocent party to suffer the greatest loss. If he (Fages) insists that he has suffered from my outrage, then keep me imprisoned at the disposal of the priest who can restrain me more or less according to his nature. He will not, however, close the doors to my honor and noble birth. These doors shall remain open to receive a lawful defense and Your Honor's protection.

I humbly beg you to agree to hear this petition in the form that is presented. Justice will grant me a pardon. I swear to accept what I am given. The laws that protect me will save me from poverty. I will not give up my rights during the course of the proceedings of my case.[5]

Soler, who undoubtedly knew the couple—the ruling gentry of California was a very small social circle—seems to have accepted Eulalia's account. He wrote Fages two days later, warning the governor that his behavior "cannot be tolerated," and offering to act himself as an intermediary in reconciling the couple. Still, at least until May, Pedro Fages claimed himself the injured party, a victim of his wife's outrageous, vilifying and very public accusations.

When exactly they were reconciled is not known, but reconciled they were, for in October of 1785 "the Prisoner of Mission San Carlos" was a prisoner no longer. Instead, she was writing to Mexico City on her husband's behalf, requesting that he be relieved of his duties because of poor health, and that the family be allowed to return to Mexico City. Eulalia Fages returned to Mexico in 1790, followed by her husband, Pedro Fages, a year later. Four years after that he died, leaving the fiery Doña Eulalia Fages a widow at the age of thirty-six.

In 1786 Mission San Carlos played host to the French explorer Jean Francois Galaup de la Perouse, on an expedition from the French government to determine just how much of a hold, military and political, the Spanish had on California. Perouse's observations of the mission were likely the most complete made to date by any European power other than Spain. Those observations are interesting, coming from a representative of the nation which would hold itself out as championing the rights of man. Perouse has nothing but high praise for the Franciscans who chose this life. "It is with the same truth that I shall paint these men, truly apostolic, who have abandoned the idle life of a cloister to give themselves up to fatigues, cares and anxieties of every kind. They are so strict with themselves that they have not a single room with fire though the winter is sometimes rigorous and the greatest anchorites have never led a more edifying life."[6]

As to their methods, he is less sympathetically inclined. He makes an unfavorable comparison between the missions and the slave plantations of his own country in Santo Domingo. "With pain we say the resemblance is so perfect we have seen men and women in irons or in the stocks; and even the sound of the lash might have struck our ears that punishment being also admitted though with little severity." He arrives at what seems an obvious conclusion: "...the progress of the faith would be more rapid and the prayers of the Indians more agreeable to the supreme being if they were not under constraint." But his final comment illustrates his conflicts: "I know that these men have few ideas and still less constancy and that if they are not regarded as children they escape those who have taken the trouble to instruct them. I know also that reasonings (sic) have almost no weight with them, that it is absolutely necessary to strike their senses..."[7]

Aside from his dichotomous social policy views, the French explorer likely gets credit for introducing the potato to California. He refers to the fact that, "Our gardener gave to the missionaries some potatoes from Chili, perfectly sound...I believe this root will succeed perfectly around Monterey." [8]

70

Six years later, Mission San Carlos hosted yet another famous visitor from the Age of Discovery. In December of 1792, the English explorer and navigator Captain George Vancouver, on a voyage with much the same objectives as his French predecessor, called at Monterey. Vancouver's observations of the Spanish occupancy of California reveal an almost angry frustration that Spain has asserted control over this rich territory so easily. Vancouver makes an observation that the United States and not Great Britain would exploit in just fifty years: "The Spanish monarchy retains this extent of country under its authority by a force that, had we not been eyewitnesses of its insignificance in many instances we should hardly have given credit to the possibility of so small a body of men keeping in awe and under subjection the natives of this country, without resorting to harsh or unjustifiable measures. The soldiers are totally incapable of making any resistance against a foreign invasion, an event which is by no means improbable."[9]

When Vancouver visited San Carlos, work on the stone church had just begun. One of Vancouver's crew members sketched the mission and its grounds as the work was progressing. It was Father Lasuen who began work on the "stone church" that Serra had envisioned more than twenty years earlier. Mission San Carlos was one of the few missions that actually had a trained architect for its design and building. The architect was Manuel Ruiz, from San Blas, Mexico. He was originally hired to build the Royal Chapel at the presidio in Monterey, and he agreed to design the mission at San Carlos as well. The similarity between the two buildings, both in use today, is marked.

From 1810 until approximately 1833, the history of Mission San Carlos, as with all the missions, was the history of Mexico; that is, a long, bloody war for independence followed by a series of civil disputes, as the birth pangs of a new republic.

These events had an impact on all of the missions, but in particular on Mission San Carlos, since San Carlos was the headquarters of the now-considerable Franciscan presence in California. In 1825, Mission San Carlos found itself at the center of the "loyalty oath crisis" that followed Mexican Independence and that embroiled all of Spain's Franciscan sons. The underlying issue causing conflicts between the Franciscans and the new government of Mexico was that which always follows a violent separation from the mother country: questions of loyalty and trustworthiness. The Franciscans were, almost without exception, privileged members of the upper strata of royalist Spain. They had been sent to the New World and to California with specific authority and privileges from the crown. There can be no serious suggestion now that the Franciscans could or would have agitated for the overturning of the new Mexican government, but the fear was real in 1825. That fear, coupled with the fact that the Franciscans were, for all purposes, in sole possession of the most valuable and extensive holdings in California, made their undoing inevitable. The Franciscans came under a series of interdictions and restrictions. Almost all were ordered deported, although few actually were. At least two of their number decided on their own to leave the ungrateful new government. A few were held under arrest, and ultimately they were dispossessed of all of their holdings.

Governor Louis Arguello ordered all public and clerical officials to take an oath to the new Republic. In residence at San Carlos was the then-president of the California missions, Father Vincente Francisco de Sarria. Father Sarria refused to take the oath. "My Venerable Sir and Master," he wrote, "After reflecting on the oath we are ordered to take to the federal constitution of the United Mexican States…I have decided that I cannot do it without violating what I owe to anterior obligations of justice and fidelity…" The term of the oath which Sarria found repugnant to his role as a Franciscan was one that required the deponent to "take up arms, or use their influence in favor of taking up arms for differences of political opinion." Father Sarria found that phrase incompatible with his vows as a Franciscan priest. Sarria left it to the individual conscience of the priests serving under him to decide whether they took the oath or not, and few of them did.

Sarria's position of authority and the genuine respect he enjoyed, not just within his order but among the secular authorities, made his intransigence unacceptable to the Mexican government. President Guadalupe Victoria ordered Governor Arguello to arrest Sarria and deport him to Mexico. Sarria was arrested, but never returned to Mexico. Instead he was held under house arrest at San Carlos until 1828, when he was allowed to take up residence at Soledad, where he remained until his death in 1835.

Mission San Carlos was actually secularized in 1834. The mission land was sold right up to the walls of the church; the monks at San

Carlos had to obtain an easement so they could go in and out of the church without trespassing on the land they and the neophytes had developed and that now belonged to others.

Shortly after secularization, the Franciscans left San Carlos. They had no authority over the Indians, and no land to be worked. Governor Pico, in 1845, declared the property abandoned and ordered it to be sold at auction. There were no takers. The building sat empty and falling into disrepair. Father Sadoc Villarasa, the pastor at Monterey, became concerned about the decaying state of the mission roof and began moving the artwork and artifacts to the *presidio* chapel in Monterey. His foresight paid off, for just a year later in 1851, the mission roof collapsed and the interior of the church was left open to rain and the deprivations of raiders. Had this been an adobe, and not a stone church, the walls would have soon crumbled into nothing.

In 1859, President James Buchanan returned the church to the possession of the Catholic church in California, but nothing was done with the ruins until about 1882, when Father Angelo Cassanova, the pastor at Monterey, took an interest and began plans for its restoration in time for the centennial of Junipero Serra's death in 1884.

Father Cassanova's zeal was admirable but his skills in restoration questionable. He replaced the collapsed roof with a steep-pitched shingled roof, which gave the old Moorish architecture the look of a misplaced New England church.* That roof remained until 1931, when Harry Downie, considered by many to be the second founder of Carmel Mission and its second patron saint, was hired to restore the church to its earlier glory. Originally hired in 1931 to reconstruct the reredo at San Carlos, Mr. Downie ended up devoting virtually the rest of his life to restoring and preserving not just Carmel, but several of the California missions. He spared himself not at all in his efforts, salvaging and using as much original material as possible and faithfully restoring the church and its interior from original drawings and plans. Historic preservation and restoration has made great strides in the past eighty years, and today Downie is sometimes criticized for not more carefully documenting and noting the ruins on which he based his work. Supposedly he once said, "I did it the way they would have done

---

* It is this awkward representation of a California mission that Junipero Serra is holding in his hand in the Statuary Hall of the United States Capitol.

it, if they'd had a little money." Imperfect as Mr. Downie's work may be by today's standards, had it not been for him it is likely that the Carmel Mission we enjoy today would be much less than it is.

Mission San Carlos Borromeo today:

Mission San Carlos Borromeo is located at 3080 Rio Road, Carmel, CA, 93923. (831) 624-3600.
http://www.carmelmission.org

The mission we see today is the seventh church built for Mission San Carlos Borremeo. Its predecessors range from crude log-and-thatch, temporary shelters to the existing church, completed in 1793. Mission San Carlos Borromeo is one of the four California missions that has been designated a basilica by the Catholic church.

Before going into the mission complex, there are a few items of interest on the outside. From the parking lot in front of the gift shop, look to the hills to the east. You should be able to see an area of white stone halfway up the hillside. This is the quarry that provided the stone blocks for the mission.

The fountain in the front courtyard of the mission is an interesting monument to the magnetism the missions seem to exert on almost all who come into contact with them. When the church was finished in 1793, it had a fountain located in its forecourt, as did many of the missions. That fountain disappeared during the mission's long period of neglect in the late 1800s. When the mission was restored, a new fountain—the one you see there today—was built. In 1984, on the 200 year anniversary of Junipero Serra's death, a special mass was celebrated at the mission by all of California's bishops. On that occasion, a local family returned to the mission the original fountain, which had been in their possession for more than a century. That fountain is presently in the garden to the east of the church, against the church's walls. There are plans to restore this original fountain to its original place in front of the church.

The cemetery to the right of the main entrance has its own interesting features. Buried here, generally in anonymous graves, are more than 200 Indians who labored to build the church and who died in large measure from the diseases the Spanish brought. It is startling to realize that these people, whose own structures were woven of reeds and branches, built stone upon stone so solidly that, after two hundred years of use, abuse and neglect, their church is still standing. Carmel Mission, and Missions San Juan Capistrano, Santa Barbara and San Gabriel, are the only missions of the twenty-one built of stone and not adobe.

The mission's most striking features are the unequal towers and the ornate window over the door. The towers do not represent a finished and an unfinished one, as is often mistakenly thought, but were designed to be disparate. (Manuel Ruiz, the architect at Carmel, was clearly a man not afraid to make a statement with his designs.) The church is a mixture of Spanish and Moorish architecture. There are nine bells in the higher of the two towers. They were cast at different time, dates ranging from 1690 to 1885. Most of them are original to the mission, although the oldest one was donated to the mission in the early twentieth century.

The "star" window over the main entrance has been the subject of endless speculation. It is not representative of any traditional Catholic symbolism. It is a design not found in any other California mission.* Does this beautiful window at Carmel represent a star? Or the four compass points? Or a cross? Is it a Native American design incorporated into the church? Most interesting of all is the theory that was it not meant to be any of these, but simply an ornate rectangle, which was mistakenly placed forty-five degrees off center. If the window was rotated forty-five degrees in any direction, it would fit perfectly between the two cornices below the window on the front of the church wall. It would then be a rectangular window with ornate corners. Supporting this theory is the fact that the College of San Fernando in Mexico City where Junipero Serra and Fermin Lasuen spent many years has this exact type of window, but placed so that they are rectangles—some with a vertical axis, and some with a horizontal axis, but all rectangular. Error or not, the "star" window is a beautiful accent to the exterior of Mission San Carlos, and is now commonly accepted as the defining element of the mission.

---

* There is very small window of the same design at Mission San Rafael Archangel. That building is a replica built in 1949. There is no evidence that the original building had such a window.

The interior of the church shows the positive influence a professional architect had on the design and aesthetics of the building. The
walls themselves begin curving inward to form the arch of the ceiling.
Were it not for ornate moldings two-thirds of the way up, it would be
hard to tell where the walls end and the ceiling begins.

The artwork and stations of the cross are a mixture of originals, salvaged from the abandoned church in the 1840s, and contributions to
the church as it restoration evolved. The original reredos, the decorative back piece with niches for statutes behind the altar, was destroyed
or stolen when the roof of the abandoned church collapsed in 1851.
The reredos in place today was reconstructed by Harry Downie as part
of his restoration of the church in the 1930s. It was he who, from a
few fragments recovered from the ruins, determined that the reredos
was similar to the one at Mission Dolores, based on which he modeled
his restoration. The reredos at Mission Dolores had in turn been assembled from pieces shipped from the mother church of San Fernando
in Mexico City.

The steps leading up to the altar are the originals. The largest single
step is more than ten feet wide and consists of one single slab of stone.
One can only imagine the labor, sweat, and crushed fingers that went
into the placing of that stone in 1793, with no power other than human
and animal.

From the main church itself a carved archway on the left leads into
a small chapel added about 1815. This chapel is often referred to as the
"Mora Chapel," for the bronze and marble sculpture which dominates
it. The monument—it cannot properly be called a sarcophagus, since
there are no remains in it—was sculpted in 1923-1924 by Jo Mora, an
artist famous for his depictions of early California life. While originally it was planned for the interment of Serra's remains, that plan
was abandoned because of an overwhelming sentiment on the part
of the parishioners that Father Serra had been interred, exhumed, re-
interred and exhumed quite enough. Serra's remains are where Lasuen
placed them beneath the altar floor. Mora's monument depicts all four
of the priests who are buried at Carmel Mission. Father Serra is obviously the recumbent figure on the casket. At his head stands Father
Juan Crespi. Mora used some artistic license here, for Crespi had pre-
deceased Serra by more than two years. Mora certainly did not cast
Crespi in that position by mistake; the dates of the deaths of virtually

all of the Franciscans are well-recorded. There has been the suggestion made that if you look carefully at the rendition of Father Crespi in this scene, it suggests he is shown as welcoming into eternal reward his longtime friend who is coming to join him. On the right side of the casket kneels Father Lasuen, with his arms crossed across his chest. Lasuen would succeed Serra as president of the missions. We know that Lasuen was not present at Mission San Carlos when Serra died, but Mora wanted to depict these three lifelong friends, who left Spain together and began a new age in a new world, together at the death of their leader. The final figure is Father Julian Lopez, who served at the mission barely three months before he died of tuberculosis, only thirty-five years old. Look carefully at the hands of Father Lopez. His passport papers show that Father Lopez, on his departure for California, was missing the index finger of his right hand. This is likely a fact Jo Mora was not aware of, for in the sculpture, all of the fingers are intact. The small animal at Serra's feet in the scene is not a dog, but a young bear cub. Although the "Bear Flag Republic" of California was sixty years in the future when Serra died, Jo Mora, again exercising some artistic license, felt compelled to depict the birth of the new state as connected to the death of the founder of the old one. All of the men depicted in this tableau were born in Spain, left a life of comfort and security, and traveled to the new world to do what they saw as God's bidding. They all died in their work, and all are buried at Mission San Carlos.

Finally of note in the Mora Chapel is the ornate statue of the Virgin Mary looking down on the tableau. This statue is an exquisitely-rendered depiction of Mary as queen, holding the Christ child as king. The statue has an interesting history and travels behind it. It was originally given to Inspector General Jose de Galvez by the archbishop of Mexico City in 1769 as the conquest of California began thus its nickname, *La Conquistadora*, "The Conqueress." It was placed in Mission San Diego and was there for a year. In 1770, Serra took it with him to the founding of Monterey, but later that same year returned it to Galvez who was now in La Paz. In 1775, Galvez returned the statue to Junipero Serra who placed it on the main altar at Carmel. As originally rendered, the statue was without a crown, and in 1802 Captain Juan Bautista Matute, in gratitude that his ship had survived a storm, had a silver crown placed on the Virgin's head. When the mission was secularized and ultimately abandoned, the statue was kept safe by the Cantua family, the last of the resident Indians at San Carlos Borromeo. For some reason someone decided to remove the child Jesus from Mary's arms and placed him in the arms of his father, St. Joseph, whose statue was located at the *presidio* chapel in Monterey. In 1876 one of the Cantua daughters, now Señora Maria de Dutra, took the statue into her home in Monterey, where it was garbed in her wedding dress and carefully tended by the family for fifty years.

We next hear of the statue in 1925, when it was inherited by Tulita Westfall. Twenty years later Ms. Westfall returned the statute to the mission. On her return to Mission San Carlos, it was noted that *La Conquistadora* had gained a set of beautiful gold acorn earrings. Although she originally occupied a place of honor on the main altar, upon her return she was placed in the side chapel. Here her child was reunited with her. St. Joseph, at the *presidio* chapel, was not left bereft. Harry Downie went to Mission Santa Cruz on the other side of Monterey Bay, took the Christ child from the statue of St. Joseph there, placed it in St. Joseph's arms in Monterey, and carved a replica for Santa Cruz. *La Conquistadora*, with her two-hundred-year history of ups and downs and her ultimate survival, is a fit representative for the entire California mission story.

In addition to the church at Carmel, which is still an active parish in the Diocese of Monterey, the mission contains reconstructions of the first library in California; a kitchen and dining room; and Junipero Serra's cell. The reconstructions come from timbers salvaged from the original mission. Serra may never have actually slept in this particular cell, but Serra's life is certainly reflected here.

While at Mission San Carlos, and indeed at any of the missions, look carefully at the artwork and religious paintings. You will quite often note a decided Asian-looking cast in the features of the figures represented. Pronounced cheekbones and epicanthic eyes are common. At Mission San Carlos in the Muneras Family Heitage Museum, the painting of a very Asian-looking Immaculate Conception, topped by a very Asian Trinity, are particularly noteworthy examples. There are some very practical historical reasons for such depictions. In the 1700s the Spanish had a well-established pan-Pacific trade. Their "Manila galleons" after trading in China, Japan and the Philippines, took the "great circle route" back to the Americas. This course gave them a landfall in North America at about the midpoint of the California coastline. Once the Spanish began colonizing California, all of the ships were required to make a stop at Monterey. Here they would drop off reproductions of famous religious paintings that were produced in China and shipped all over the Spanish world. It seems as if even in the eighteenth-century one of the principal items Asian countries offered for export was cheap reproductions.

Mission San Carlos - star window.

Cemetery, statue of Virgin.

"The Death of Serra"

Reconstruction of Serra's cell.

Fountain and tower.

Endnotes

1   Englehardt, Zephyrin. *The Franciscans of California.* Harbor Springs: Holy Childhood Indian School, 1897.

2   Ibid., 64

3   Tibesar, Antoine. *Writings of Junipero Serra, Vol IV*. Washington, D.C.: Academy of American Franciscan History, 1955.

4   Bancroft, Hubert Howe. *The Works of Hubert Howe Bancroft, Volume XVIII, History of California, Vol. I.* San Francisco: A.L. Bancroft & Company, Publishers, 1884.

5   Beebe, Rose Marie, and Senkewicz, Robert M. *Lands of Promise and Despair Chronicles of Early California 1535-1846*. Berkeley: Heyday Books, 2001.

6   Bancroft, *The Works of Hubert Howe Bancroft*, 436.

7   Ibid., 437

8   Ibid., 431

9   Ibid., 529

Lands Never Trodden

Chapter 6

SAN ANTONIO DE PADUA

L *a Mision de San Antonio de Padua* (The Mission of Saint Anthony of Padua), the third mission, was founded on July 14, 1771. The mission is named after a thirteenth-century Franciscan priest, Saint Anthony of Padua, who started his priestly life as an Augustinian. However, in 1220 he was taken to view the bodies of some Franciscans who had been martyred in Morocco. Anthony was so moved by their deaths that he decided to become a Franciscan and hopefully attain martyrdom himself. He did indeed become a Franciscan, but he never achieved martyrdom. St. Anthony has become the saint to invoke for finding lost articles, likely based on an incident when a novice at his abbey absconded with a psalter belonging to Anthony. Anthony prayed for its return and a suddenly conscience-stricken novice returned it forthwith. Generations of Catholics and very likely quite a few non-Catholics have invoked his help in finding misplaced items: "Tony, Tony, look around, something's lost and can't be found!" In the Catholic church the feast day of Saint Anthony is celebrated on June 13.

This mission is another testament to the initiative and optimism of Junipero Serra. Having established his missions at San Diego and Monterey, his next task, according to his original charge, was to establish one "halfway between the two." This would have been the mission San Buenaventura, but political and military troubles made that site impractical for the time. Junipero Serra was not one to waste any time or energy. He went to plan b, which he undoubtedly developed one evening after an unsuccessful argument with Governor Fages over providing troops and manpower to found San Buenaventura. San Buenaventura was put on hold, so Serra ventured into the Santa Lucia Mountains and established San Antonio. Only two years after founding the mission at San Diego, and while Carmel was still very much being built, San Antonio de Padua was founded.

San Antonio, perhaps more than any of the other missions, is a testimony to the assistance given by the natives to the Franciscans. When Junipero Serra returned to the mission a year later in 1772, he credits food from the Salinan Indians with keeping his two missionaries from starving. In charge of this mission, were Fathers Miguel Pierras and Buenaventura Sitjar. Pierras and Sitjar were an ambitious pair. In less than two years, San Antonio had a church, a house for the priests, workshops, and lodgings for soldiers and for some of the converts. Sitjar, as we shall see, was a tireless worker with a talent for success in whatever he put his hand to. He was, in addition to a preacher, liturgist and administrator, a musician, linguist and hydraulic engineer, the latter three all self-taught skills. Sitjar was to spend the rest of his life at San Antonio.

As was repeatedly the case, the initial site picked for the church and the final location of the mission today are different. Construction was originally begun at the juncture of San Miguel Creek and the San Antonio River. In drought years the creek dried up and in winter floods, the river washed out the mission. Two years later, in 1773, the mission was moved further north to the present location and a new building begun. A year later the mission listed sixty-seven cattle in its inventory.

On May 16, 1773, San Antonio became the site of the first Christian marriage in California. Juan Maria Ruiz, a soldier from Sonora, Mexico, twenty-five years of age, and Margaretta de Cortona, twenty-two years old, a Salinan woman of Mission San Antonio, were married in the as-yet unfinished church.

The natives of the San Antonio valley seemed to have accepted the *padres* in a much more open fashion than was noted at other sites. Besides the fact that the assistance of the natives at San Antonio kept the two missionaries there from starving to death, there was little in the way of hostile action towards the Spanish. The most serious incident occurred in August of 1775. A recently-converted catechumen was shot with an arrow as he was leaving mass. While this was likely a personal attack on the individual, it was characterized by the military as an attack on the mission. Captain Fernando Rivera, never one to let a challenge go unanswered, sent troops from the *presidio* at Monterey to capture the culprits, who were flogged, placed in stocks, flogged again and released. The injured man recovered and Rivera's heavy hand and arbitrary justice did not seem to set relations with the natives back.

It wasn't until 1776 that the first adobe church was completed. That same year, Colonel Juan De Anza, guiding a group of settlers to San Francisco, stopped at San Antonio. The expedition's diarist, himself a Franciscan priest, described the site as very good, but the natives as dirty and *"embarrassingly primitive in their mode of dress;"* i.e., naked. San Antonio was the first of the California missions to have a tiled roof.

Padre Sitjar was by all indications one of the more benign and amiable missionaries. He was genuinely interested in the Indians and their culture. In addition to the daunting tasks necessary to founding a working complex in the middle of the wilderness, Sitjar somehow found the time to develop a 400-page "vocabulary and phrase book of the Indians of San Antonio Mission." His work detailing the Telame and Mutsun languages is still studied by linguists and ethnologists trying to recreate the vanished languages of central California's native people.

In 1778, Father Sitjar had the neophytes begin what was eventually to be a very ambitious system of irrigation, a system that would turn out to be the most complex and most enduring of all of the mission water systems. Much of it is still visible today, and some of it is still in use today. Although they were away from the river's floodplain in their new location, they were also too far away to easily use its water. Father Sitjar designed and had the neophytes build a dam on the San Antonio River, three miles from the mission. From that site, a series of ditches, flumes and conduits carried water to a reservoir adjacent to the mission complex. Once the water was on the mission ground, more ditches moved the water through a complex system of *lavanderias*, drainage fields, a millrace, a two-story grist mill and finally to the wheat fields. The full works took almost twenty years to complete, but some of those irrigation ditches built by the local natives still water California's fields. This work is considered one of the most impressive engineering accomplishments in California's early history. From all available records, Sitjar never had any formal training in hydraulics or engineering, and for sure none of workmen had any previous experience. Buenaventura Sitjar died on September 3, 1808, after a brief but painful illness. By its description, the fatal malady was undoubtedly appendicitis.

San Antonio in 1779 was one of the first missions to assign positions of authority to the native population. The Franciscans acceded to this arrangement, not because they were in the forefront of empowerment of the Indians, but because they saw it as a way to stave off complete abrogation of their authority over the Indians, and because Governor de Neve ordered it. Even once appointed, the native leaders—either *alcades* (mayors) or *regidores* (one who manages)—were seriously limited in their power. Most limiting of their authority was the fact that they were appointed by Franciscans and not chosen by any process of the people they supposedly governed. They themselves were subordinate to the Franciscans, and subject to corporal punishment on order of the priests. Conversely, they were not allowed to bring any charges against the Franciscans. Their primary role, it seems, was to operate as the link between Indians and the Franciscans in matters of faith and morals. They maintained order and discipline in the mission communities and did not hesitate to impose corporal punishment themselves. They communicated to the mission Indians the rules of conduct, particularly in matters of sexual mores according to the Catholic church. It was this last issue, that of imposing seventeenth-century Spanish moral values on the California natives, that led to a spectacular crime of passion at Mission San Antonio.

While there are unfortunately many records of abuse, rape and murder of women at various missions—sometimes by husbands, sometimes by frustrated lovers, sometimes by Spanish soldiers—Mission San Antonio has the distinction of being the site of the murder of a husband by an apparently sexually outraged wife. One Eulalia (no last name given, and not to be confused with Eulalia Fages from Mission Carlos), had been married to her husband Juan for several years. In December of 1800 she reported that the late Juan had died by choking while smoking. The Spanish soldiers suspected otherwise, and Eulalia and several men were placed under arrest. Eventually it was determined that Eulalia, her lover Primo, and his brother Ventura had killed Juan one night while they were away from the mission. Eulalia and Primo had been carrying on a well-known affair for many years. Each of them had been previously punished for their derelictions, Primo with a flogging and Eulalia by having her hair shorn.

Although their desire to be together, frustrated by the fact that each was married, was the primary motivation for their crime of passion, there is also evidence that Eulalia was that all-too-common phenomenon in Spanish California, a sexually abused woman. Eulalia's ultimate revenge for the abuse was, as she testified, to tear his testicles from his body. Whether or not there is the possibility of "death by testicular torsion" is unknown, but certainly Juan's final minutes were not pleasant, and when his body was recovered his testicles were indeed partially torn from his body. This is the second Eulalia to make her mark in mission history by demanding retribution from an erring husband. Like Eulalia Fages, she was clearly not a woman to be trifled with in affairs of the heart. Governor Fages, lamenting his woes with his Eulalia twenty-five years earlier, would undoubtedly have considered himself a fortunate man had he known of the type of revenge this Eulalia would extract on her husband.

Justice as rendered to the perpetrators in this case took some shortcuts from the usually meticulous adherence to judicial procedure under Spanish rule. None of the defendants had legal counsel; it is doubtful if they could have understood what was happening. Procedural requirements were brushed aside and the review by higher authorities was clearly not pursued with much rigor. On December 31, 1801, Primo and Ventura were found guilty of homicide and were sentenced to be hanged. Since there was a dearth of hangmen in Spanish California, they were instead executed by firing squad, and are buried in the cemetery at Mission San Antonio. Eulalia was found guilty as an accomplice to the crime and was sentenced to six years at hard labor, which she served at the mission *monjera* (the quarters for unmarried women in the mission).

In 1801, Mission San Antonio was also the site of the first autopsy in California. Father Francisco Pujol, in residence at San Antonio, had been asked to go to Mission San Miguel to assist the *padres* there who had suddenly been taken ill with a debilitating malady. On this mission of mercy, Father Pujol was stricken with the same illness and, while the priests at San Miguel recovered, Father Pujol died shortly after his return to San Antonio. Poisoning was suspected, so an autopsy was performed. The autopsy on Father Pujol was at least inconclusive. On opening the abdomen, "the stench that came out left no room for further examination." This less-than-scientific observation somehow led to the conclusion that father Pujol had been poisoned.*

A new church was begun in 1810 and completed in 1813. This is the only one of the California missions with a barrel-vaulted *españdana*, which was added to the completed church in 1821. Interestingly, San Antonio de Padua in California is remarkably similar in design to another Mission San Antonio, likely the most famous mission in the entire United States: Mission San Antonio de Valero, in San Antonio, Texas, better known as the Alamo. San Antonio in Texas had the same arched façade and vaulted *españada*.

Mission San Antonio was secularized in 1834. The church itself and its immediate lands remained in the hands of the Franciscans, but with no land to work and no herds to maintain, a steady decline began. Many, if not most, of the mission churches have interred in their walls or floors the remains of Franciscans who labored there. In 1835, San Antonio had the distinction of having interred, to the left of the altar, a priest who had never served there. Father Vicente Sarria had been serving at Mission Soledad when, on May 24, 1835, he died an apparently protracted and painful death. While Sarria was *in extremis*, word was sent to Father Mercado at San Antonio to come and perform the last rites. Mercado arrived shortly after Sarria died, and because Mission Soledad was at that time mostly abandoned except for Father Sarria, Mercado made the decision to have Sarria's body carried thirty miles to San Antonio for internment.

In 1845, Governor Pico offered the mission holdings for sale for $8,200. There were no takers. Infrequent and half-hearted attempts at maintaining the mission were made by various of the priests assigned there, perhaps the most notable being that of Father Dorotea Ambris, not a Franciscan but a secular priest of native origin who had been born in Mexico and ordained at Santa Barbara. Father Ambris came to the abandoned mission in 1851 and stayed, doing his best for thirty-one years.

In 1863 the church and thirty-three surrounding acres were returned to the Franciscans by President Abraham Lincoln. Father Ambris continued his work with a small contingent of natives he had attracted to his church. When Father Ambris died in 1882, the mission truly

---

*   This unfortunate "poisoning" at San Miguel and its fallout are discussed in detail in the chapter on San Miguel.

fell into disrepair. Much of its artwork was moved to Mission San Miguel for safekeeping. Mission San Miguel, the nearest mission to San Antonio, still contains many of the latter's paintings and statutes. As was generally the case with the abandoned missions, the roof tiles were most vulnerable to pilferage. Once the roof tiles were gone, the adobe walls quickly melted in the winter rains. For most of the rest of the nineteenth century the mission crumbled until only the façade and a few walls remained.

On June 13, 1903, the feast day of Saint Anthony, the California Historic Land Marks League chose San Antonio as its poster child for a campaign to restore the missions, and the task of renovation of all the missions began. For many years thereafter, every June 13, a celebration was held in the old ruins. Candles were sold for a dollar each and the money was used for restoration of the mission. Harry Downie, most famous for his work at Mission San Carlos, also supervised much of the restoration work at San Antonio.

The process of restoration at San Antonio must have given the mission aficionados a taste of the trials the Franciscans faced two hundred years earlier. Torrential rains in the fall washed out the work accomplished during the summer, and the earthquake of 1906 undid virtually everything that had been accomplished. For another forty years, little more than maintenance was done on the crumbling ruins. In 1939, the United States Army acquired most of the surrounding land from the Hearst family and established the Hunter-Ligget Military Reserve, where the mission is located today. Fort Hunter Ligget is still in operation as a training ground for armored and mechanized forces. In 1947 a disheartened fan of Mission San Antonio lamented, "Hope for restoration is finally dead."

But San Antonio, like most of the California missions, just would not die. In 1948, with the help of a grant from the Hearst Foundation, serious work on reconstructing the mission began. The original adobe walls, which now were little more than melted piles of mud, were used to form bricks for new walls. Period tools and techniques of the eighteenth-century were used in rebuilding the mission, as were the original timbers and as much wood as could be salvaged. On June 4, 1950, the reconstructed Mission San Antonio was rededicated. The mission continues today as an active Catholic church of the Diocese of Monterey.

Mission San Antonio today:

Mission San Antonio is located on the Hunter Liggett Military Reservation, 23 miles Southwest of King City off of Highway 101. Although it is located on a United States army base, it is available and open to the general public. PO Box 803, Jolon, CA, 93928. (831) 385-4478
http://www.sanantoniomission.org

San Antonio is today considered one of the best-restored of all the missions. Its location, in the oak-covered valley largely unchanged from the way the Franciscans found it, gives the visitor an opportunity to savor the sense of what life in the original missions must have been. In fact, the population of the mission environs is less now than it was at the mission's height.

San Antonio is one of the missions where the visitor may find more of interest in the grounds than the buildings. The grounds at San Antonio show much of Father Sitjar's original irrigation works. The planning and work that went into this system is impressive. When grade did not work to their advantage in moving water, the Indians built above-ground mill-races that allowed them to create their own grade. Very well-constructed underground piping systems were developed using pipes designed with one end wider than the other so that they would fit together. The sections of pipes, as they were laid in the ground, were protected from the shifting of the earth by fired roof tiles laid over them, and by a crushed-pottery bed. The grist mill at San Antonio is one of the few surviving at the California missions. It was one of the earliest water-powered industrial ventures in California. The water source was an artificial lake three miles away from the works. Although at present the mill is not working, its wheel and internal workings are clearly observable. Prior to the construction of this mill, all grain was ground by hand, individual women using mortars and pestles to grind whatever was needed for their own family. With the implementation of the water-powered mill, the mission natives began producing grain for the community at large and even for sale beyond the mission complex. These water mills were the first commercial industries in California.

Clearly visible is the stone floor of the long-disappeared threshing mill, as well as tanning vats and washing pools. The Franciscans had an extreme appreciation for the economies of water. Water brought to the mission grounds was conducted through a series of works. A sophisticated state-of-the-art filtering system, using sand and charcoal, was used. From the filtering tank, water was distributed in a sanitary, hierarchal order. First to receive the water were the wells and ponds for drinking and cooking. From there, it went to pools for bathing and laundry, next to the tannery, and it was then diverted to turn the mill and finally returned to the earth and, ultimately, the water table, by being directed in the gardens and fields. Virtually all of this complex— some sections in better repair than others—is easily visible today.

Two of San Antonio's most famous artifacts are also two of its most mysterious. In the courtyard in front of the mission are two figureheads, purported to represent Saints Peter and Paul. Supposedly they were presented to the mission by grateful sailors from a ship that had survived a terrible storm off the California coast. The sailors had prayed to Saint Anthony for deliverance; he is not only the saint of lost articles, but the saint to invoke for protection from shipwrecks, since he himself survived one. When their ship survived the storm, they presented the ship's figureheads to Mission San Antonio. There are a few problems with this story. First, in the seventeenth and eighteenth centuries, ships' figureheads were almost always female. Saints of either gender would never be used as figureheads by the devout and superstitious Spanish sailors. Their position on the ship's prow was a punishing one, and a saint would never be subjected to such exposure. Next, a ship may have had a figurehead, and it may even have been that of a saint. But ships *never* had two figureheads. Finally, the two heads at San Antonio are not carved in the fashion of a ship's figurehead, which would presuppose the head coming at an angle from the body, so that it could be fitted to the sloping prow of the ship. The two figures at San Antonio appear to be heads from a straight, up-and-down body, if ever there was a body attached.

In the church itself the painted borders of oak leaves and acorns were restored from photos taken in the late 1800s. Father Doroteo Ambris, who served as pastor from 1851 to 1882, would never allow any photographs to be taken of the interior of the church. Fortunately, one photographer persisted, and finding out one day that Father Ambris was away, he snuck into the church and took at least one picture. This picture proved invaluable in the reconstruction of the church that began in 1906.The ceiling beams and carved wooden doors are the originals, as are most of the statues. Above the altar is Michael the Archangel, and in the center below him is Saint Anthony, the mission's patron. Flanking Saint Anthony are two other Franciscans: Saint Bonaventure and the order's founder, Saint Francis of Assisi. On the right side of the altar is Saint Joseph, and on the left, Saint Mary.

Buried at the mission are Father Sitjar, one of the founding priests; Father Sancho, who served from 1804 to 1830; Father Doreto Ambris, who devoted thirty years of his life to maintaining the mission after secularization; Father Pujol, the possible victim of lead poisoning in 1801 and California's first autopsy subject; and Father Sarria, who died at Mission Soledad but who was interred in San Antonio.

Mission San Antonio was for many years an archaeology study site by students at the nearby California State University in San Luis Obispo.

Mission San Antonio - facade.

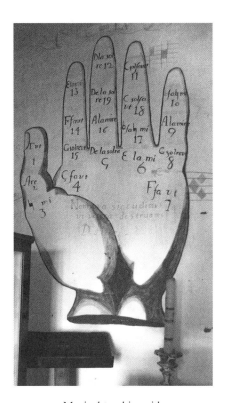

Musical teaching aid.

Mill race.

LANDS NEVER TRODDEN

Chapter 7

SAN GABRIEL ARCHANGEL

L *a Mision del Santo Principe el Arcangel, San Gabriel de los Temblors* (the Mission of the Holy Prince of Archangels, Saint Gabriel of the Earthquakes), the fourth mission, was founded on September 8, 1771. "Of the earthquakes" is not part of The Archangel Gabriel's usual title. It was appended to the mission from the name given to a nearby river when Portola's men, traveling the area in 1769, experienced four earthquakes in one day.

Mission San Gabriel is named after Gabriel the Archangel. Gabriel is the archangel who is the herald, recognized in the world's three great monotheistic religions. In the Jewish Old Testament, Gabriel appears to Daniel and interprets his dream for him. In the Christian New Testament it is Gabriel who brings to Mary the message that she is to be the mother of the savior. In the Koran, it was Gabriel who revealed the Quran to Mohammed. In the Catholic church, the feast day of Gabriel (and of all of the archangels) is celebrated on September 29.

With the founding of San Gabriel, Serra now had four missions, spread over almost five hundred miles, under active construction. He put in charge of this fourth mission Fathers Pedro Cambon and Angel Somera. Cambon's journey to his assignment at San Gabriel is a testament to the complexities of travel in serving the California missions. Cambon left Cadiz, Spain, in 1769, and arrived at the College of San Fernando in Mexico City on May 27, 1770. He left San Fernando in October of 1770 and sailed for California, arriving in San Diego on March 12 and in Monterey on May 21. Within three weeks, Serra had assigned him to the new mission planned at San Gabriel and had him return to San Diego by ship. From San Diego, Cambon once again headed north, this time by land and with an armed escort.

Arriving at the site chosen for the mission, the band was confronted by a group of hostile natives. According to Palou in his biography of Junipero Serra, one of the missionaries unfurled a large painting of the Blessed Virgin as Our Lady of Sorrows. "He had scarcely done this when they all subdued by the vision of this beautiful image, threw down their bows and arrows and came running hastily forward. The two captains threw down at the feet of the Sovereign Queen the beads and trinkets which they wore about their necks as a sign of their greatest respect and also to indicate that they wished to make peace with our company."[1] Palou, the first biographer of Junipero Serra and a very early historian of the California missions, can be a little over-the-top in attributing miraculous attributes to common place happenings. On Serra's initial trek across Mexico, Palou credits their safety on one occasion to the personal intervention of the Holy Family. The banner of Our Lady of Sorrows, though, may have been the first-ever representational depiction of the human form the natives had ever seen. It is by any description a beautiful painting, still on display at Mission San Gabriel.

Serra, in picking Cambon and Somera to found San Gabriel, picked men of not only demonstrable obedience but of some initiative as well. They did not like the original site designated by Serra, so they decided to cross the San Gabriel River and move on another nine miles, locating the mission near what is now the town of Montebello. In 1771 there was no way to easily communicate this decision nor receive permission from their superior. The Franciscans who settled California did not accomplish what they did by being cautious or unsure of themselves. Cambon was only thirty-three years of age. He had been in California only six months, and yet he did not hesitate to make a decision that flew in the face of his explicit instructions. As far as we know, his decision was never challenged by his superiors.

San Gabriel got off to a slow and troubled start. Within a month of the mission's founding, there was a serious incident involving some soldiers and the Indians. One of the soldiers' pastimes involved going to the native settlements and literally lassoing women, who were then raped on the spot. The poor women were doubly damned in these cases, being forced to undergo a long period of purification after being violated by the Spanish. Children born of such a union were strangled at birth.[2] In one of these forays, one of the soldiers picked the wife of one of the tribal leaders as his victim. The outraged husband gathered some supporters and sought retribution for the crime. In the ensuing confrontation, Spanish weaponry easily prevailed against the natives, and the aggrieved husband was killed. Then, adding insult to injury, the soldiers cut off his head and displayed it on a pole at the gate of the crude stockade at the entrance of the mission. An ironic end to this ugly incident was that the widow of the murdered man eventually brought her son to be baptized in the new faith the Franciscans were promoting. It seems as if the Indians had little to learn, and perhaps much to teach, about the Christian ideals of love and forgiveness.

Two years after the founding of the mission, Fathers Somera and Cambon were still living in shelters of brushwood and thatch. Their clothes were pitiful rags, and they were existing on three tortillas a day. Had it not been for the natives of the region, they likely would have died. Only seventy-three baptisms had been performed.

The scurrilous behavior of the soldiers assigned to San Gabriel was one of the reasons Junipero Serra made one last trip to Mexico. In 1773, Junipero Serra traveled to Mexico City to discuss with Viceroy Bucarelli the deteriorating situation between the missionaries, the soldiers and the Indians, the outrages at San Gabriel being of primary importance. In Serra's words, "not even the boys were safe from soldiers." Justifiably or not, Serra laid the blame for the soldiers' behavior at the feet of their commander, Pedro Fages. Again, Serra's abilities as politician are obvious. Despite the fact that Pedro Fages had been governor for three years, during which he had sent regular reports to Mexico City, Bucareli accepted Father Serra's representation that the root of the problem was Pedro Fages's inability to control his troops. Fages was removed from command.

In 1775, Father Fermin de Lasuen suggested that San Gabriel be moved, primarily to avoid the annual flooding of the Los Angeles River*. While avoiding floods was the primary motive for moving the mission site, the selection of the new site may have been a very coolly calculated one. A year earlier, Captain Juan Bautista de Anza had arrived in the valley after a three-month trek from Mexico, through present day Arizona. Lasuen was astute enough to understand the signifi-

---

*   Viewing the Los Angeles River today, for most of its length a dry, unappealing, concrete ditch, it is hard to believe it ever could have posed a flood threat.

cance of this: at the new site, San Gabriel would be at the crossroads of the two main routes from Mexico to California, *El Camino Real* and De Anza's new trail. *El Camino Real* had been the original route into California. This route necessitated crossing the Gulf of California, and then either an arduous land journey from Baja California to Alta California, or taking a ship up the coast. The ships currently in use were so small that they would be impractical for moving colonists and their livestock to the new land. If families and the livestock necessary to begin a new colonial venture were to travel from Mexico, a route that did not necessitate travel by sea had to be found. *El Camino Real* served the soldiers and the missionaries well, but it would not do for permanent colonization. Families, livestock and the necessities of permanent residence could not be moved by sea. An alternative route was needed. A route from northern Mexico proper into California had long been sought, and Captain Juan Bautista de Anza accomplished this in 1774. De Anza was guided on the new route by an escaped neophyte from Mission San Gabriel. Sebastian Taraval, a Cochimi Indian from Baja California, had been bought from his home to Mission San Gabriel. He cared not at all for his life at the mission and escaped to the east, together with his wife and a brother. Taraval was the only one of the three who survived the journey to Arizona. When de Anza learned of his feat, he recruited Taraval as a guide for a trip back to San Gabriel. After more than two months of traveling, they reached San Gabriel and the well-established *El Camino Real,* on March 22, 1774. De Anza's trail became a proven land route from Mexico to California.

With the information gained on this first trip, de Anza was able to convince Viceroy Bucareli that actual colonization of California, not just establishment of missions, was feasible. In October 1775, he left Tubac, Arizona once more, now with a party of men, women, children and livestock, with the objective of founding *presidios* and new missions north of Monterey. This was no small undertaking. De Anza had, in addition to his soldiers, approximately 200 settlers, many of them women and children, 300 cattle, 300 horses and 120 mules. They were carrying six tons of provisions. The first night out one of the women went into labor, and before the trip was over, seven more children were born. One has to marvel at the fortitude of women, far advanced in a pregnancy, who would undertake such a trip. The party crossed the Sierra Nevada in December and celebrated Christmas on the western slope. De Anza was upbraided by Father Font, who was accompanying the expedition, because in honor of the occasion the captain had given the party a cask of brandy and the bedraggled travelers had gotten royally drunk. De Anza was nonplussed at the charges, and Father Font had to be satisfied with preaching a sermon against drunkenness at his next mass.

De Anza and his party reached Mission San Gabriel on January 4, 1776, thus enshrining Mission San Gabriel as the crossroads of the two main routes from Mexico to California. The mission was obviously doing quite well, because it was able to feed and replenish his large expedition. De Anza, after a brief detour to visit the recently-attacked Mission San Diego, returned north to eventually establish the first European settlement on San Francisco Bay in March of 1776. De Anza's trail would become part of the Santa Fe trail when the United States began its westward expansion.

Located at this important juncture, San Gabriel served not just the local Indians but traders, trappers, soldiers, settlers and adventurers of every ilk. San Gabriel and its attached lands were huge by any standard. All of the land encompassed in the present day counties of Los Angeles, San Bernardino, Orange and Riverside County—well over million acres—originally belonged to Mission San Gabriel. Aside from the cattle ranching, common to most of the missions (San Gabriel at one time listed over 26,000 head of cattle on its inventory), San Gabriel's perhaps most enduring agrarian legacies were its vineyards and orchards. At its height, San Gabriel produced not just wine and oranges but 18,000 bushels of wheat, as well as olives, beans and cattle and leather goods.

With growth in both its industries and population, a new church was needed. Construction of the church we see today, using stone and fired brick, was begun in 1779 and completed in 1805. This is perhaps the only one of the California missions that was built under the direction of a Native American master. Miguel Blanco, originally from Baja California, directed the work and used as one of his chief assistants a neophyte from San Gabriel named Remigio. Originally, the plan called for a vaulted ceiling, but early on it became apparent that limitations imposed by using local building material would not allow it, so a flat design was substituted. Father Antonio Cruzado oversaw the construction of this "most Moorish" of all of the missions. Father

Cruzado was educated in Cordoba, Spain. Architectural experts have noticed a striking similarity between Mission San Gabriel and the cathedral in Cordoba. That cathedral was a Muslim Mosque until the expulsion of the Moors from Spain.

With the erection of San Gabriel came the building of California's first hospital. Fifty years later, that hospital was to prove critical to the wounded at the First Battle of Caheunga Pass. The church was dedicated on February 21, 1805. Into this new church were moved most of the furnishings and artwork from the then-existing church. A new altar and reredos were received from Mexico City.

Perhaps Mission San Gabriel's greatest claim to fame involves not the mission complex itself, but one of its outlying communities. In 1781, a group of *padres*, some neophytes from San Gabriel, and some recently-arrived families from Mexico set out from San Gabriel and moved nine miles west to found *El Pueblo de Nuestra la Reina de Los Angeles* (The City of our Lady Queen of the Angels). Los Angeles was founded. The church they founded is located in Old Town Los Angeles, and still serves as an active parish.

San Gabriel's troubles with the natives of the region were not over. In 1785, plans for an attack on the mission were uncovered. The success of the attack depended largely on the element of surprise, and once the plot was uncovered it was doomed before it ever began. One of the main participants in the planned attack was a woman shaman named Toypurina, and to this day the attack is generally referred to as "Toypurina's Revolt." While it is clear that Toypurina was a key player in the attack, it is not clear that she was a leader.

Toypurina was believed by the natives to possess supernatural powers, including the power to predict the future and, perhaps most important for staging a revolt, the power to kill people from a distance. She was enlisted to use her powers against the Franciscans by one of the converts, a neophyte named Nicolas Jose. Nicolas Jose had some six years earlier been involved in a failed uprising, testifying at his trial for "Toypurina's revolt" that he had been one of the people imprisoned after that earlier effort. Despite this, he had actually been appointed an *alcalde* at San Gabriel; clearly Nicolas Jose was a man of some innate leadership abilities. He was able to convince Toypurina and at least two other chieftains, as well as people from eight widely-spaced *rancherias*, that the time was ripe for revolt.

The trial of the malefactors is an intriguing view of the Spanish sense of a fair judicial proceeding. While it shows high regard for faithfully recording the questions posed and the answers of the accused, it also includes as a prelude to the testimony the somewhat chilling charge to "use effective means of persuasion to put pressure on them to answer the following list of questions truthfully."[3] What those "means of persuasion" were, we can only guess. When Toypurina herself was questioned as to the reason for the attack, her answer was startlingly straightforward, telling her interrogators not once but twice that it was ". . . because she was angry with the Fathers and with all the others at the mission because we are living here on their land." [4]

Nicholas Jose and two other chiefs were convicted and imprisoned at the military *presidio* in San Diego for a term of six years. Several other of the participants were flogged and released. Toypurina was initially ordered to be banished from San Gabriel and imprisoned at San Antonio, but it appears as if the banishment was never carried out.

She was now an outcast from her own society because of the failure of her alleged powers during the revolt, and especially because of the harsh punishment meted out to some of the men after the revolt. She was actually in fear of violence from her own people, and was forced to align herself with her former enemies. She was in the early stages of pregnancy at the time of the uprising, and a son was born while she was in captivity. She had him baptized on May 12, 1786, and she herself was baptized less than a year later, taking the name Regina Josefa. Her son died shortly after his first birthday. Two years after that, in 1789, she appears in the records of Mission San Carlos Borromeo, apparently no longer under imprisonment. At San Carlos she married a soldier from the Monterey *presidio*, one Manuel Montero. They had three children. Toypurina Regina Josefa Montero died in 1799 after a very full and exciting life, but at the young age of only thirty-nine. She had gone from Indian shaman, to leader of a rebellion, from a banished convict to a respected matron of Spanish California.

Toypurina has recently enjoyed a bit of a resurgence as a historically significant figure in California history. There is a depiction of her as a shaman in one of the commuter train stations in Los Angeles. Isabel Allende has cast her in the role of Zorro's mother in her 2005 novel of that name.

In 1812, the earthquake that destroyed San Juan Capistrano and damaged all of the existing missions toppled the bell tower at San Gabriel. The ruins of that tower are still in evidence at the right front of the church. The tower was never replaced. In its place the *campanero* we see today, with its six bell alcoves, was built on the opposite side and end of the church in 1828.

In 1814, San Gabriel and several of the other missions reached out to the *asistencia* in Los Angeles and began the construction of a new church in the growing metropolis. In fact it was the city fathers of Los Angeles who, with now almost a thousand occupants in their city, asked that a bigger church be built. San Gabriel provided materials, labor and even some of its bells to the new Queen of Angels Church in Los Angeles.

Through decades of political squabbling, ecclesiastical mandates and military maneuvering, one of the most significant people in San Gabriel's history was not a politician nor a priest nor a soldier but the delightfully named Eulalia Perez de Guillen Marine, a midwife and sacristan.* Most of Doña Perez's early history, including the date of her birth, is unknown. Señora Perez was interviewed in 1877 as part of a "living history" project undertaken by the indefatigable Hubert Howe Bancroft. During that interview Senora Perez indicates that she does not know the date of her birth. When she died in 1878 there was speculation regarding her age with guesses ranging from 112 to 140. She was almost certainly a centenarian. However old she was, she clearly lived much of California's early history and became an institution at Mission San Gabriel, beginning around 1821.

We do know Eulalia was born in Loreto, in Baja California. At the age of fifteen she married a sergeant in the Spanish army. Her husband, Miguel Antonio Guillen, was transferred to San Diego after several years at the *presidio* in Loreto. In San Diego she began practicing as a midwife for the wives of the soldiers. She apparently traveled to *presidios* and missions north of San Diego, for she tells of being a survivor of the collapse of Mission San Juan Capistrano in the

---

* Eulalia was obviously a *very* popular female name in eighteenth century California. The name is of Catalan origin, and legend has it that in the third century a Spanish girl by that name was martyred by burning for refusing to renounce her faith. As popular as it may have been in Alta California, it does not make even the top one-thousand girls names in the United States today.

earthquake of 1812. She recalls being pregnant at the time and being knocked down by people as they tried to escape the crumbling church.

For about four years, her husband was posted to San Gabriel, and Eulalia and their children accompanied him. There must have been something about San Gabriel which resonated with her, for Mission San Gabriel would weave in and out of her history for the rest of her life. From San Gabriel the army returned the family to San Diego. Her husband had been ill for some time, and shortly after the return to San Diego he was discharged. On his discharge, they returned once more to San Gabriel. Shortly after this move, Miguel died and Eulalia was forced to relocate her family again to San Diego. In 1821, Father Jose Sanchez, one of the priests at San Gabriel, wrote to one of his confreres at San Diego and specifically asked if Doña Perez could return to San Gabriel. She did return, this time for good, until her death in 1878. Her many years of service to the church as "keeper of the keys" was recognized in allowing her to be buried in the church, certainly a singular honor for a laywoman in the nineteenth century Catholic church. A white marble bench marks her grave on the right side of the church.

One can hardly say the words "California missions" without including the word "romance" in the sentence, and Mission San Gabriel was the site of one of California's most famous and, at the time, most scandalous romances. In 1826, an American sea captain named Henry Fitch fell in love with Josefa Carillo, the daughter of a prominent *Californio* family. He began a courtship, wrote a formal letter of proposal to her father, converted to Catholicism, changed his name to Enrique and set a wedding date. On the day before the wedding, Josefa's uncle, who had acted as Fitch's godfather at his baptism, appeared and ordered the wedding halted. The order came from Governor Echeanida, who may have had intentions toward Josefa himself; but more likely, he was acting on the prevailing hostility to all Americans as they increasingly encroached into Mexican California.

Enrique and Josefa fled to a ship, which had the unfortunate name the *Vulture*. They were assisted in the flight by her cousin Pio Pico, who himself would become the governor of California four years later. From the *Vulture,* the couple boarded Fitch's ship, the more prosaically named *Maria Ester,* and this ship took the two lovers to Chile. Enrique and Josefa were married by a Catholic priest in Valparaiso, Chile on

July 3, 1829. A year later they returned to California with a month-old son. All was forgiven by family, but not by church nor secular authorities, which for all practical purposes were one and the same. Mr. and Mrs. Fitch were subjected to an ecclesiastical trial testing the validity of their marriage. While the marriage was upheld, because of certain irregularities Captain Fitch was ordered to give a bell of at least fifty pounds' weight to the church of Our Lady of the Angels. It is this bell that is reportedly hanging at the top of the tower at San Gabriel. While the wonderful story of the Fitch's romance, elopement, trial and subsequent long married life is all true, that particular bell cannot be verified as coming in payment of Enriques's penance. Enrique, while at least nominally a Catholic, was not a man much cowed by church authorities, and most evidence is that he never paid the penance. A letter written by him after the trial rants with the wonderful phraseology, "So all those busybodies who had too much to say about my marriage being unlawful may go to hell and f—k spiders..."[5]

In 1826 Jedediah Smith, the American mountain man, arrived to avail himself of the famous mission hospitality. Smith was another traveler who was led to the mission by two of San Gabriel's neophytes who had previously escaped.* Smith stayed at the mission for more than six weeks, apparently free to come and go, but when word of his stay reached Governor Echeandia, he was arrested and detained for ten days.

At the end of that time the governor ordered Smith to leave California immediately and directly. Mountain men had virtually no respect for any authority or government, and instead of leaving California, Smith headed up the Central valley to continue his trapping. As did so many who came after him, Smith formed a decided attraction to California. He returned repeatedly over the next several years, almost always to face temporary detention by the now-paranoid Mexican government. Governor Arguello was convinced that Smith and men like him had designs on his territory. His fears were a little premature, but indeed in just twenty years they would prove to be well-founded.

San Gabriel, because of its strategic location, found itself as the locus of several battles, both political and military. In the unsettled

---

* The repeated willingness of "escapees" to return to the missions they had just fled only adds to the confusion of trying to sort out the conditions under which they lived at the missions and the circumstances of their leaving.

years following Mexico's independence from Spain, the area around San Gabriel became a battleground in the struggle for control between those faithful to the new republic and those who wanted to establish a new independent government of Alta California. The Battle of Cahuenga Pass was an almost comic last gasp of the romantic *Californios*. It was fought between local citizens and the forces of Governor Manuel Victoria.

The two sides met at Cahengua Pass on December 5, 1831. The total population of Los Angeles in 1830 was less than fifteen hundred people, so it takes no stretch of the imagination to derive that many of the assembled combatants on either side would have been related to those on the other side. The predictable outcome was that after the first volley, not a single casualty was suffered on either side. The troops had all fired over the heads of their opponents. The battle now devolved to a *mano a mano* contest between Captain Romualdo Pacheco of the governor's troops, and Captain Jose Maria Avila of the rebels, each on horseback and armed with a lance. This contest, too, was a draw until a frustrated Captain Avila drew his pistol and shot Captain Pacheco dead. Governor Victoria, outraged at this unchivalrous act, responded in kind and shot Captain Avila. One Captain Portilla from the rebel forces responded by driving his lance through Victoria's face. Victoria was horribly wounded, but survived the battle that apparently ended at his injury. He was taken to the hospital at Mission San Gabriel, the only one in California at the time. He recovered from his wound but resigned as governor and returned to Mexico.

In 1834, San Gabriel was stricken with two blights. A literal blight destroyed the majority of the mission vineyards, and the blight of secularization struck its near-fatal blow to the mission as an institution. As was so often the case, secularization achieved no measurable good. The mission Indians shortly all but disappeared.

If Doña Eulalia Perez had been a stellar example of a holy and sainted woman at San Gabriel, in 1836 there arrived a woman of a completely different stripe. Doña Maria Felix was the wife of Don Domingo Felix, a wealthy *ranchero*. Doña Maria became enamored of one Gervasio Alipas. When confronted by her husband and asked to abandon her lover, Doña Maria sought refuge at Mission San Gabriel. The missionaries really had no choice but to return her to her husband when he came to the mission and demanded the return of his "property," for such a married woman was in 1836. Don Felix placed his erring wife on his horse in front of him and began the return trip to his *rancho*. Unfortunately, the persistent Gervasio was lying in wait. The story is that he lassoed Don Felix and dragged him from his horse. To do that without dragging the young lady as well would have been a feat of very accomplished roping. Not only did Don Felix end up stabbed to death, but Doña Maria assisted in hastily covering the body with earth and leaves. When the body, some bloodstains, and the footprints of a man and a woman were discovered, the two lovers were quickly arrested.

The citizenry was outraged at the crime and its circumstances. An *ad hoc* vigilante committee met and demanded that a public example be made, with death to the murderers. The *ayuntamiento* (town hall officer) refused but the mob was not to be denied. The crowd forcibly entered the jail, took the two prisoners out and summarily executed them. On April 7, 1836, Doña Maria del Rosario Villa de Felix had the dubious distinction of being the first woman executed in California, and certainly the only one ever executed by firing squad.

In 1841, a complaint was made that the caretaker of the mission had established a dram shop and a brothel on the formerly sacred grounds, and Governor Pio Pico in 1846 turned San Gabriel over to two Americans, Hugo Reid and William Workman, in settlement of debts he owed.

Turmoil over the leadership of California continued, though, and on February 19, 1845, the Second Battle of Cahuenga Pass was fought. It was a farcical repeat of the first, again contested by the forces of an unpopular governor, this time Manuel Micheltorena, and again by a citizens' army, this time led by Juan Bautista Alvarado. The two armies were so ill-equipped that each was forced to chase after the cannonballs of the other so that they could be fired back. The end result of two days of artillery exchange was one horse and one mule killed. Once again, the governor, Micheltorena, decided that governorship of this ungovernable state was not worth it, and retired to Mexico.

Though the mission was now owned by private parties, the Franciscans continued on until 1852, when Father Jose Jimeno retired to Santa Barbara. The title granted to Reid and Workman was ultimately ruled as invalid, and the property returned to the Church in 1859. In the interim, though, furnishings, timbers, and building materials were harvested for use in the growing town, and the mission compound shrunk to little more than just the church building itself. This was staffed and maintained by a variety of orders of priests, and its surviving outbuildings used as schools and seminaries.

There was one final military battle in San Gabriel's future. In 1847, the Battle of Rio San Gabriel was fought between American and Mexican forces within the shadow of Mission San Gabriel. The objective was the city of Los Angeles, held at the time by Mexican forces. In an hour-and a half battle, and suffering only eight casualties, the Americans regained control of Los Angeles and ultimately Alta California. A year later, in 1848, the Treaty of Guadalupe Hildago concluded the Mexican-American War and ceded California to the United States.

In the 1850s, the vineyards that San Gabriel developed, and the burgeoning wine industry, drove the last nail into the coffin of the local native population. Grape growing and wine processing is a very labor-intensive industry, and the only pool of readily available labor was the large number of Indians dispossessed from the former mission holdings. They had planted, tended and harvested the mission's grape crop and they were the only local laborers skilled in the trade. They were hired by the local vineyard owners to prune, maintain and harvest their vineyards and process the wine. They were generally paid, at the end of each week, in brandy instead of money. They would spend the weekend in drunkenness and fighting, be arrested by the sheriff on Sunday afternoon, and jailed. On Monday morning, they would be bailed out by the vineyard owners who would pay their fines to the sheriff and take the Indians, as payment for the bail, as workers for the next week. As one observer noted:

> Los Angeles had its slave mart, as well as New Orleans and Constantinople—only the slave at Los Angeles was sold fifty-two times a year as long as he lived, which did not generally exceed one, two, or three years, under the new dispensation. They would be sold for a week, and bought up by the vineyard men and others at prices ranging from one to three dollars, one-third of which was to be paid to the peon at the end of the week, which debt, due for well performed labor, would invariably be paid in "*aguardiente*," and the Indian would be made happy until

the following Monday morning, having passed through another Saturday night and Sunday's saturnalia of debauchery and bestiality. Those thousands of honest, useful people were absolutely destroyed in this way.[6]

In 1886, Father Joaquin Bot came to San Gabriel and "updated" the mission by enlarging the windows and installing a new ceiling. The new ceiling, while it may have been state-of-the-art in 1886, was completely out of sync with the mission's original style. He also repainted the interior, and in the process undoubtedly covered some priceless artwork by native artisans on the walls.

Mission San Gabriel today:

Mission San Gabriel is located at 428 South Mission Dr., San Gabriel, CA, 91776. (626) 457-3048.
http://www.sangabrielmission.org

Mission San Gabriel, while it may have operated in much-reduced circumstances, is one of the few California missions that has never been without an active congregation, and it has never suffered the indignity of being subjected to another use. The building we see today is in large measure the building that was begun in 1791. As with all of the missions, it has undergone a series of restorations and renovations, some unfortunately with little regard for the original design. The ceiling we see today hides the original beams erected when the mission was built, and is more a Victorian, rather than Moorish, design. The hammered copper baptismal font, holy water font, and baptismal shell are all from the original furnishings of 1771.

San Gabriel is one of the four California missions built of stone and not adobe. The style of the mission, towering and fortress-like, could not have been built of adobe. The capped buttresses are unique among all of the missions. Architectural experts have noticed striking similarities between Mission San Gabriel and the cathedral in Cordoba, Spain, which was a former mosque. The credit for this most "Moorish" of all of the missions goes to Father Antonio Cruzado, who was the primary overseer of the construction of San Gabriel and who was educated in Cordoba.

The *campanero* contains six bells of varying ages. The bells at all of the missions have their own appeal and romanticism, and San Gabriel's bells perhaps even more than most. Almost every one of them carries a romantic if unverifiable tale. The topmost bell—one of two in the tower that were cast in 1828 by the Holbrook Company of Massachusetts—is the bell that Captain Fitch supposedly purchased as his penance for his illegal marriage to Josefa Carrillo.

On the second tier, the middle bell is the other of the Holbrook bells. The right-hand bell in this middle tier was one of the mission's original bells. It disappeared in the 1870s, and was returned to the mission from the Baldwin Ranch in 1930. The left-hand bell was cast in 1795 in Mexico City by Paul Ruelas. Inscribed in Latin on this bell are the words *"Ave Maria, Purisima"* (hail Mary, most pure), which was the angel Gabriel's greeting to Mary in Luke's Gospel (Luke 1:28). One story of this bell tells how a young man in Mexico City threw a silver coin into the mold while the bell was being cast. Years later, as a Franciscan priest at San Gabriel, the first time he heard the *angelus* rung on the mission's bell, he recognized the tone of the bell that held his silver.*

The left-hand bell on the bottom tier was also cast in Mexico City in 1795 by Paul Ruelas. The largest bell, in the lower right position, weighs over a ton. When rung, it could be heard in Los Angeles, eight miles away. Its crown-shaped top should denote that it is a "royal bell," but the bell has been dated from around 1830, nine years after Mexico won its independence from royalist Spain. This massive bell supposedly contains all the gold and silver jewelry of a young lady in Spain who, on hearing that her lover had died in Alta California, threw her ornaments into the cauldron where the bell destined for San Gabriel was being cast. Who could remain unmoved, even three hundred years later, when hearing these bells rung?

The side entrance to San Gabriel was originally the main entrance to the church. As you step out of that door the pavement you are standing on is covering the *El Camino Real.*

---

* The *angelus* was an observance of the Roman Catholic church marked by the ringing of church bells at dawn, noon and dusk, when the faithful would pause to recite a short litany of prayers commemorating the angel Gabriel's announcement to Mary that she was to be the mother of Christ.

One of San Gabriel's most attractive displays are the stations of the cross in the church. These fourteen stations represent the most complete single work of European-style art ever completed by Native Americans. They were originally created as church decorations at Mission San Fernando, twenty-five miles to the north of San Gabriel. When that mission was suffering from the worst deprivations of secularization and abandonment in the 1850s, the paintings were moved for safekeeping to Our Lady Queen of Angels in Los Angeles. In 1893, they were exhibited at the World Columbian Exposition in Chicago, and then returned to Los Angeles and next displayed at a chamber of commerce exhibition in 1902. For many years after that, they disappeared from public display to a basement storage room. When they were finally sent to San Gabriel for permanent display, for twenty years they were hung in an outside corridor and suffered some degradation as a result.

The paintings are not just a wonderful reminder of the skill of a Native American painter. Although viewed by some as crudely executed, it must be remembered that they were done by a people who until thirty years earlier had only flat, one-dimensional drawings as their representative art. A careful examination gives significant insight into the culture that gave rise to them. Originally they were attributed to a single artist, a baptized member of the Chumash tribe known only as Juan Antonio. Recent research, though, shows slight differences in technique and brushstrokes, suggesting that several different artists worked on them. If this is true, the paintings are all the more remarkable because they demonstrate that it was not just a singularly talented native, but several very talented ones who completed the works. The paintings are rendered on sailcloth canvas, and native plants, seeds and clays are used as dyes, pigments and fixatives.

The artist or artists were undoubtedly working from paintings that already existed, perhaps in a prayer book or religious text used for instructing the Indians. Almost immediately one is taken with the decided Asian cast to many of the figures in the paintings. Epicanthic eyes and ornate, oriental-style headgear predominate.

The artists' personal empathy with the scenes they are depicting is obvious. They may have been depicting scenes from first-century Jerusalem, under Roman occupation, but they were clearly projecting their own experiences of the nineteenth century under Spanish occupation. The soldiers have a universally cruel, dark and Latin look. In the fourth station, there is an interesting depiction of Mary, the Mother of Jesus. She is shown as a small, perhaps pre-teen girl. This may have been a reflection of the artist's sense that no mature woman would be a virgin, as Catholic doctrine insists. In the sixth, the sympathetic bystanders lifting the cross from Christ are certainly Indian, as is the kneeling Veronica. Yet, all of the Indians in the scene are not kind ones. One of Christ's tormentors wielding a whip or flail appears to be an Indian, perhaps their view of the *alcades* appointed by the Franciscans to punish the neophyte misbehaviors. As with all art, the beauty is in the eye of the beholder, but the story is in the heart of the artist. We can only surmise what was in the heart of the anonymous artist or artists, but we can still enjoy the beauty of their art.

The banner of the Virgin Mary, now more than three hundred years old, that so impressed the Indians at the founding of San Gabriel is on display in the church sanctuary to the left side of the altar. The copper baptismal font is from the original mission built in 1771. It is estimated that more than 25,000 faithful have been baptized in this font.

Mission San Gabriel - "The Moorish Mission."

Endnotes

1   Palou, Francisco. *Life and Apostolic Labors of the Venerable Father Junipero Serra, Founder of the Franciscan Missions of California.* Translated by C. Scott Williams. Pasadena: George Wharton James, 1913.

2   Bancroft, Hubert Howe. *History of California, Vol. I* N. 29. (San Francisco: A.L. Bancroft & Company, Publishers, 1884).

3   Beebe, Rose Marie, and Senkewicz, Robert M., trans. "Revolt at Mission San Gabriel, October 25, 1785." *Boletin, The Journal of the California Mission Studies Asson.* 24, No. 2 (2007): 16.

4   Ibid., 18

5   Fitch, Henry to J.B.R. Cooper, Letter, 9 January 1831. BANC MSS C-B 30:17 *Documentos para la historia de California, 1780-1875.* The Bancroft Library, University of California, Berkeley.

6   Bell, Horace. *Reminiscences of a Ranger or Early Times in California.* Los Angeles : Yarnell, Caystile & Mathes, Printers, 1881.

Chapter 8

SAN LUIS OBISPO

The History Of San Luis Obispo de Tolosa

L   *a Mision de San Luis Obispo de Tolosa* (the Mission of Saint
      Luis Bishop of Toulouse), the fifth mission, was founded on
      September 1, 1772. It was named for the "boy bishop," Louis
of Toulouse. Louis had been born to one of France's and Europe's
most well-connected families, in 1274. His father, King of Naples,
was taken prisoner in Italy during a war with King Pedro III. He secured his release by giving his three sons as hostages. Louis and his
brothers were taken to Barcelona, placed under the care of the Franciscans, and held for seven years. It could not have been an entirely unpleasant experience because on his return to France, Louis renounced
all claims to royalty and took the Franciscan vows of poverty, chastity
and obedience. He was then consecrated bishop of Toulouse at the age
of twenty-one. Louis may have renounce his rights to royal preroga-
tives, but clearly his family connections did not hurt his ascension in
the ecclesiastical hierarchy. Louis was a conscientious and dedicated
bishop, devoting his energies and the wealth of his position to caring
for the poor during his brief episcopacy. He died at the very young age
of twenty-three. His feast day is celebrated in the Catholic church on
August 19.

San Luis Obispo provides a great example of the interdependence
of the missions, and of the mutual support they provided. Before anything was built at San Luis Obispo, it became known that two earlier
missions, Carmel and San Antonio, were starving. A very large and
disturbing population of bears was troubling the settlers at San Luis
Obispo. The Franciscans at San Luis Obispo extended an invitation
to those at San Antonio and Carmel to come and harvest some of the

pests. A three-month campaign of bear hunting at San Luis Obispo resulted in an impressive nine thousand pounds of bear meat being shipped to the other missions.

As with most of the other missions, Serra selected the site, dedicated a crude structure as a church, and turned the day-to-day tasks over to a subordinate, in this case Father Jose Cavaller, who was joined a year later by Father Domingo Juncosa. Father Juncosa lasted a scant two years before retiring to Mexico City in 1774. Serra noted that Juncosa was seeking retirement because he could not stand to be in the company of the "scandalous conduct of the soldiers." Serra himself had noted before leaving San Luis Obispo that he and Father Juncosa had once stumbled upon a soldier actually in the act of raping an Indian woman. They interfered with the commission of the crime, but such occurrences were all too common.

Father Cavaller was of sterner stuff; he stayed at San Luis Obispo until his death in 1789. It was Father Cavaller who built the first permanent church, of logs roofed with tiles. In 1785, he replaced that church with an adobe one, and in 1788 he began the construction of the present church, which was completed in 1792. San Luis Obispo is one of the very few missions that has the distinction of sitting at the same site where it was originally dedicated. Unlike most of the missions, it has never been moved.

The records of San Luis Obispo are a testament to the fortitude and dedication of the Franciscans, but it was the assistance of the natives that saved them. When Serra left Cavaller with two Indians and five soldiers tasked with building the mission, their provisions consisted of fifty pounds of flour, three pecks of wheat and a barrel of brown sugar. They could not have survived to accomplish their task had it not been for the good graces of the natives who provided them with seeds and venison.

San Luis Obispo may have survived in its early days due to the friendliness and help of the local natives, but as the mission developed and Spanish influence spread, the inevitable discord with the native populace arose. The site of San Luis Obispo was an area of some contention between the Chumash and the Yokuts tribes. Shortly after the completion of the first church, the compound found itself caught in the literal crossfire of these two warring groups of natives, as flaming arrows were launched towards the thatched roofs. The roofs and

114

wooden buildings were extremely vulnerable to fire, and almost all of the buildings except the church were destroyed. These attacks occurred with some frequency over the next several years; whichever group was not currently in residence at the mission saw it as a refuge for its enemies. Each time the indefatigable Franciscans rebuilt. Not a group of men who ever saw any problem as unsolvable, in 1790 they began experimenting with tile roofs. Using locally available clay, they worked it in pits, formed rectangles and, while the clay rectangles were still wet, shaped them over shaved logs. When sun-dried and baked, the tiles were not only fireproof, but waterproof, and lasted virtually forever. There are still original tiles from the mission existent and in use today.

Soon tile roofs became the standard for all of the California missions, but whether or not they were the innovation of the *padres* at San Luis Obispo is a matter of debate. Credit for the first manufacture of these tiles is claimed by both San Luis Obispo and San Antonio de Padua even to this date. Because San Luis Obispo had the misfortune of suffering frequent destruction by fire, the general consensus is that it was there that a light finally went on, and the *padres* concluded, "Let's stop roofing with thatch and put tiles up there." However, Father Maynard Geiger, a Franciscan historian and biographer of Junipero Serra, states that it was at San Antonio de Padua that the clay tiles were first used. There is a letter from Junipero Serra written in 1781 discussing tiled roofs at San Antonio, and all the evidence is that the first tiled roof at San Luis Obispo was not completed until around 1790. It seems as if San Antonio does indeed get the credit for being the first to install these iconic mission tiles.

These roof tiles, which were the salvation of the missions in 1790, indirectly led to their rapid deterioration in the 1830s. The tile roofs are very heavy; probably, from an engineering perspective, too heavy for the wooden trusses supporting them. At San Luis itself, after an earthquake in 1868, the roof tiles were removed to relieve strain on the structure. While the missions were in use, the beams were constantly being inspected, reinforced and repaired. Once the missions were abandoned, though, the wooden beams weakened, decayed and collapsed under the weight of the tiles. The demise of several of the missions, notably Carmel, San Fernando, Santa Cruz and San Antonio, is well documented as beginning with the collapse of the roofs.

Once the roofs were gone, the interior and adobe walls could not long stand against coastal California's autumn and winter rains.

San Luis Obispo was the setting for one of several tragic examples of the problems caused by imposing rigid, eighteenth-century, Spanish Catholic precepts of morality on the native people. Most of the native Californian tribal groups had strict marital and sexual codes, but their codes were not those of Catholic Spain. Among the California natives, generally pre-marital sex was not forbidden, and marriages were not necessarily lifetime commitments. Such practices were of course abhorrent to the Franciscans, and their unremitting efforts to impose their own standards on the native populace often led to violent and unpleasant encounters. In June of 1796 these efforts led to a murder and a trial that highlighted some interesting aspects, good as well as bad, of Spanish jurisprudence.

In that month, one Silberio (no last name is given*) murdered his wife Rebecca. When the sordid facts were bought to light, it seems that Silberio had for some time been carrying on an affair with a widow named Rosa. In the closed society that was mission life, the affair was somewhat common knowledge. In response to the affair, the *padres* had been negotiating a marriage between Rosa and a widower, hoping to put an end to her scandalous conduct. It was one thing to have Silberio commit adultery with a widow; it would be entirely something else for him to continue his activities with a woman married to a member of the community. Likely by the mores of the native Californians, had it not been for the Franciscans, Silberio would have been permitted to put aside his first wife with proper compensation and take up a life with Rosa. Obviously this would not be allowed under the rules of Catholicism. To Silberio, it seemed there was only one answer: He would dispose of his wife and himself marry Rosa, before the Franciscans could complete their matchmaking.

Silberio initially claimed that his wife had been killed by a bear, but it soon became obvious that her injuries were inflicted by a knife. Silberio and Rosa were both tried for murder. Among his defenses, Silberio asserted that he had acted only on the orders of Rosa. Rosa, obviously a woman of some acumen, pointed out to no avail that she

---

* Almost without exception, neophytes were christened with only a proper name. Since none of the native California tribes had familial names, there was no familial name that could be attached to the baptismal name.

was not his wife and thus could not have ordered him to do anything. Both were convicted of murder. Rosa, who by all evidence was nowhere near the unfortunate victim when the crime occurred, could not have murdered her. At worst she may have been an accomplice or an accessory, but in the eyes of the Spanish tribunal, murder it was.

Despite this somewhat cavalier attitude toward the elements of a crime, there now appears a remarkably enlightened view of crime and punishment in eighteenth-century Spanish California. First, the accused had members of the Spanish military appointed as counsel for their defense. They were not men at all trained in the law, and the defense was inadequate, but still the concept was recognized. Next, on conviction for murder in eighteenth-century California, one would expect a sentence of death by hanging. In the case of Silberio and Rosa, however, the commander of the *presidio*, Felipe de Goycoechea, immediately recognized that a punishment so severe could not be imposed on people who, in his words, could often not even remember the name they had been given at baptism. Goycoechea sent the case to the governor of California, who sent it to the viceroy in Mexico City, who had it reviewed by the Supreme Court of Mexico.

The Supreme Court recommended that the accused should be given at least some immunity from a crime and a legal system they probably did not understand. Ultimately, Silberio was sentenced to eight years of hard labor at the *presidio* in San Diego, and Rosa to eight years as the housekeeper for the commander of the *presidio* in San Francisco. In each case the imposition of an exile, hundreds of miles from their homes, community, and most of all each other was probably the most onerous aspect of the sentence.

It was at San Luis Obispo that Father Luis Martinez staged the parade of ducks, chickens, geese and turkeys that Helen Hunt Jackson depicted in one of the most memorable passages in her book *Ramona*. *Ramona* is pure fiction, but Father Martinez was in fact a long-serving *padre* at San Luis Obispo from 1798 to 1830, the era covered by the novel. Father Martinez, who is remembered as a lovable but somewhat bizarre monk, is one of a very select group of Franciscans who spent their entire missionary career at one mission.

In 1818 Hippolyte Bouchard, an Argentinian pirate (or privateer, depending on one's political and national inclinations) began terrorizing the California coastline. Bouchard was a Frenchman, born in St.

Tropez. In 1809 he settled in Argentina and adopted that country as his own. He served in the Argentinian navy and was the first Argentinian to circumnavigate the globe. He was chartered by the Argentinian government to seize property from Spanish vessels. Inevitably his wanderings took him to the California coastline. On October 8, 1818, Governor Sola, who had been told that Bouchard's ships were headed for California, sent out a dispatch that warned of absolute impending doom:

> All articles of value, such as sacred vessels and church ornaments must be boxed forthwith and sent away . . . Stores of provisions must be collected for the four *presidios*. Women and children must be ready to retire at the first warning to the places designated, with neophytes enough to prepare food for them. All livestock . . . must be driven inland as far as possible. . . Invalids, settlers, and *rancheros* must come forthwith to their respective *presidios* or hold themselves in readiness to obey the commandants' orders. Immediately on sight of a vessel a flying company must be sent out to reconnoiter all points and see that each man has 500 cartridges. Two thirds of all gunpowder . . . must be removed to the interior and spikes must be prepared for the guns in case of abandonment. Two mounted couriers for the speedy transmission of despatches(*sic*) must be stationed at each of some twenty five points. . .[1]

On and on through two pages of grim warnings the governor's missive went. His warnings sat unnecessary and probably unheeded for almost a month, but on November 20, Bouchard's vessels came into view. For the next several months, Bouchard staged sporadic raids at several of the California missions. His activities caused disturbances at Monterey, Santa Cruz, Santa Barbara and San Juan Capistrano, but, never to the extent one would have expected based on the governors warning.

Father Martinez from San Luis Obispo personally formed a volunteer army of neophytes and traveled with them as far south as Santa Barbara and San Juan Capistrano to assist in the defense of those communities. There is no record that he and his ragtag group of volunteers ever saw any action, but he gained personal recognition from the vice-roy in Mexico City for his services.

When Mexico gained her independence in 1821, Martinez's service, which had been rendered to the Spanish Crown, along with his outspoken criticism of the new Mexican government, made him particularly suspect with regard to his loyalties to the new republic. In his heart, Martinez was undoubtedly an unregenerate royalist. He had written frequent letters making politically injudicious comments. According to one historian, "Of all the *padres*, Martinez of San Luis Obispo was the most outspoken and independent in political matters, besides being well known for his smuggling propensities. Echeandia deemed his absence desired for the good of the territory and had issued a passport which had not been used."[2]

Independence for Mexico brought only instability to those in Alta California. From her independence in 1822 until cession to the United States in 1846, Californians were ruled by twelve different governors. Each governor brought to the office questions of loyalty, form of government and, frequently, armed rebellion. In 1829 Joaquin Solis and a group of mutinous Mexican soldiers midway between Santa Barbara and Monterey stopped at Mission San Luis Obispo. They were fed and sheltered by Father Martinez, probably not so much out of Christian charity, and certainly not with any sympathy for their ill-fated mutiny, but most likely because he was confronted by a large group of armed, unruly men who demanded hospitality. Given Martinez's well-demonstrated lack of respect for the new government, sheltering mutineers was all that Governor Echeandia needed to rid himself of the outspoken *padre*. Echeandia ordered Martinez arrested and bought to the *presidio* in Santa Barbara. A military trial found him guilty of disloyalty to the Mexican government and he was deported to Spain, via Lima, Peru, on March 30, 1830. He died in Madrid in 1833.

San Luis Obispo was secularized in 1835, and the inevitable decline began. Four years later, there were only 170 Indians living in the mission environs. In 1845, San Luis's Obispo's property, other than the mission itself and its immediate land, at one time a thriving enterprise valued at almost $100,000, was sold by Governor Pio Pico for $510. The church itself remained under the control of the Franciscans.

During the Mexican-American War, Mission San Luis Obispo was the locus of several significant incidents, if not battles. Because of its location and the fact that it was a well-built complex, the mission found itself attractive to both sides for use as a headquarters of local operations. John C. Fremont, a captain of the United States Army Topographical Corps, had been in and out California for years, perhaps on a mission of discovery, perhaps on a mission of provocation; the record is very murky. What is clear is that on December 14, 1846, Fremont, now decidedly an American soldier engaged in a war with Mexico, launched an assault on Mission San Luis Obispo, where he had been told a large number of Mexican troops were waiting for him. After a one-day siege, the embarrassed Fremont discovered only the priests and some women and children cowering in the church. He withdrew and, to his credit, posted sentries to guard the church from further intrusions. Fremont returned to the church a few days later to use it as the venue for a court martial. In occupying the town of San Luis Obispo, Fremont's troops had captured Jose de Jesus de Pico. Señor Pico had been previously captured in the fighting in Los Angeles. He had been released on parole* with his promise not to engage in further hostilities. Because he was captured this second time as an combatant in San Luis Obispo, he was deemed to have violated his parole. A hasty military tribunal was assembled in the church, and Señor Pico was tried and sentenced to be shot, the only time a sentence of death was ever pronounced in any of the missions. Richard Owens, a longtime, well-trusted friend of Fremont, intervened and prevented the execution. Pico, after his reprieve, joined the American force and proved to be a valuable source of information on the activities of Mexican troops.

The mission or what remained of it was returned to the Franciscans by the United States government in 1859. It went through several reconstructions, not all of them beneficial. After an earthquake in1868, the roof tiles were removed and replaced with shingles to relieve the strain on the structure. The adobe walls were covered with white siding to protect them from the elements and a shingled tower with cupola was installed. For many years after these unfortunate improvement

---

* Because of the fluid character of war on the frontier, neither side had any sort of permanent encampment, and thus no place to hold prisoners. Under these circumstances, it was common practice to release captured prisoners "on parole" with their promise that they would not again take up arms against their enemies.

the mission looked more like a New England meeting house than a Spanish church. Finally in 1934 it was restored to its original form.

San Luis Opispo today:

Mission San Luis Obispo is located at 728 Monterey St. (PO Box 1461), San Luis Obispo, CA, 93401.
http://www.misssionsanluisobispo.org

Mission San Luis Obispo today sits almost ten feet above street level, in the heart of downtown San Luis Obispo. Originally it was *at* street level, but as the town grew around the mission, the street was re-graded several times, each time slightly lower than the existing grade, until today the church sits well above the street it fronts.

San Luis Obispo embodies the fact that while the missions—in par-ticular the first nine missions—were all envisioned by one man, they are not standardized in their ultimate design. There is certainly a "mis-sion style," and marked similarities from one to the other, but they are by no means cookie-cutter buildings. Every one of them has its own unique characteristics. In the case of San Luis Obispo, there are sev-eral unique features. The interior of the church is in a very distinctive "L"-shaped design, with seating for the congregation not just in front of the altar but to the right. It is the only mission built in this fashion, and seems to anticipate by two hundred years the post-Vatican II de-sign so common in newer Catholic churches today. San Luis Obispo is the only one of the missions that incorporates the bell tower into the vestibule. As you walk in the front entrance of the church, you are walking directly below the mission bells. Finally, on close examina-tion it can be seen that the colonnaded walkway along the side of the mission is different than any of the other mission colonnades. Many of the missions have this colonnaded cloister walk; it is probably *the* defining feature of the missions, and it was the air conditioning of the seventeenth century. Look carefully, however, at San Luis Obispo's colonnade. The pillars are of Doric design and define square spaces, rather than the expected arches.

There are three bells in the mission's *campanero*; two of them were cast in Lima, Peru in 1818, and the third in 1878 in San Francisco, from the broken remnants of two other bells that had been damaged in their trip from Lima to California. The largest of the bells is in the center and weighs 1,800 pounds. The doors at the church entrance are from the original mission, while the scrollwork above them is of modern application. Inside the church we see the original floor and roof beams. The painted embellishments on the walls are recent, but the painted "eyes" on the roof beams are original and are one of the building's most interesting features. The painting of the church's patron, St. Louis, is oil on canvas, and was done by the Mexican artist Jose de Paez; it has been in the church since 1774. Paez, who was a friend of Junipero Serra's, has his artwork in several of the earlier missions.

The baptismal font is copper and while of a different design, seems to be the same workmanship as at San Antonio. The first entry in the baptismal registry is in Father Serra's handwriting. The museum at San Luis Obispo, which is housed in the former priests' quarters, contains some of the mission's original roof tiles, vestments and candelabra, as well as extensive photographs of mission life one hundred years ago.

There are two graves in the church. Buried beneath the sanctuary is Father Jose Cavaller, the mission's first priest and the man responsible for building it. On the left wall of the church, just inside the front entrance, is a more interesting grave. Entombed here is Adeline Eliza Dana. Adeline was a child who, as far as can be determined, had no special place in the mission's history except as a member of the congregation. She died at the age of five and was originally buried in the mission graveyard. Her plot, however, turned out to have a very high water table and her casket persisted in rising to the surface. This disquieting process was finally ended by entombing her in the wall of the church.

Mission San Luis Obispo - fountain.

Endnotes

1   Bancroft, Hubert Howe. *History of California*, Vol. II. San Francisco: The History Company, 1886

2   Ibid., Vol III,   98

Chapter 9

SAN FRANCISCO DE ASIS

The History of San Francisco de Asis

*L*a *Mision de Nuestro Padre San Francisco (*The Mission of Our Father, Saint Francis), the sixth mission, was founded on June 29, 1776, five days before the United States of America declared its independence from Great Britain. Its patron, Francis of Assisi, is the founder of the Franciscan order. He was the son of well-to-do Italian merchants. At the age of twenty, he was a soldier in the war between Umbria and Perugia. He was taken prisoner and held for a year. Upon being released, he planned to continue as a soldier but fell seriously ill, and in a long period of convalescence had a conversion and a prophetic vision of Christ, wherein Christ told him to "rebuild my church." He gave up his former lifestyle, rejected his family's substantial wealth, and began a life, first of hermitage but ultimately of reconstruction of the Catholic church, which had become a center of wealth and power. Francis urged the church to return to Christ's mission of love and compassion for the poor. He soon had gathered around him more young men (and ultimately a separate order of women, the Poor Clares) who vowed themselves to poverty, chastity and obedience. Francis's ideals took quick root, and in his lifetime he traveled not just all over Italy but to Spain, Egypt and Palestine. He was largely successful in his attempts to reform the faith before he died in 1226. At his death, his order consisted of thousands of members in Italy, France, Spain, Germany, Hungary, Egypt and Palestine. Today, the Franciscans have a presence on every continent and are the second largest order of professed Catholics. Saint Francis's feast day is October 4.

The mission was originally founded on the bank of a small creek which Juan de Anza had named *Arroyo de los Dolores,* "Creek of the Sorrows," because it was discovered on Good Friday.* The creek and the small lake which fed it have disappeared, both being filled in as San Francisco boomed during the gold rush. The name "Dolores" remained though the creek did not, and even today the Mission San Francisco de Asis, now on the edge of downtown San Francisco and situated on Dolores Street, is commonly referred to as "Mission Dolores." It is probably the only one of the missions with an "official" nickname. It calls itself by that name on its web site, in its publications, and on the historical marker in front of it.

Mission Dolores was one of the few missions founded on a site picked by the military. Generally the Franciscans were first on the scene and they picked the site for both the church and the *presidio.* In the case of Mission Dolores, Captain Juan de Anza arrived at the bay on March 28, 1776, after his colonizing trek from Mexico and picked sites for both the mission and *presidio.* De Anza left a small contingent of troops in place and almost immediately returned to Mexico. After Junipero Serra performed the dedicatory ceremonies at Dolores, Father Francis Palou, one of his former students in Mallorca and one of the original group of Franciscans in California, was put in charge of building the mission. Father Pedro Cambon was Palou's assistant in the venture. Although they immediately started building a crude structure, work on a permanent building was not begun until October of 1776. That church was a wooden structure plastered with mud; it served for six years.

In 1782, work on the present church was started. It was dedicated in 1791. *"Dolores"* was an apt nickname for St. Francis's mission, because the mission in its early years was plagued with sorrows. A year after its founding, Mission Dolores could claim only three converts from the native population. As always, there was trouble between the soldiers and the natives, generally as a result of the disregard the former showed for the women of the latter. In his writings, Father Palou describes a series of confrontations between the natives and the soldiers within months of the missions' founding that led to the death of one native and the serious wounding of another. Additionally, Mission

---

* Good Friday was in that era referred to as "The Friday of Sorrows" by the Spanish.

Dolores, with its cold, damp climate, was about the last place in the world where a policy of enforced confinement in close quarters—for such was life for the natives in the mission scheme—should have been attempted. The Spanish plan for colonization included a de facto policy of enclosure of the natives. The area's famous fogs were not at all romantic to the missionaries trying to treat, in their primitive hospital, the Indians who had been infected with the newcomer's diseases. These double "crimes" of California's colonization—introduction of virulent disease and confinement in close unsanitary quarters of the natives—had a devastating impact on the natives, and the mortality rate among the natives at Mission Dolores was higher than at any of the other missions. The mission's early history is a steady recitation of measles, smallpox and cholera, all diseases to which the natives had no resistance. Fear of the diseases the Spanish brought resulted in an effective boycott of the mission by the natives for most of its first year. When Father Serra returned to Mission Dolores for its first anniversary, he celebrated Mass for an underwhelming congregation of seventeen people, and that included the resident friars and soldiers from the *presidio*.

In 1786, Father Palou returned to Mexico, where he would complete his paean to his close friend, Junipero Serra. This seminal biography of Junipero Serra, *Relación Histórica de la Vida del Ven. P. Fr. Junipero Serra*, was published in Mexico City in 1787. The book had been largely written in San Francisco, and is generally viewed as the first book ever written in California.

On leaving San Francisco, Palou put Father Cambon in charge. Despite ill health, Father Cambon stayed until 1791 to see the new church completed, and then resigned from missionary work and returned to Mexico. Captain George Vancouver visited the mission in 1792 and described the wool processing and looms at work, as producing "very adequate cloth." San Francisco's cloth products were so desirable that at one point the governor of California prohibited their export to Mexico. Tile and brickwork from the mission was used extensively in the ongoing maintenance of the *presidio*. But these industries could only be maintained with Indian labor, and the Indians at the mission had no desire to live in the dank, unsanitary quarters offered them. They made repeated attempts to escape the mission environs as quickly as they could. They were dragged back by the soldiers and then punished, with floggings, stocks and chains, by the priests.

Father Cambon's replacements, Fathers Antonio Danti and Martin de Landaeta, were men who would add to the sorrows of Mission Dolores. Father Danti was, by all descriptions, cruel and harsh, and Father de Landaeta was, by most descriptions, insane.

In 1795, Father Danti led a punitive expedition across San Francisco Bay to recover a group of Indians who had decided to leave the mission. There is every indication that the impetus behind their decision to flee was disease and death at the mission, plus harsh treatment by Father Danti. When the runaways were located they resisted capture, and seven members of Danti's party were killed. Danti tried to suppress this grim news but the word got out, and Governor Diego de Borica ordered that no further such campaigns be attempted. Borica himself believed that the missionaries were unduly harsh in their treatment of the natives, going so far as to write a letter to Father Lasuen, the president of the mission, suggesting that such was the case. Father Lasuen admitted that the charges "may have been true" but he asserted that the matter "had been corrected."

Despite the governor's prohibitions, a year after Father Dantis' debacle Father de Landaeta sent another expedition to recover fleeing natives. This attempt was no more successful than the earlier one, although there was apparently no loss of life this time.

This latest foray bought to Governor Borica's attention not just the problems of Indians versus Spanish, but an apparently seething internal conflict between the Franciscans on the treatment of the Indians. It was one of the Franciscans, Father Jose Maria Fernandez, a fairly recent arrival at Mission Dolores, who wrote the governor regarding this latest expedition. Father Fernandez was outspoken and perhaps injudicious in his accusations against his fellow Franciscans, but Borica could not ignore his complaint. He launched his own expedition to the east side of the bay and returned with almost one hundred captive Indians. Although his intent was primarily to demonstrate to the Indians that the Spanish were not to be trifled with, he used the opportunity to gain some intelligence from the captives in hope of finding out the cause(s) of the defections. The testimony of these unfortunates, even if interpreted with the most jaundiced eye, reveals a mission life that can only be described as hellish:

Tiburcio was flogged five times by Danti for crying at the death of his wife and child. Magin was put in the stocks when ill. Tarazon visited his country and felt inclined to stay. Claudio was beaten by the *alcade* with a stick and forced to work when ill. José Manuel was struck with a bludgeon. Liberato ran away to escape dying of hunger as his mother, two brothers and three nephews had done. Otolon was flogged for not caring for his wife after she had sinned with the vaquero. Milan had to work with no food for his family and was flogged because we went after clams. Patabo had lost his family and had no one to take care of him. Orencio's niece died of hunger. Toribio was always hungry. Magno received no ration because, occupied in tending his sick son, he could not work.[1]

Borica was an efficient administrator and a conscientious servant of the Spanish Crown. He sifted the evidence and the testimony and concluded that the treatment given the Indians at San Francisco was more than harsh and in fact was cruel.

After almost two years of investigation Fathers Danti and Landaeta were returned to the more controlled atmosphere of the Franciscan College in Mexico City. Presumably they joined the long tradition of unbalanced eccentrics terrorizing the halls of higher education that continues to this day in universities throughout the world.

While there was clearly no love lost between the Indians of the region and the Franciscans of Mission Dolores, love apparently found a way to bloom between one of San Francisco's most privileged daughters and a Russian count. As has been mentioned, the Russians had long had designs on California, and although they never were in a position to seriously challenge Spanish supremacy, they continued to probe for possibilities from their base in Alaska. In 1806, Count Nikolai Petrovich Rezanof arrived in San Francisco, ostensibly seeking supplies for the Russian post in Sitka. Rezanof admits, though, in his journals that one of the things he is interested in is determining the adequacy, or inadequacy, of the Spanish military in the area.

Whatever his true motives, Rezanof is remembered not for his diplomatic or intelligence-gathering efforts but for giving the mission one of its very early love tragedies. While being entertained at Mission Dolores, Rezanof became enamored of another guest, Maria de la Concepcion Marcell Arguello. Despite the fact that she was but fifteen, and while he was forty-two, he pursued an engagement. He swore his true and undying love and asked her parents for her hand. Initially opposed to—in fact, likely outraged at—the proposal, her parents refused. Petrovich persisted and the parents eventually relented, but with a very serious caveat. Petrovich must obtain the consent of both the Russian czar and the Russian Orthodox church, and the Arguellos would have to obtain the consent of their own king and the Catholic church. Perhaps the family was simply taking the path of least resistance with an imposing Russian count and a headstrong teenage girl, figuring that all of the bureaucratic and religious hurdles would never be cleared, and the marriage would never take place. On the latter point they were correct, but not in the manner they had planned.

In May of 1806, Count Rezanoff left for St. Petersburg with a lock of Maria's hair around his neck. It was anticipated that his trip to Russia and back would take about two years. Ten months later while traveling through Siberia, the count suffered a series of injuries and died. It was two years before the waiting Maria learned of his death. Maria never married; she took the veil and became a Dominican nun, Sister Mary Domenica Arguello, and died fifty years later, still faithful to her Russian count.

It wasn't until 1808 with the arrival of Father Ramon Abella that the mission and its enterprises began to thrive. By 1810 Mission Dolores could boast of eleven thousand sheep and eleven thousand cows. Twenty looms were in operation and the congregation was over one thousand strong. Father Abella stayed twenty-five years.

In 1817, the Franciscans, finally recognizing the unhealthy situation at Mission Dolores, opened an *asistencia** and hospital in San Rafael across the Golden Gate, and began transferring neophytes from Dolores to the *asistencia.* San Francisco sits directly in the path of a major gap in California's Coast Range, through which wind and fog pour regularly. Although less than twenty miles apart, the difference in weather between the two locations is dramatic. It wasn't long before

---

* An asistencia was a smaller church attached to one of the missions. It was meant to provide access to religious services for those neophytes who lived too far away from the mission church.

the *assistencia* became the preferred site, and the population of Mission Dolores began to decline.

Dolores may be the only mission once threatened with extinction by one of its own Franciscan priests. Father José Altimira arrived at Mission Dolores in 1820. He was no more a fan of the foggy, damp climate than were the natives. Initially, Father Altimira began lobbying for the permanent closure of the mission and removal of all of its operations to the more benign climate of San Rafael. Eventually, though, he decided that another mission should be built still further north in Sonoma, and that both Missions Dolores and San Rafael should be closed. Father Altimira initially followed appropriate protocol and went to Mariano Payeras, the president of the California missions then in residence at La Purisima. Payeras had long been concerned about Russian encroachment on Spanish territory in California, so he very likely may have expressed support for the idea of a mission not far from the Russian establishment at Fort Ross. There is, however, no record that Payeras gave Altimira the go-ahead for his plan. Altimira nonetheless took the unprecedented step of next going directly to the legislature in Monterey with a detailed memorandum outlining his proposal. In April of 1823, the legislature approved the plan in total and authorized the closure of Dolores and San Rafael, and the establishment of a new mission in Sonoma. This intrusion of the civil authorities into the administration of the missions caused a significant three-way *contretemps* between the civil authorities, church authorities and the Franciscans. This controversy is treated at length in the chapter on Mission San Francisco de Solano, but suffice it to say here that it was yet another example of the difficulties the Franciscans faced in trying to serve two masters. Ultimately a compromise was crafted. It allowed the construction of a mission in Solano, but left Dolores and San Rafael intact.

The priests at Mission Dolores were very much caught up in the loyalty oath controversy when Mexico won its independence from Spain. While the president of the Franciscans in California refused to swear the required oath, he left it up to the individual Franciscans as a matter of conscience for their own individual decision. At San Francisco, a conflicted Father Estenaga initially refused to take the oath, but did celebrate the new republic with a special mass.

In 1833, the mission was put in the charge of Father José Quijas, an Indian native of Ecuador who had been ordained a priest. This was the only one of the California missions ever put under the authority of a Native American. Quijas was at Dolores only a year before he was moved north to San Rafael.

The following year, Mission Dolores was secularized and turned over to private interests. While the church was never abandoned, virtually all of the mission land surrounding it sat untended until the Gold Rush of 1849 put habitable land in San Francisco at a premium. The mission environs became the booming city's playground. Saloons, brothels, cheap hotels and bear-baiting pits surrounded the church. The rapidly-expanding city and its system of streets consumed most of the mission quadrangle. The church cemetery became the city cemetery, and in it were buried some of early California's most famous and infamous citizens, including California's first governor under Mexican rule, Don Louis Arguello who, along with Father Altimira, would have closed Mission Dolores. James P. Casey, hanged by San Francisco's notorious vigilantes in 1856, has one of the cemetery's most conspicuous markers. San Francisco politics were apparently as convoluted then as they are now. Casey, who by every account shot an unarmed man because he had revealed that Casey was an ex-felon, was also a member of the San Francisco Board of Supervisors and captain of the Crescent Fire Company No. 10. Over his grave, the members of his company have erected a monument with the plaintive epitaph, "May God forgive mine enemies."

In 1876, on the 100-year anniversary of the mission's founding, a large Victorian-style church, the Basilica of Mission Dolores, was built adjacent to Mission Dolores. The *convento*, or priests' quarters, from Mission Dolores was sacrificed to this edifice. The building was in the process of being enlarged in 1906 when the famous San Francisco earthquake and fire occurred. The new building was so badly damaged that it had to be abandoned; the original mission survived, largely intact, with a few broken statues and fallen angels.

It wasn't until 1916 that any real attempt was made to rehabilitate the mission, and unfortunately a large part of that rehabilitation was the towering basilica, which now overshadows the original mission. Still, in the center of San Francisco stands Mission Dolores, the oldest building in the city and the oldest intact church nave in all of California.

Mission San Francisco de Asis today:

Mission San Francisco de Assisi is located at 16th and Dolores Sreets, 3321 16th Street, San Francisco, CA, 94114 (415) 621-8203. http://www.missiondolores.org
Nickname: Mission Dolores

The church today at the corner of 16th and Dolores was the second Mission San Francisco, moved in 1782 from the original Dolores Creek location. The mission is now dwarfed by the Mission Dolores Basilica, completed in 1918. The basilica is a beautiful and inspiring structure, but to visit the Mission San Francisco de Asis, you have to visit the small structure with the Doric columns to the left of the basilica's towers. Mission Dolores is the oldest building in San Francisco, having survived all of San Francisco's earthquakes and fires. The chapel at Mission Dolores and the one at Santa Barbara are the only two buildings in the entire mission chain where we can say with certainty that Junipero Serra worshiped.

The mission at San Francisco is one of the smallest of the California missions. It appears even smaller than it is, since it abuts the towering basilica. The three openings above the balcony on the second level contain the original bells hung, from rawhide thongs. Because of their age and probable fragility, the bells are now rung only during Holy Week.

Its interior differs little from its original appearance. The redwood ceiling beams are the original ones created by Indian workmen. The decoration painted on these beams is dazzling and unique to San Francisco. Eye-catching, geometric patterns of red, gray, orange and white present an immediate impression that is almost dizzying. A careful study of these decorations reveals that they are the same interlocking design and colors as can be found in native basketry. The columns along the front third of the church and on the altar *reredos*, although they appear to be marble, are actually artfully painted wood. The *reredos* itself was built in Mexico City and brought to the mission in pieces. It was this *reredos* that served as the model for the reconstruction

133

of the *reredos* at San Carlos Borromeo. The statues in the *reredos* represent, on the upper row, Saint Anne, the mother of Mary, and Mary as Our Lady of the Angels. Below are Saint Francis, for whom the mission is named, Saint Joachim, the father of Mary, and the Archangel Michael. The statue of Michael is incongruous because there are three archangels, Michael, Rafael and Gabriel. Each of them has been identified with certain attributes. Michael is the warrior archangel. Rafael is the healer, and Gabriel is the herald. It was Gabriel who announced to Mary that she was to be the mother of God. Gabriel would thus be the logical archangel to depict in a tableau that clearly honors Mary. All of the other statues have a certain connection to Mary, the Mother of God, a significant personage in Catholic theology. However, Michael the warrior does not. Is it supposed to be Gabriel the herald? Did the builders of the mission not have their angels straight? Angelic confusion or not, the workmanship of the statutes is exquisite, and since they are of redwood found only on the northern California coast, they may be presumed to be the work of local artists, but their creator is unknown.

This type of workmanship, seen not just here but throughout the missions, is another tribute to the dedication of the early friars. They were not creating utilitarian buildings to serve a simple purpose; a Catholic mass can be celebrated in almost any surroundings and under any circumstances. Masses are today celebrated on the hoods of Humvees or on desert rocks. The missionaries themselves celebrated all of their early masses under crude, thatched shelters. Their goal was never to simply erect a building to practice their religious ceremonies. Their goal was to create lasting works of art and beauty, and in this they succeeded.

The arch which sets the altar off from the rest of the church has large symbols painted in each corner. To the left of the altar are the letters IHS, which is a contraction of the Greek term for Jesus. To the right are the letters AVM, superimposed on each other, which represent the Latin phrase *Ave Maria* (Hail Mary). Along the right wall is a large painting on canvas mounted on a moveable panel. In the early days of the mission, this panel was moved in front of the altar on Holy Thursday to close it off from the worshipers. It is a Catholic tradition that on Holy Thursday, after the celebration of the Mass of the Last Supper, the altar is stripped of all ornamentation and the Blessed

Sacrament removed. No masses are celebrated on the altar until the celebration of the Easter Vigil on the Saturday evening before Easter.

Mission Dolores, along with Mission San Juan Bautista, had a brief moment of Hollywood fame when it was featured in the 1958 Alfred Hitchcock film *Vertigo.* In the film, you can watch James Stewart park in front of the mission, go in the front door, and out a side door to the cemetery. It is in the cemetery that Kim Novak, as Madeline Elster, visits Carlotta's grave. The mission and the cemetery in the movie are in fact the cemetery at Mission Dolores, but Carlotta's grave was a prop created by Alfred Hitchcock.*

Vertigo is of course a purely fictional story, but Kim Novak's bête noir, Carlotta, is very loosely based on a real-life Carlotta, whose tragic history is part of the European colonial efforts in the new world. Carlotta was the wife of Maximilian, the short-lived French emperor of Mexico. In its revolution against Spain, Mexico borrowed heavily from various European powers. In 1861, President Benito Juarez suspended interest payment on these debts. In response, France, who was one of those creditors, with the support of Great Britain and Spain sent an expeditionary force to Mexico. In April of 1864, the French installed Maximilian, a Belgian prince, as emperor of Mexico. Despite the fact that the French invasion of Mexico was a flagrant trampling of the Monroe Doctrine, there was little the United States could do, being fully occupied at the time by the Civil War. Most historians agree that Maximilian tried to be a conscientious and reform-minded ruler but the Mexican people wanted nothing to do with this foreign usurper and the United States never would recognize his rule and this encouraged the "revolutionaries" against him. Although he sent his wife to safety, out of the country he himself refused to flee. He was captured and died in front of a firing squad, supposedly with the cry of "Viva Mexico" on his lips. As Maximilian and his rule came to a violent end, Carlotta began a life of pitiful wandering, apparently never understanding nor accepting that her husband was dead. Carlotta died in 1927, but in Belgium, not San Francisco.

Although Carlotta is not buried in the graveyard at Mission Dolores, much of California's early history is. The cemetery contains

---

*   For many years after the movie was released, "Carlotta's tombstone" placed by Hitchcock was left in place because so many people came to see it. It has since been removed.

the remains of Native Americans, Spanish and American soldiers, adventure-seekers from all over the world and, of course, priests. Also buried here are the first Mexican governor of California, Luis Antonio Arguello, and the early pugilist, "Yankee" Sullivan, from whom the more famous John L. Sullivan took his name.

Mission Dolores - the oldest building in San Francisco.

Endnotes

1   Bancroft, Hubert Howe. *History of California, Vol. I.* San Francisco: A.L. Bancroft and Company, 1884.

Chapter 10

SAN JUAN CAPISTRANO

The History of San Juan Capistrano

*L**a Mision de San Juan Capistrano de Sajivit** (The Mission of San Juan Capistrano of Sajivit), the seventh mission, was originally founded on October 30, 1775, near an Indian settlement known as Quanis Sajivit, which gave the mission its last name.

The mission was named after St. John of Capistrano, a German by birth, Italian by nationality, who died in Hungary. John was a lawyer who became a Franciscan priest relatively late in life. He was asked to go to Belgrade to give spiritual guidance to the city then under a siege by Mohammed II. Less than three years earlier, the Muslim army had conquered the much more heavily-defended and strategically important Constantinople. The fall of Belgrade and Vienna was seen as all but inevitable. At the Battle of Belgrade, John actually commanded the left wing of the Christian army against the Muslims. John's army, comprised primarily of peasants, not only defeated the Muslims but set in motion the process of the Muslim retreat from Europe. His feast day is celebrated in the Catholic church on October 23.

San Juan Capistrano is one of two missions that were actually *founded* twice. While several of the missions were started, stopped, and started again or relocated from site to site, San Juan Capistrano, along with Santa Barbara, actually had two formal founding ceremonies.* Originally, at the direction of Junipero Serra, Father Fermin de Lasuen and Father Gregorio Amurrio were assigned to build the mission. Amurrio arrived at San Juan Capistrano on the same day that

---

*   When Santa Barbara was founded, the new governor of California, Pedro Fages, could not be present, so twelve days later another dedication ceremony was held with Governor Fages in attendance.

137

news of the attack on San Diego was received. Fearing a wide-spread revolt throughout California, work on San Juan was stopped, the bells buried, and the site abandoned at the direction of Sergeant José Ortega, who was in charge of the soldiers at San Juan. A year later, when calm, if not peace, once more came to the Spanish settlements, Father Serra himself returned to the site, had the bells excavated, and once more founded San Juan Capistrano, on November 1, 1776. Thus San Juan Capistrano, while it was originally the sixth mission founded, is listed as the seventh. Father Lasuen was now serving as personal minister to Governor Rivera, so Serra appointed Father Pablo Mugartegui to serve at San Juan with Father Amurrio.

Father Mugartegui notes that in October of 1778, they moved from the original site to a new site approximately three miles to the west for a better access to water, as was so often the case. With adequate water assured, California's wine industry began at Mission San Juan Capistrano in 1779, with the planting of the first *"Criolla"* grape vines. There were grape plantings at all of the missions, including the very first one at San Diego. These earlier vineyards were primarily for the local production of sacramental wine; it was at San Juan Capistrano where vineyards as a commercial venture were instituted. In 1783, a winery and a distillery for producing brandy were completed.

While all of the missions had thriving agricultural and agrarian works, San Juan Capistrano boasts one of the few industrial complexes in the missions, and certainly the first one in California. In the 1790s San Juan Capistrano had a series of forges and metal working shops. The native Californians were introduced to the Iron Age five hundred years after it began, by the Franciscans at San Juan Capistrano.

In 1782, a new church was dedicated. It is still there today and is named as the Serra Chapel, because it is one of only two buildings in California where it is known for sure that Junipero Serra celebrated the sacraments.* This building would serve as the mission church for almost fifteen years, have a hiatus of ten years and then, after a tragic

---

* Mission Dolores in San Francisco is the other one. As with much of the mission legacy, this claim "Serra worshiped here" is argued back and forth between Mission Dolores and San Juan Capistrano. San Juan Capistrano does not dispute that Serra offered Mass at San Francisco, but their position is that it was not a finished church but a building under construction at the time, whereas when he said mass at San Juan Capistrano it was a completed building, the same one in existence today.

earthquake in 1812, regain its status as Mission San Juan Capistrano, a status it continues to enjoy to this day.

In 1796, work began on a much larger church, in order to accommodate the growing congregation. This church was the largest of all of the California missions. The dome over the transept was almost five stories high, and the bell tower approximately twelve stories. For a building as large and as complex as this one would be, the Franciscans did not overextend themselves, and hired a professional stonemason, Isidro Aguilar. Adobe would have been totally inadequate for a building of this scale. Sandstone was quarried six miles away and transported on ox carts to the building site. Almost ten years went into this effort, and unfortunately the master stonemason died in the sixth year. Here the Franciscans did overextend themselves, deciding to carry on the work without professional guidance, assuming that they had learned enough from the master while he was alive. There were documented irregularities in the walls as they were built, and although Aguilar had designed a church with six domed arches, a seventh was added to compensate for some less-than-accurate measurements. Finally, in 1806, the largest and most magnificent church in California was dedicated. An awful price would be extracted six years later for those less-than-accurate measurements. On December 8, 1812, just at the end of the first mass of the day the earth shook, the bells rang out on their own as the walls swayed, and the bell tower and ceiling collapsed. The bell tower toppled onto a nearby native settlement, and the domed ceiling failed and dropped tons of stone on the worshipers.* Virtually all of the southern California missions were damaged by the quake, but San Juan Capistrano, probably because of faulty construction, suffered the only known deaths. Although there was a half-hearted attempt to rebuild, it was soon recognized that the priests lacked the expertise for such a structure, and that perhaps it was that very lack of expertise that had led to the disaster of 1812. A church that took ten years to buld was six years later left a mass of rubble in a matter of seconds. There had been some dissension among the Fran-

*   There is an unverifiable legend that attending mass that day was a young lady named Magdalena. She and her lover Teofilio had been carrying on a secret affair and she had gone to mass that day to offer penance. When the earthquake struck, Teofilio rushed into the church to save her. When the rubble was cleared, Teofilio and Magdalena were found in each other's arms. Supposedly the ghosts of the two young lovers still haunt the ruins.

ciscans from the day the church was planned. Some of them felt that a church of such grandeur was not fitting to their mission or their order. It was seen as ostentatious and out of character with the Franciscan creed of simplicity and poverty. The earthquake and the destruction of the church was viewed by this minority as God's retribution for pride.

The earthquake was the most destructive of a series of earthquakes that continued for a month. For many years, 1812 was referred to as *"el ano de los temblores."* Every one of the existing missions suffered damage, some to the extent that they had to be replaced by new structures. Here was yet another challenge for the Franciscans. Hostile natives, harsh living conditions, sickness and disease were all part of the rigors they had anticipated when they began their task. An earth that shook and trembled for a month straight had never been contemplated. Anyone who has ever been in an earthquake will remember the absolute feeling of helplessness when it becomes clear that it is not the wind, not a storm, not water nor fire nor any other bound force, but the very earth itself that is threatening. That feeling in reality only lasts for seconds or at most minutes, but remains for a lifetime. Imagine such a feeling for day after day, or worse, in the darkness of night. Imagine hearing from your *confreres* both north and south, that the same thing is occurring with them. Is this the final cataclysm? The end of the world? Can anyone survive this?

They did survive, but housed now in a much more modest and practical structure. There was finally an acceptance that this most magnificent, and some said pretentious, church was not meant to be. "Serra's Chapel," which had been used for grain storage, once more became the church. That chapel remains today as Mission San Juan Capistrano. The still-magnificent ruins of the stone church remain as starkly beautiful reminders of the folly of casually seeking magnificence.

San Juan Capistrano was one of the missions that suffered the deprivations of privateer Hippolyte Bouchard. In 1818, he assaulted the mission compound with a company of men and several field pieces. Bouchard overcame resistance by an outmanned and outgunned military force, and the mission and its stores, particularly wine and brandy, were ransacked. One of Bouchard's officers noted that the march back to the ship was considerably less orderly than was the march to the mission, because of intoxication. Several buildings were damaged, including the storehouse and the governor's residence.

140

In 1826, Governor Echeandia used San Juan Capistrano as a model for his plan of secularization and the emancipation of the Indians from Franciscan control. Despite a less-than-enthusiastic acceptance of the plan, not just from the Franciscans but more importantly from the Indians themselves, the plan continued. When secularization did come about in 1834, the mission assets were valued at something approaching $55,000 dollars. However, when the mission and its lands were sold in 1845, the entire property went for just over $700. The fact that the purchaser was the brother-in-law of then-Governor Pio Pico did not seem to be cause for much concern. The purchaser, Don Juan Forster, and his family actually lived in the former friars' quarters for twenty years. In 1865, Abraham Lincoln returned the property to the Catholic church. Fitful efforts at restoring it were made from time to time, but it wasn't until 1895 that the Landmarks Club initiated serious efforts toward its restoration and preservation. However, no one did more to restore San Juan Capistrano than Father Saint John O'Sullivan.

Father Saint John O'Sullivan ("Saint" is his name, not an honor bestowed by the Catholic church,) arrived at San Juan Capistrano on July 5, 1910. He was suffering from tuberculosis and had received an invitation from another priest to visit San Juan to see if California's salubrious climate might help him. San Juan Capistrano was Father O'Sullivan's salvation, and Father O'Sullivan became in large measure San Juan's salvation. For twenty-three years, enjoying the benefits of the dry climate, Father O'Sullivan labored at San Juan and oversaw its restoration and preservation. One of his first tasks was to restore the Serra Chapel, that once more was being used as a storehouse. In the restoration, the chapel had to be enlarged by raising the roof of the apse to accommodate the beautiful gilded altar and backdrop you see today.

Father O'Sullivan assured San Juan Capistrano a spot in California's pop culture when, in 1911, he officiated at the wedding of silent film star Mary Pickford in the mission chapel. The mission had been the backdrop for the first movie ever made in Orange County, *Rose of the Golden West*, starring Miss Pickford.

Father O'Sullivan was also responsible for the mission's garden, one of its most attractive features. It must be remembered that the original missions were workplaces meant to produce economic gain to the Spanish empire. A quiet, contemplative garden for strolling, such as we see today at San Juan Capistrano and many of the other missions, was not part of the mission complexes. Where the garden is today was originally part of the mission work area, containing mills, forges and workshops. Father O'Sullivan died in 1933 and is buried in the cemetery at San Juan Capistrano.

Mission San Juan Capistrano today:

Mission San Juan Capistrano is located at 26801 Camino Capistrano/Ortega Highway, San Juan Capistrano, CA; PO Box 697, San Juan Capistrano, CA, 92693. (949) 234-1300.
E-mail: miawrence@missionsjc.com
Nickname: The Mission of the Swallows

San Juan Capistrano is today a wonderful blend of well-restored gardens, grounds and buildings, and aged and imposing ruins from the earthquake of 1812. The church itself is Serra's Chapel, the oldest continuously-used building in California, enlarged and improved after the huge church was destroyed. As mentioned, it is one of the places we know for sure where Junipero Serra officiated at Mass.

The spectacular golden altar is actually a fairly recent addition. It was added as part of the restoration of the mission in 1924. At an estimated three hundred years old, it is far older than the mission it graces, and in fact is older than any of the missions. It was originally built and likely used for an unknown church in Spain. In 1906, the bishop of California purchased it for the Los Angeles cathedral. It was never installed in the cathedral and in 1924 it was donated to San Juan Capistrano. The backdrop was so tall that the roof of the chapel had to be raised. Should you care to count, you will find fifty-two angel faces carved in this piece, one to give praise for each Sunday in the year.

In the center niche is a statute of Saint John of Capistrano, holding a crusader's banner, although the warrior Saint John was not actually a participant in any of the Crusades. To his left and right are Saint Francis, Saint Clare, Saint Peter, and Saint Michael the Archangel. There are two side altars, one dedicated to Saint Joseph, the other to the Virgin Mary. While the Native Americans did most of the decorating at all of the California missions, San Juan Capistrano is likely the only one with a depiction of one of their pagan gods. Likely while the building was being used as a storehouse, or perhaps during a long service, one of the congregation sketched an outline of the god Tobet, venerated by the Tongva and Luiseno peoples, on one wall of the Serra Chapel. Undoubtedly Tobet was put there surreptitiously and never noticed until the chapel's restoration. Thankfully, the restorers realized the artistic and historic importance of this piece of graffiti and have left it in place

When visiting San Juan Capistrano, one is torn between spending time in the wonderfully-restored chapel, the beautiful gardens, or the magnificent ruins, the remains of the great stone church that collapsed with a huge loss of life in 1812. They are breathtaking in their crumbling grandeur. To view the remaining arches and towering walls and to realize that they were built in the eighteenth century with no power except human or animal is to gain new respect for the Franciscans who envisioned such a project, and for the natives who crafted it.

There can be no discussion of San Juan Capistrano without a discussion of its famous swallows. For years, the swallows nested at the mission in large numbers. Their comings and goings were celebrated in story and song, and with various festivities. They are not the more familiar barn swallows, but rather cliff swallows *(petrochelidon pyrrhonota)*. As such, they nest on the sides of stone walls. If the stone walls are those of a building, and if the niches and crevices conducive to the building of a nest are most common over doorways, swallow nests can be unpleasant attachments for people coming and going. Of course, there could not be a story about birds and the followers of Saint Francis without some element of the miraculous to it. In the case of San Juan Capistrano, the story goes that when one of the early monks noticed a storekeeper in the town knocking the nests of the birds off his building, he invited the homeless birds to the mission where there was "room for all." The swallows accepted his invitation and have stayed at the mission ever since. The myth of the swallows is that they leave for their journey to South America on October 23, the feast day of the mission's patron saint, and that they return each spring on March 19 the feast day of Saint Joseph, the patron saint of the entire California mission project. It is a fact that around those dates the swallows do begin and end their migratory journey. Every year there is a huge festival at San Juan Capistrano generally on the weekend closest to March 19, the feast day of Saint Joseph. There is food, dancing, open-air markets and a parade to celebrate the return of the swallows. The swallows do return in the spring but great flocks of them appearing from over the ocean on March 19 has never happened. In fact, in most recent years the swallows have made very disappointing appearances at the festival held in their honor. No one is quite sure what has brought about the change in their migratory habits. Like so many other recent phenomena both positive and negative, climate change is the most frequent suspect. Another theory suggests that modern architecture, particularly freeway overpasses, offer a more attractive nesting environment than adobe walls, and the swallows have no incentive to return to their old haunts.

Buried in the church at San Juan Capistrano are Father Vincente Fuster, Father Jose Barona and Father Vicente Pascual Olivia. Father Fuster took a somewhat circuitous route to his final resting place. As one of the founders of San Juan, when he died in 1800 he was buried in the then-existing church. When the more grandiose church was finished, he was moved to that edifice. When that church was destroyed in the earthquake, he was returned again to Serra's Chapel, where he lies today.

A few blocks to the west of Mission San Juan Capistrano is Mission Basilica San Juan Capistrano, which was built in 1982 as a somewhat smaller replica of the original mission. If you want a sense of what Mission San Juan Capistrano looked like before the 1812 earthquake, walk the few blocks to the west and visit the Basilica.

Mission San Juan Capistrano - bells.

Ruins of 1812 earthquake.

Ruins.

LANDS NEVER TRODDEN

Chapter 11

Santa Clara de Asis

The History of Santa Clara Asis

*L*a *Mision de Nuestra Madre Santa Clara de Asis* (the Mission of our Mother Saint Clare of Assisi, the eighth of the missions, was founded on January 12, 1777. Santa Clara was the first of the missions to be named after a woman. Saint Clare was born in Assisi, Italy, around 1193, just ten years after the birth of Assisi's most famous son, Francis, the founder of the Franciscan order. Clare's family, like Francis's, was wealthy and influential. Clare was a child much taken with religion, and as a young woman, she became enthralled by the preaching and message of Saint Francis and decided to follow his example. At the age of eighteen, on Palm Sunday, she showed up at the Franciscan community, had her hair shorn, exchanged her clothes for a dress of sackcloth, and made a vow to become a nun. Her brothers, who had already found Clare's sanctity a bit over the top, literally stormed the altar and tried to drag her from the church while she clung, wailing and beseeching, to the church tapestries. Drama and tumult notwithstanding, Clare prevailed and after taking the veil, she founded an order of nuns, the Poor Clares, an order that to this day continues its work of service to the poor all over the world. Plagued with ill health, Clare was frequently confined to her bed, which kept her from attending mass. One Christmas day while ill in her bed, Clare supposedly saw and heard the mass being celebrated in the distant church, on the wall of her cell at the foot of her bed; and so, Clare became the patron saint of television. Her feast day is August 11.

Mission Santa Clara, along with San Diego, San Francisco and San Buenaventura, was originally sited not by the Franciscans, but by the Spanish military. Mission San Francisco and its *presidio* secured the ocean side of San Francisco Bay, but it soon became clear that given the size of the harbor, security would be needed on the eastern and southern end of the huge bay. Eventually two missions were built on that eastern shore, Santa Clara at the southern end and San Jose to the north.

Junipero Serra appointed Father Tomas de la Peña and Father Jose Murguia to establish the mission. (Father Murguia was originally scheduled to be in the initial trip to San Diego in 1769. He was to be the chaplain on the *San Jose* when it sailed for California. Before he could join the ship, though, an epidemic broke out at Mission San Jose del Cabo in Baja California. Murguia was sent there to assist its stricken priest. The *San Jose* sailed for California without him, and was never heard from again.) Father de la Peña picked a site for the church building on the Guadalupe River, and on January 12, 1777, the mission was founded. Murguia was sixty-two, a very advanced age in 1777, when he accepted the daunting task of founding a new mission in Alta California. He remained at Santa Clara until his death five years later.

It was from Mission Santa Clara that one of the persistent myths surrounding Junipero Serra arose. To this day there are people who insist that Junipero Serra *walked* every mile of the considerable distances he covered in his fifteen years in California. It was a chance encounter at Mission Santa Clara that gave the myth wings. Serra's friend and his first biographer wrote:

> We arrived on the 11th of October at the Mission of Santa Clara, and at the very same hour the Venerable Father Junipero also arrived. He had suddenly resolved to visit these missions in order to make confirmation…ignoring his malady and putting all his trust in God. But he arrived so badly fatigued that he could hardly stand, as in two days he had traveled twenty-seven leagues.* And when the officers and the surgeon saw his foot with the ulcer they said that it was just a miracle that he had been able to walk. But he had *indeed made that journey.* . . . coming from the south and we from the north . . . [1]

---

* Twenty-seven leagues is more than seventy miles. This amount of travel by anyone in two days has to be questioned. Palou offers no factual information (e.g., where Serra began) regarding the distance.

This one recorded instance of Junipero Serra traveling by foot a prodigious distance under very difficult circumstances has somehow become an article of faith by mission *aficionados*: that Junipero Serra made all of his thousands of miles of travel on foot. This, despite the fact that Serra in his own writings many times refers to traveling by horseback or mule, or even by ship.

Santa Clara was one of the missions that got off to a very rocky start with the native population. First, several of the soldiers' mules were stolen, and when an avenging force arrived from the *presidio* in San Francisco, the unfortunate Indians were caught in the act of eating the contraband. A confrontation ensued, and as usual in the conflict between firearms and arrows, the firearms prevailed. Three of the natives were killed and several others taken prisoner and flogged. Shortly after this unhappy affair, one of the all-too-frequent epidemics broke out at the mission, carrying away many of the native children.

Father de la Peña, whose full name was Tomas de la Peña Saravia, was not by any means one of the more stellar members of the Franciscan order. Almost from the outset, he proved to be not just difficult but impossible to deal with when it came to controlling the lives of the Indians. Once again, the Franciscans' efforts to impose their standards of conduct and morality on the native population caused not just resentment and rebellion but—as the following case illustrates—confusion and consternation. In 1781, an unbaptized Indian woman named Yumen came to Father de la Peña and expressed her desire to marry one Sebastian. Yumen and her parents were open with the priest, telling him that she had been married previously but was now divorced. De la Peña, exhibiting a well-known Catholic prejudice regarding marriage after divorce, refused to allow the marriage.

Yumen worked as a maid for one of the ladies in the nearby town of San Jose. Her employer must have been a very well-educated eighteenth-century Catholic, for she told Yumen that in accordance with the doctrine of the "Pauline Privilege," if she was baptized in the Catholic church, and her former husband was not, the first marriage could be annulled and then she could be married in the Church. The "Pauline Privilege" is an obscure doctrine that allows for the dissolution of a marriage contracted between two non-baptized persons if one of the two, but not the other, seeks baptism and converts to Catholicism. It is based on a somewhat convoluted reading of Paul's first letter to the

Corinthians (1 Corinthians 7:10-15),* thus the name "Pauline Privilege." Yumen set about to make her case fit the circumstances as detailed by St. Paul. She had herself baptized, took the name Pelagia Maria, and once more petitioned de la Peña to marry her and Sebastian. De la Peña was obdurate, not only refusing to perform the ceremony but harassing the couple to the extent that they fled to San Francisco. Fleeing from one mission to another was pointless; in San Francisco, both were arrested, returned to Santa Clara, and flogged for apparently trying to do the right thing.

Yumen's troubles were far from over. Father de la Peña, not satisfied with just frustrating her efforts to marry a new husband, was determined to restore her to the old one. Her first husband, Pedro Huajolis, had been baptized in the midst of this contratemps. Subsequently, on July 2, 1785, Pedro Pablo Huajolis and Pelagia Maria (Yumen) were married at Mission Santa Clara. The insufferable Father de la Peña's efforts notwithstanding, Yumen was not going to submit to his machinations. Yumen's view was that she was tricked and forced in to marrying Huajolis, and that she had never consented to the marriage. She later gave written testimony that neither she nor Pedro wanted the marriage, it was never consummated and that after the ceremony, she returned to her family and Pedro returned to his wife, whom he had acquired some time earlier, a marriage that for some reason did not seem to bother de la Peña.

De la Peña's issues with the natives were not limited to matchmaking. Father de la Peña has the dubious distinction of being the only Franciscan in the early history of the missions accused of murder. In 1786, a group of fifteen neophytes at Mission Santa Clara lodged a formal complaint that de la Peña regularly and cruelly punished the Indians for routine infractions. Although corporal punishment of the Indians was unfortunately an accepted practice at all of the California missions, in de la Peña's case there were charges that he had actually killed not one, but *three* Indians, one by kicking him in the head after

---

*   "If a brother has a wife who is an unbeliever, and she is content to live with him, he must not send her away; and if a woman has an unbeliever for her husband, and he is content to live with her, she must not leave him. This is because the unbelieving husband is made one with the saints through his wife and the unbelieving wife is made one with the saints through her husband."

knocking him down, one by beating him to death and one by breaking his neck. Investigations ensued at both the civilian and ecclesiastical levels. Interestingly, one query common to all of the investigations was whether or not Father de la Peña had, in his punishments "drawn blood or otherwise seriously harmed the Indians." There was no concern in anyone's mind about corporal punishment; just how violent that punishment may have been.

The civilian investigation was conducted by Governor Fages. Fages himself had been present on one occasion when de la Peña hit a young boy so hard on the head that his ears began to bleed. Not surprisingly, at the conclusion of his investigation, Fages made a report in which he concluded that de la Peña was not fit to serve as a missionary.

Unfortunately (also not surprisingly), the investigation by Father Fermin de Lasuen, the president of the Franciscans at the time, not only absolved de la Peña, but charged his accusers with perjury and calumny. The two conflicting views were argued and debated for many years, with judgments made, appeals filed and more investigations conducted, not just in California but in Mexico as well.

In June of 1786, Father Lasuen wrote an almost twenty-page report and appeal on the matter. Lasuen gives second hand information from a variety of soldiers who had served at Santa Clara, none of whom had anything but glowing reports to give of de la Pena's behavior. Lasuen saved his most compelling arguments for the end of his letter, raising the defense of clerical immunity. Even if the accusations are true, he asserts that there could be no further proceedings against the erring priest because the governor's investigation was not conducted in secrecy as required by Spanish law and thus the whole matter would have to be viewed as totally invalid. This appeal did not work, and the investigation dragged on until 1791, when the viceroy declared de la Peña unfit to be a missionary, and ordered him to be recalled to Mexico. De la Peña's superiors were still unconvinced, and perhaps fearing more than anything a precedent of allowing civil authorities to control the activities of the Franciscans, requested that they be allowed to conduct further investigation of the matter. At the conclusion of their investigation, de la Peña was once again found innocent of the charges. The wheels of justice in this case had ground so exceedingly slowly that Father de la Peña was now seen by detractors and defenders alike as completely demented, one side citing the charges against him as the cause, and the other seeing it as proof that he had always been too unstable to be a missionary. He was ordered back to Mexico on August 12, 1794, and thus the charges were effectively dropped.

De la Peña was replaced by Father Benito Catala, fortunately for the natives a man more renowned for his piety than his cruelty. He was often referred to as "the holy man of Santa Clara." Father Catala arrived at Santa Clara in 1794 and remained there until his death thirty-six years later. Despite the fact that he was severely crippled with arthritis, Father Catala was an extreme aesthetic, fasting until noon each day and never consuming meat, eggs, fish or wine. When his infirmities prevented him from standing to preach, he gave his sermons while seated at the foot of the altar. Father Catala's reputation for piety and holiness prompted the first archbishop of San Francisco, Joseph Alemany, to petition the Vatican to consider Catala for sainthood. Although the petition for canonization was accepted in 1884 and advanced through the first of several steps, it has lain dormant since 1909. The "holy man of Santa Clara" does not seem to be slated for official sainthood in the Catholic church.

In 1794, two other priests, Father Jose Viader and Father Manuel Fernandez, came to the mission. By all of the available evidence, these two were unfortunately more in the mold of the vindictive Father de la Peña than the holy Father Catala They were additional trials the neophytes of this mission had to face.

Father Viader was a capable but boisterous and tumultuous priest. He was chastised at least once for not just ordering the flogging of an Indian woman, but for inflicting the punishment himself. It was this sort of behavior that occasioned an attack on Father Viader by three Indians seeking revenge for his highhanded treatment. Father Viader managed to best them all and, in a turn of events indicative of the man's personality, sought friendship with the men and actually converted one of them, Marcelo, who became the mission's *major domo* for many years. Whatever his temperamental issues, Viader is another example of the faithfulness and obedience of the Franciscans. He was not happy in California, and repeatedly petitioned for permission to return to Mexico, in 1820 importuning, "For the love of God, let my permission arrive."[2] Permission was not forthcoming and Viader, like so many of his contemporaries, stayed true to his vow of obedience and remained at Santa Clara until 1833, when the mission was handed over to a different province of the Franciscans.

Viader's partner, Father Fernandez, was a man cut from a slightly different cloth. His superior once noted that ". . . I am told that nothing suits him; and I notice that none of the missionaries who have known him like him."[3] He stayed at Santa Clara only four years, and was given permission to return to Mexico because ". . . he is possessed of an insurmountable boredom and a repugnance for the country and for laboring in it."[4]

The site for Santa Clara had been picked based on the ready availability of water. Two years after its founding, the water became all too available, and the log church was destroyed by a flood. A second but temporary log church was built at the same location. It wasn't until 1781 that they were satisfied with a site high enough to be out of the flood plain, but close enough to allow them to bring irrigation water to their fields. A third church was built, not of logs but of adobe, and was completed in 1784. Faithful Father Murguia, who had been the church's mainstay from its humble beginnings, was never to enjoy the beautiful church he designed. He died just four days before its dedication. Junipero Serra himself dedicated the church.

Santa Clara was another of the missions visited by George Vancouver on his 1792 expedition. Vancouver discussed the industries of cloth making and tanning, which were mainstays of the mission. He noted that the cloth at Santa Clara was of better quality than that obtained at San Francisco.

As in much of California, missions and *pueblos* that were many miles apart at their founding now meld invisibly one into the other. The towns of Santa Clara and San Jose are examples of this, with Mission Santa Clara located at what is now the edge of downtown San Jose. This kind of proximity led to conflicts between the *padres* and the civic authorities. Typical of this was the complaint made by the *padres* in 1777, when the town and mission were both being founded, that their land and their water and grazing rights were being encroached upon by the inhabitants of San Jose. One attempt at easing tensions was undertaken in 1795, when Father Catala had more than two hundred Indians embark on a project of lining both sides and the center of the *alameda,* the four-mile piece of roadway between the town and the mission, with willow trees. For years, these trees were the defining element of a beautiful and gracious carriage ride between the two institutions. Subsequent street widening has resulted in the destruction of almost all of these trees. As late as the early 1980s, some of these 150-year old trees were still present, but the last one was removed in 1982

Thirty-seven years after its founding, Mission Santa Clara was a thriving enterprise with 1,400 native people living on its lands. The mission cattle numbered around 8,000, and there were 2,000 horses in its herds. 65,000 bushels of cereals and grains were harvested annually.

In 1812, the mission was seriously damaged by the earthquake that did so much damage to all of the then-existing missions. Despite the damages, the church continued in use until 1819, when a fourth church was built. In 1825, a fifth church was built. This church had a ceiling decorated by Agustin Davila, a famous Mexican artist who contributed his talents to several of the missions.

Several Indians from Santa Clara took part in what is now known as the "Estanislao Revolt," one of the more serious attempts to throw the interlopers out of Alta California. California was a territory of the Mexican government when, in 1829, Estanislao, an *alcade* at Mission San Jose, decided he no longer wanted to be confined to the mission way of life. He left San Jose with several other neophytes and fled to the San Joaquin Valley.* By the next spring, several Indians from Mission Santa Clara joined him, and Estanislao had a force of several hundred. Attempts to capture and return them initially met with the failure and defeat of the Mexican soldiers. In a subsequent engagement, one of the rebels, an unnamed unfortunate identified only as a "Christian Indian from Santa Clara," was captured. The Mexican soldiers had their Indian auxiliaries form a semi-circle, place the prisoner at the center of this arc, and begin shooting him with arrows. Seventy-three arrows in his body later, the man still was not dead. A Mexican soldier shot him in the head to bring the grisly affair to an end.

Santa Clara was one of the last missions to be secularized, but in 1836 the inevitable blow came. Mission Santa Clara escaped the worst ravages of secularization, but when the decree was carried out it was

---

*   Stanislaus County and the Stanislaus River, flowing down the western slope of the Sierra Nevada, are named after him.

a prime example of the disconnect between the ideal and the practical. At Santa Clara, 66,000 acres was distributed, 12,000 to Indians and 54,000 to others. The church building remained in the Franciscans' hands, but all other land and buildings were appropriated. The church at Mission Santa Clara was never abandoned, and always had a priest in residence, sometimes good priests, oftentimes very bad priests.

Arriving in 1844, Father José Maria del Refugio Suarez del Real was one half of a somewhat infamous pair of brothers in the Franciscan order. Each of them had a reputation for drunkenness and licentious living. Father del Real came to Santa Clara with a reputation for scandalous conduct well-established from his previous posting at Monterey. He was known to his superiors to have lived at various times, and sometimes contemporaneously, with three different women. He maintained the women and his children by them in houses he built with mission funds. James A. Forbes, British Vice Counsel in Monterey, himself baptized into the Catholic Church by Father Suarez de Real, described him as "reeking with concupiscence... [the] padre had the woman he lived with, and from whom he had several children ... across the street from the Mission church." [5] Apparently "sins of the flesh" were not the only failings of Father del Real. Forbes leaves a dark hint that the priest was suspected of poisoning another priest sent to investigate his behavior.

Something about Santa Clara seems to have drawn the worst of the Franciscan order. Besides Father del Real, Father José Vinals (1794) and Father Jesus Maria Vasquez del Mercado (1839-1844) were all accused, with some fair amount of evidence, of fathering children while at Mission Santa Clara.

Mission Santa Clara played a very small part in the Mexican-American War. On May 13, 1846, the U.S. Congress approved a declaration of war with Mexico. The immediate issue leading to the declaration was a strip of land between the Nueces and Rio Grande rivers in Texas. The war and its consequences would have a dramatic impact on California, the other major Mexican territory. For several years there had been, an increasingly large number of American citizens settling in the Santa Clara Valley. In January of 1847, a force of United States Marines and volunteers under Captain Ward Marston engaged in a brief skirmish at Mission Santa Clara, with Mexican forces led by Don Francisco Sanchez, a prominent rancher in the Santa Clara Valley. Sanchez was holding several Americans he had taken prisoner when the news of hostilities between Mexico and the United States reached him. After a desultory and inconclusive battle, a truce was arranged and prisoners exchanged. Sanchez returned to his ranch, Marston to San Francisco; and the Santa Clara valley, along with the rest of California became part of the United States at the end of the Mexican-American War in 1848.

In 1851, the first bishop of San Francisco appointed a Jesuit priest, Father John Nobili, as pastor at Santa Clara. Father Nobili had been trying to found an institution of higher learning in California. In May of 1851, the decrepit mission Santa Clara became the site of California's first college, Santa Clara College. That same year the Methodist church founded Wesleyan college in Stockton, California, but because Santa Clara started actual instruction before Wesleyan College—now the University of the Pacific—Santa Clara claims the distinction of California's first institution of higher education, although Weslyan College was granted a charter in 1851 and Santa Clara did not get its charter until 1855. What is not in doubt is that Santa Clara awarded the first bachelor's degree given in California, to one Thomas I. Bergin. In 1912, Santa Clara College added schools of engineering and law and changed its name to University of Santa Clara. In 1985 it became Santa Clara University, supposedly so that there would be no confusion in initials with the University of Southern California.

In 1926, a fire started in the attic of the church at Mission Santa Clara. At first it burned slowly, giving the priests and the community time to rescue much of the artwork. What could not be saved was Davila's painted ceiling. There were, however, photographs of this priceless artwork, and when the mission was rebuilt in 1929, Davila's work was reproduced from these photographs. Davila also painted the ceiling at Mission San Jose, and that work was lost when an earthquake destroyed that ceiling. As far as is known, the only surviving piece of Davila's entire body of work is a baptismal font at Mission San Jose.

Mission Santa Clara today:

Mission Santa Clara is located on the campus of Santa Clara University, 5000 East Camino Real, Santa Clara, CA, 95053; (408) 554-4023. http://www.scu.edu/visitors/mission

Mission Santa Clara is nestled into the campus of its offspring, the University of Santa Clara, a Catholic university offering undergraduate, masters, doctoral and law degrees to more than eight thousand students. The University is also the home of the California Mission Studies Association, a non-profit corporation dedicated not just to the preservation of the missions, but of all to the Hispanic-period historic resources in California. Interestingly, the university and consequently the mission itself is staffed by the Jesuits, the same order whose expulsion from Spanish territories in 1766 opened the way for the Franciscans to be tasked with the duty to establish the California missions.

As you approach the church you will note eight white crosses on the lawn in front of the church. These crosses are a reminder that the rigors of missionary work continue today. They commemorate the deaths in 1989 of six Jesuit priests and two of their staff in El Salvador. They were murdered by members of the Salvadoran army for their attempts to bring social change and justice for the poor to El Salvador. Twenty years later the president of El Salvador, Mauricio Funes, announced that his government would posthumously bestow its highest honor, the Order of José Matías Delgado, on the six Jesuits. President Funes, in announcing the honor, said that he and other members of his cabinet considered the men "eminent Salvadorans who rendered extraordinary service to the country." Of the six priests killed, only one was a native Salvadorian, the others having arrived as young seminarians from Spain, much as had their Franciscan predecessors two hundred years earlier in California.

The statues on the front of the church are depictions of Saint Clare, the mission's patron, in the central position above the door; Saint Francis to her left; and John the Baptist to her right. These are bronze reproductions that replaced the original ones, carved of wood, that are now inside the church.

The mission bells have their own interesting history. In 1784, when the first permanent mission was completed, King Carlos of Spain sent a complete set of bells to the mission and requested that they be rung each evening at eight-thirty to commemorate the deceased members of his family. One of these original bells remains, in slightly revised form: the bell was actually broken in the 1926 fire, but Alfonso XIII of Spain had it recast. It continues the tradition that began more than 200 years ago, and is rung every evening at eight-thirty.

Because of the devastating fire in 1926, none of the church interior is original. Virtually all that remains is a portion of an adobe wall, exposed in the Saint Francis chapel, so that one can see at least a bit of the workmanship now almost 200 years old. Santa Clara was one of the few California missions whose artwork was at least directed, and in large measure undertaken, by a professional.

The Mexican artist Augustine Davila originally painted the vaulted ceiling. The ceiling today is a reproduction based on photographs taken of his work before the church burned down. These photos show almost playful figures against an ornate background.

Davila came to California at the age of twenty-nine. Santa Clara was his first, but not his only, artistic endeavor. All that survives today of all his works is a hand-carved baptismal font at Mission San Jose. The ceiling at Santa Clara was considered his masterwork. Of particular interest in the ceiling painting is the depiction of the Holy Trinity as three male figures—seemingly contemporaries—sitting down for some talk and conviviality. These "three *amigos*" of Santa Clara, with their prominent placing above the altar, are one of its most charming features.

Davila's personal life was at least as flamboyant as his artistic renderings. At the age of thirty-two, he married a thirteen-year-old girl. They had four children, and in 1848 he was killed by a neighbor in a dispute over chickens.

There are other interesting works of art in the mission, including the murals of Saint Francis and Saint Dominic above the altar. To this day the myth persists that Francis and Dominic, the founders of two of the largest orders in the Catholic church, were friends. In fact, while the two were contemporaries, they never met. The story of their friendship was perpetuated by the official church in an attempt to put an end to an unseemly rivalry that had grown up between the two orders. It seems to have worked, because it is rare that in a church founded by either of the orders that you will not see portrayals of the other.

In the baptistery at the back of the church is a painting of the Holy Family. This painting was done in 1889 by Italian artist Giuseppe Riva, and it is based on an earlier work by Murillo. The painting was commissioned by a Captain Francisco Raggio for his brother Father Aloysius Raggio, who was a pastor at Santa Clara in the late 1800s. The painting was completed in fulfillment of a promise made by Captain Raggio, who had served in the French Foreign Legion, and who had made a promise to God that if he ever got home alive from what at the time was French Indo-China, he would pay for a magnificent work of religious art. The painting was rescued from the 1926 fire and re-hung in the reconstructed church.

On the left side of the church near the altar is the Guadalupe chapel. This chapel contains a reproduction of the iconic image of Mary as Our Lady of Guadalupe. Above it is another image of Mary, as Our Lady of Refuge. This painting is also one that hung in the original church and was saved from the fire. It was painted by a former mission Indian known only by the name of Eulalio. He is one of the few native Californians to have received training as a professional artist in Mexico, and so his painting, done in the mid-1800s, is considered Mexican art, and not native Californian.

Buried in the church are Father Magin Catala, "the holy man of Santa Clara," Father John Nobili, the Jesuit who founded the University of Santa Clara, Father Peter de Vos, another Jesuit, and James Murphy, the son of a pioneer family who founded the nearby town of Sunnyvale.

Mission Santa Clara - altar

Endnotes

1   Palou, Francisco. *Life and Apostolic Labors of the Venerable Father Junipero Serra, Founder of the California Missions.* Translated by C. Scott Williams. Pasadena: George Wharton James, 1913.

2   Geiger, Maynard. *Franciscan Missionaries in Hispanic California – 1764-1848: A Biographical Dictionary.* San Marino: Huntington Library, 1969.

3   Kenneally, Finbar. *Writings of Fermin Francisco de Lasuen, Vol. I.* Washington D.C.: Academy of American Franciscan History, 1964

4   Ibid., Vol. II, 97

5   Forbes, James Alonzo to Zephyrin Englehardt, letter, 30 December, 1905. Santa Barbara Mission Archive Library.

Chapter 12

SAN BUENAVENTURA

The History of San Buenaventura

*L*a *Mision del Glorioso Obispo Cardenal y Doctor Serafico de Iglesia, San Buenaventura* (the Mission of the Glorious Bishop, Cardinal and Angelic Doctor of the Church Saint Buenaventura), was the ninth mission and the last mission founded by Father Junipero Serra. He had arrived in California in 1769, and on March 31, 1782, he founded this, his ninth mission. Two years later he died at Mission San Carlos Borromeo.

Mission San Buenaventura is named after St. Bonaventure. Bonaventure was born John di Fidanza in 1221. It is not clear how his name got changed from John to Bonaventure, but legend has it that as a child he was cured of a serious illness by St. Francis himself, who on seeing the child cured, cried *"O buono ventura!"* (roughly, "What good luck"). Since Bonaventure was born in 1221, and Francis died in 1226, it is possible that this actually did happen. Bonaventure became a Franciscan priest at an early age. He rose to the position of cardinal, and is considered a Doctor of the Church for his prodigious exegetical and theological works. His feast day is July 15.

In the mission "master plan," if there ever actually *was* a mission master plan, Mission San Buenaventura was supposed to be the third mission built. San Diego and Monterey were chosen as first and second because of their harbors. Once these were secure, the narrow Santa Barbara channel was seen as strategically important and a mission at that site would secure it. Present-day Ventura was the ideal location. For years, other demands and the always-present politics between Madrid, Mexico City, and Monterey put impediments in the way. A steady diet of war in Europe was draining the Spanish Crown, and made expenditures for the Alta California missions a low priority. A decision was made by Viceroy Bucareli to change the California model to that of the territory to the east, present-day Arizona. That is, no longer would missions be built with an eye to founding industries manned by natives, and there would be only one priest assigned to each mission. The Franciscans would not accept these new regulations without a fight, and while the fight occurred, with San Buenaventura as the focus, they filled their time in building six other missions up and down the coast. In early 1782, Governor de Neve agreed in principal to the founding of a mission at San Buenaventura, under the new model. He planned to accompany Serra to the site chosen. De Neve had his plans changed when he was dispatched to assist Pedro Fages in his battle with the Yuman Indians. While de Neve was away, Serra took the opportunity of taking off on his own and founding Mission San Buenaventura, of course on the California model that was essentially his brainchild, and not on the de Neve model. By the time de Neve returned, the work was well along, and although undoubtedly unhappy by what was a deliberate challenge to the civil authorities by Serra, he made no objection and allowed the mission to be completed.

Father Pedro Cambon, who had Mission San Francisco to his credit, was put in charge of the new mission. Father Cambon was in ill health. He had recently returned from the Philippines and was supposedly in California to recuperate, but like many of the Franciscans, he would never refuse what he saw as his duty, nor any request from Junipero Serra. Three months later, Father Cambon was relieved by Fathers Francisco Dumetz and Vicente Santa Maria. Father Cambon stayed at San Buenaventura until 1791. One of Father Cambon's lasting legacies was an aqueduct to bring water from the Ventura River to the mission grounds. Even after he left, the work on the canal continued. The Chumash Indians constructed the magnificent aqueduct which allowed the mission to grow a wide variety of fruit and grain. The aqueduct was so well constructed that it lasted almost sixty years, and might still be in use today had it not been washed out in a flood in 1862.

In 1800 the church itself was finished and as work continued on other buildings of the complex, San Buenaventura became the site of one of the most infamous and sad criminal cases in all of Spanish California. An eighteen year old soldier, Jose Antonio Rosas, was seen by two Indian girls to commit a "heinous crime" with one of the mules in the mission compound. Commandante Goycoechea instituted proceedings. Despite a remorseful confession and a plea for mercy from his attorney, Rosas *and the mule* were both sentenced to death. (It is not clear if the mule was represented by counsel.) The sentence was hanging and burning, but since there was no hangman in California young Rosas was executed by firing squad and his body was then burned, to purify it before it could be buried in holy ground. The mule met the same gruesome fate (without the benefit of being buried in holy ground). This sad case is a reminder of the differences in moral values between the era of the missions and today. Acts which today would be seen as at most deviant or unnatural were considered crimes of the highest order in the eighteenth century. Present-day critics of the mission system and the standards it imposed must keep these different standards in mind. It must be noted that the prosecutor in this case was not the Church, but the military. Even more interesting is that in this entire sordid affair someone did not forget to find the mule complicit in the crime. Are there any circumstances in today's world where the mule would be seen as anything other than an instrument of the moment?

Ten years after its completion, the church was largely destroyed by fire. The priests began work on a more substantial church of adobe and fired brick. Father Santa Maria died before the new church was finished. Initially, he was interred in the remains of the burned church, which had been repaired enough to serve the day-to-day needs until a new church was built. When the new church was dedicated in 1809, his remains were transferred to it.

At the dedication of the new church, very little of the interior decoration had been completed. Most of this work was completed between 1810 and 1811, and there are records documenting the fact that many of the paintings, murals and artwork were done by Native Americans. In particular Juan Pacifico, a Chumash Indian, was an apprentice in this task. Juan Pacifico has been given credit for producing "marbleized pilasters and cornices, painted side altars, urns, terraced dado borders, swags with pendant bouquets, leaf and window surrounds."[1] Unfortunately in one of the many renovations done at San Buenaventura, Juan Pacifico's decorations were covered over. There is still hope that, given recent advances in art renovation, they may someday once again see the light of day.

For the new church, an altar had been sent from Mexico with pillars painted to resemble marble, and gold paint highlighting cornices and latticework. The stations of the cross were from Mexico as well. The altar candelabra and crucifixes were solid silver. The main crucifix was full-sized, with a life-sized figure of Christ, and the statue of Saint Bonaventure on the main altar was brought from the Philippines.

In 1812, the same earthquake that destroyed San Juan Capistrano caused significant damage to San Buenaventura. Although the church stood, structural damage was so evident that for three years services were held in a temporary building. Ultimately the church was reinforced and rebuilt and, despite the best efforts of an overzealous priest to modernize it in the late nineteenth century, it is still essentially the original church from more than two hundred years ago.

Mission San Buenaventura in its early years seems to have had a benign and peaceful relationship with the local natives. In1819 that came to an end. While the coastal-dwelling Chumash, native to the area, tended to be a docile group, their kin, the Mojave from the Colorado River, were not. A group of Mojave coming for one of their periodic trading visits with the coastal Chumash took umbrage at a preemptive detention imposed on them by the Spanish soldiers when they arrived at San Buenaventura. Two Spanish soldiers and ten Indians were killed in the ensuing melee, and relations between the Indians and the missionaries there were forever poisoned.

In 1826, Mission San Buenaventura acquired the unpredictable Father Jose Altimira. Father Altimira was the obstreperous priest who, three years earlier, had embroiled his order and the California legislature in a controversy surrounding the founding of San Francisco de Solano. He proved just as contentious at San Buenaventura as he had at San Francisco. Shortly after his arrival at San Buenaventura, Altimira refused to take the oath promising fealty to the new Mexican republic. In December of 1826, the Mexican government ordered the expulsion of all Spanish citizens from Mexico and its territories. This decree, at least initially, caused no small amount of consternation among the Franciscans, most of whom were Spanish citizens. As events would bear out, the decree was honored more in the breach than the observance, and dozens of Spanish Franciscans remained in California, until their death almost always with the knowledge and quite often with the cooperation of the authorities.

Father Altimira, though, as he was wont to do, decided to take matters into his own hands. He surreptitiously travelled to Santa Barbara, met up with Father Antonio Ripoll from that mission, and the two of them booked passage on an American ship the *Harbinger.* They sailed for Europe on January 23, 1828, and neither, for all practical purposes, was ever heard from again. Their precipitous flight under obvious efforts at secrecy has led to yet one more of the mysteries of the missions. It was freely bandied about by the Mexican authorities that the two priests had fled with a horde of gold stolen from their missions. The fact that none of the missions ever had any substantial amount of gold did nothing to diminish this rumor. An investigation was conducted. Nothing of any value was found missing from either of the missions. It was determined that Altimira took some books and a box of cigars, and that was the extent of it. Perhaps Altimira's most serious crime was an offense against his order and his duties. He had served only seven of the ten years promised when he was assigned to California, and he left Mission San Buenaventura in the sole care of Father Francisco Suner, who was blind. Poor Father Suner, unable to celebrate Mass or maintain any of the mission records, hung on at the mission until 1831, when he died at the age of sixty-seven after service of more than twenty years in California.

San Buenaventura was secularized in 1834, and shortly thereafter, probably because the president of the Franciscans took him to task for his dissolute lifestyle, Governor Mariano Chico ordered the Franciscans to turn the mission over to a secular administrator. Chico, as well as dealing with Franciscan censure, was concerned about the volatile state of California politics and feared a revolution. He left for Mexico to plead for troops to put down the feared rebellion. Instead of troops, he received a censure and removal from office for abandoning his post.

In his place as governor was appointed Nicolas Gutierrez. Gutierrez proved highly unpopular and was deposed by a member of the California legislature, Juan Bautista Alvarado. Alvarado spent several months trying to unite disparate groups of Mexicans, *Californios* and Americans, fighting over what California should be and who should rule it. The central government in Mexico City became very nervous about the whole affair and appointed yet another governor, Jose Castro. Alvarado was not willing to accept this usurpation. He marshaled his forces and met those of Castro at Mission San Buenaventura in March of 1836. Shots were exchanged and one man killed before Alvarado and his forces retreated from the fortified mission. The retreat may have been a tactical one, for when Castro's men pursued Alvarado, they were surrounded and captured. Alvarado prevailed, not just militarily but politically, and remained governor for four years.

When the Mexican government finally asserted its authority over the fractious Californians, San Buenaventura became a political pawn. When Pio Pico became governor in 1845, he first leased and ultimately sold the holdings of Mission San Buenaventura. The new owner, Jose Arnaz, not only allowed the priest to remain in his apartment there, but actually paid the expenses of conducting services. It wasn't until 1862 that the United States government declared the sale invalid and ordered the return of the mission church and slightly less than fifty acres to the Catholic church. San Buenaventura once again became an active parish in the diocese of Los Angeles, as it is today.

The latest effort at restoration was in 1957, and had as its objective the undoing of a "modernization" done in 1893. That unfortunate effort had covered up but not destroyed many of the most attractive features of the church built in 1809. The original flooring and ceiling were uncovered and refurbished, and the windows re-cut to their original size. The ceiling beams are the originals, of pine and oak harvested from the nearby mountains and driven by ox cart to the mission. The church walls at their base are six-and-a-half feet thick.

Mission San Buenaventura today:

Mission San Buenaventura is located at Main and Figueroa, 211 East Main, Ventura, CA, 93001; (805) 643-4318.
http://sanbuenaventuramission.org
Nickname: The Mission by the Sea

The church you visit today is the original building completed in 1809, but it has been reconstructed and deconstructed several times. The structure you see today, however, is almost completely the 1809 building.

166

Immediately inside the front entrance are two wooden confessionals. These are of modern construction, from the 1957 renovation. In the museum next to the church is one of the original wooden confessionals, hand-carved by Native American craftsman. It will be noted that the original confessional was much less commodious than the 1957 reproduction. In the eighteenth century, people were much smaller than they are today. To the left of the main aisle is the baptistery, which contains a hand-hammered baptismal font, likely also the product of a Native American artisan. Over the main altar is a four-hundred-year-old statue of Saint Bonaventure, the mission's patron. To his left is Saint Joseph with the infant Jesus, and to his right is Mary as the Immaculate Conception.

To the right of the main altar is a shrine to Our Lady of Guadalupe. The painting here was done in 1747 in Mexico by Francisco Cabrero. To the left of the painting is a statue of Saint Gertrude, patron saint of the West Indies.* There is also a statue of Saint Dominic, founder of the Dominicans, and, to the right, statues of Saint Isidore, patron saint of farmers, and Saint Francis.

To the left of the main altar is the shrine of the Crucifixion. The corpus of Christ on the cross is more than four hundred years old; originally from the Philippines, it came to the mission at the completion of the church in 1809, along with the statue of Saint Buenaventura. To the right of the crucifixion scene are statues of Saint Thomas and Saint John the Apostle, while to the left are Mary as the Mother of Sorrows, and Saint Anthony of Padua.

Adorning the right and left walls of the church are the stations of the cross—fourteen paintings, all more than 250 years old, depicting Christ's final journey from his condemnation by Pontius Pilate to his entombment. These paintings have hung in the church since it was built.

There are four very old bells in the bell tower, and one fairly new one. This is the large upper bell, cast in 1956 and placed at the opening of the restored church. One bell has no date, and its origin is uncertain. Two bells are dated 1781, and one, 1825.

---

* The Spanish considered all of their holdings in the New World to be part of the Indies.

Among the interesting artifacts in the mission museum are the wooden bells. These are actual working bells, clappers and all carved from wood. The usual story behind these bells is that they were used each year on Holy Thursday, Good Friday, and Holy Saturday. These days, commemorating the Last Supper, the death, and the burial of Christ, are days of mourning in the Catholic church. Songs and celebratory sounds such as the ringing of bells are not allowed, but the faithful still must be called to the solemn services of these events; thus, the wooden bells. However, this is the only one of the California missions with such bells, and if they were used to keep solemn the three holy days we would expect to find survivors at several of the missions. It is more likely that they were constructed to serve the mission in its very early days, until more expensive cast iron bells could be obtained.

Also of note in the mission museum is a photograph of one of the parishioners from San Buenaventura with Pope Pius X. The picture was taken in 1905 when parishioner Juan Camarillo, made a pilgrimage to Rome. His was the first group of pilgrims ever photographed with a pope.

The side door of the church has over it a decorative motif which was never intended as anything more than a simple decoration, consisting of a cross connected to two curving lines. To the natives of the region however, the two curved lines represented the Ventura and Santa Clara rivers, which flowed to either side of the mission itself. The cross represented the mission and the straight line above the cross was the hills on the horizon behind the mission.

In the yard to the rear of the church there is a grotto and a statue of Kateri Tekakwitha, the first native American to be officially canonized as a saint by the Catholic church.

Buried behind the church denoted by a common marker, are Fathers Vincente de Santa Maria (1782-1806), José Senan (1806-1823) and Francisco Suner (1824-1831).

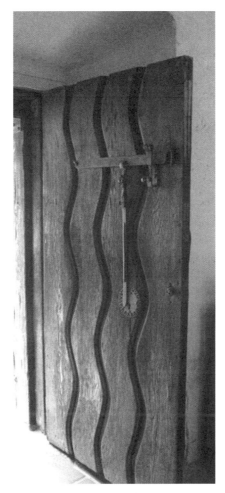

Door - River of Life pattern

Endnotes
1   Neuerburg Norman *Decoration of the California Missions.* Santa
Barbara: Bellerophon Press, 1987.

Chapter 13

Santa Barbara

The History of Santa Barbara

*L**a Mision de la Senora Barbara Virgen y Martier (*the Mission of the Lady Barbara Virgin and Martyr), the tenth mission, was founded on December 4, 1786. Mission Santa Barbara is named after Saint Barbara, a second-century woman of great beauty and great wealth. Because of her beauty, her father had her confined to a tower built just for the purpose of keeping her away from possible suitors. This overly-protective father apparently went to the other extreme when Barbara converted to Christianity, and beheaded her himself. Returning from this ghastly deed, he was struck dead by lightning. While Barbara might well have been named the patron saint of dysfunctional families, she is instead invoked as protection against lightning, and is the patron saint of artillery men (the lightning strike) and architects (the tower.) Her feast day is December 4, and this, rather than any particular association with the Franciscans, is the reason the mission was named after her. Santa Barbara was the first mission founded under the presidency of Father Fermin de Lasuen, who succeeded Junipero Serra. Lasuen would go on, like his predecessor, to found a total of nine missions.

The actual founding of Santa Barbara and who gets credit for it is another one of the wonderfully confused tales of religion, politics, and the military that gives so much color to the story of the California missions. Ardent supporters of Junipero Serra—and they are legion—claim that he should get credit for the founding of Santa Barbara, and thus "one-up" his successor with credit for ten missions. A little study of the political and military considerations in founding all of the missions needs to be done to sort this question out.

The Channel Islands are a chain of eight islands stretching 160 miles along the southern California coastline. The Spanish, early on in their attempts to solidify their hold on the Pacific coast, recognized this relatively narrow channel as of great strategic importance, and planned to protect it with missions and *presidios*. Three of the missions—San Buenaventura, Santa Barbara and La Purisima—were built along the narrow corridor of ocean between the California coastline and the Channel Islands. There was actually a suggestion in 1784 that there should be a mission built on one of the Channel Islands, Santa Catalina or Santa Cruz being proposed. The thinking was that with outposts on both sides of the channel, smuggling, always a concern to the Spanish, could be much more easily controlled. A scarcity of arable land and concerns about adequate water supplies on either of these islands caused the idea to be abandoned, and no mission was ever built on any of the islands.

The building of the three "channel missions" and the order in which they were built was a matter of much debate between Junipero Serra and the governors of California. As mentioned in the last chapter, San Buenaventura was to be the third of the California missions. In a letter written by Junipero Serra in 1770, he mentions, "The steward opened the second box. …We saw inscribed on the lid what it contained, three paintings: San Carlos, San Buenaventura and San Diego." After inventorying more of the material he goes on to assure Viceroy Galvez ". . . that the foundation of San Buenaventura will not be delayed on our part."[1] So material for the first of the channel missions, San Buenaventura, had been in crates ready to be shipped since at least 1770.

Junipero Serra's ambition and the limitations of the Spanish military came into constant conflict on this issue. Indian uprisings, not just in California but in present-day Arizona, took an extreme toll on the very sparse military presence in Alta California. In fact, Serra's nemesis Fernando de Rivera met his death on the Yuma River in 1781. All of the Spanish military governors were justifiably concerned about stretching their very limited resources too thin as the Franciscans, more or less at their own whims, founded missions here and missions there.

Finally in March of 1782, after years of discussion about the channel missions, Junipero Serra and Phillip de Neve, the governor of California, met and agreed, at least in principal, that the next three missions to be built should be San Buenaventura, Santa Barbara, and La Purisima. Thus, they would secure the two ends and the middle of the channel. They left from San Gabriel together, the civil/military and ecclesiastical powers of Alta California, to accomplish this end. On Easter Sunday, March 31, 1782, Mission San Buenaventura was founded. The founding of this one mission seems to have been the only sure thing the two groups agreed upon. On April 15 they headed north again. At the site of present-day Santa Barbara they stopped, and de Neve began the plans for a *presidio*. De Neve's site for a *presidio* was not to Serra's liking: He felt that it was not a good site for either a *presidio* or a mission. Misgivings notwithstanding, Serra officiated at the blessing of the site. Nothing in Spanish California, whether it be mission, *presidio* or *pueblo,* was founded without a mass and blessing. As part of the process, Serra initiated baptismal and marriage registers and titled them as records of "This new mission and Royal *Presidio*," thus the claim that Serra may not have *built,* but that he did *found* mission Santa Barbara. If this was the only argument to be made, it might be a compelling one, since many of the missions were founded with a religious ceremony, sometimes years before permanent building was begun.

Unfortunately for those who would give Serra credit for the founding of Santa Barbara, Serra himself offers some troubling testimony to the contrary. Without a doubt he conducted a ceremony founding the *presidio* at Santa Barbara, but it would be a stretch to give him the credit for founding the mission simply because he inscribed some journal as records for a church. De Neve was obdurate: they were founding only a *presidio* and not a mission, and "...the governor told [Serra] that he would not proceed to the founding of the Mission until the *presidio* was completed. Upon hearing this [Serra] said: 'As I am not needed here, *seeing the Mission is not to be founded* I propose to go on to Monterey';"[2] and he did. It must be noted that Serra's refusal to proceed with the construction of Mission Santa Barbara was not because of any actual obstacles placed in the way of his beginning work. It was simply because he was not willing to begin work under the conditions as de Neve laid them out.

The issues between de Neve and Serra with regard to Santa Barbara were not simple ones. First, as military commander of California, de Neve had at his disposal very few troops, probably not more than 300 for all of Alta California. Each mission founded further stretched those already strained resources. More important was de Neve's firmly-held belief that the mission system as it had been implemented for the past many years was a failure. He argued, with much justification, that in the last seventeen years and nine missions, the Franciscans had done nothing to prepare the natives for independent, productive lives in the territory. In de Neve's view, the nine missions already founded were little but institutions of serfdom for the natives and self-serving fiefdoms for the Franciscans. The natives were held virtually captive in the mission compounds and if they attempted to flee, the Franciscans expected the soldiers to pursue them and bring them back, another waste of his very scant resources in de Neve's eyes. He issued orders forbidding his soldiers to pursue Indians who had escaped from any of the missions.

By 1781, De Neve had devised, had approved, and promulgated his own plans for settling the territory. Under his plan, when a new mission was founded the natives would be left relatively undisturbed in their own villages. Rather than gather the natives into the mission compounds, de Neve's plan proposed that the missionaries would go to the native villages, where they would teach the Indians to farm and help them master the other crafts they would need to survive in the "civilized" world. De Neve's plan does seem to have been a better one than the official one of *reducción,* but Serra objected, saying the Franciscans needed more time to prepare the Indians for the change. Ironically, *reducción* was not Serra's nor the Franciscan plan for settlement of California, either: it was the official policy of the Spanish government. Spanish law was clear that this was to be policy for conquest of the *"Indies."* It was equally clear, though, that this was not to be a policy of forced reduction.

The Franciscans in general and Junipero Serra in particular were completely opposed to de Neves' suggestion that their policy should be changed. They had not the slightest inclination to give up the control they had exercised over their neophytes. De Neve was equally intent on implementing his new plan with the construction of Mission Santa Barbara. These were the terms Serra was not willing to agree to.

The Franciscans in both Mexico and California had enough influence to frustrate de Neve's plan. In 1783, de Neve was promoted to brigadier general and sent to Arizona to settle issues with the Yumans.

Once de Neve was gone, his plan for a new system had no traction. The Franciscans maintained their absolute control over the California missions until secularization. Whether de Neve's *"reglamento"* (regulation) would have made a difference in the lives of the native Californians will never be known. What is known is that when secularization finally took hold, the natives were no better prepared to face the challenges of "civilization" then they had been when Serra objected to de Neve's plan by claiming the Franciscans needed more time.

Besides the questionable founding by Serra, Santa Barbara had not just one but two founding ceremonies when it was founded several years later by Father Lasuen. On December 4, 1786, Fermin de Lasuen, now the president of the California missions, conducted the founding rites and celebrated mass. The new governor of California, Pedro Fages, could not be present for the ceremony, so twelve days later another dedication ceremony was held with Governor Fages in attendance. Construction of the actual buildings had to wait out the coast's wet winter and didn't begin until the spring of 1787. The first church was mud, adobe and thatch. From then until 1793, kitchens, workshops, outbuildings, additions and larger chapels were added. Finally the decision was made that such "tacked-on" additions would no longer serve. In 1794, a new church was dedicated. This was the first really substantial church at Santa Barbara. It was plastered adobe with a tile roof, and in addition to the main altar had six side chapels. This church served Santa Barbara until the 1812 earthquake damaged it so significantly that it had to be abandoned. In 1815, the present church was begun under the direction of Father Antonio Ripoll. When it was finished in 1820, it had only one tower. The second tower was added in 1831.

It was at Santa Barbara in 1818 that the Franciscans marshaled their own ineffectual military force, the only one of the missions to do so independent of the Spanish military. This came about due to the depravations of Hippolyte Bouchard. When it was rumored that he was approaching Santa Barbara, Father Antonio Ripoll armed several hundred Indians, gave them the somewhat puzzling name of the "Society of Urban Realists," and offered their services to the Mexican army in repulsing the invaders. It was also to the "beleaguered" Santa Barbara that Father Luis Martinez marched with thirty-five armed neophytes from San Luis Obispo. The army declined help from either the urban realists or Martinez's irregulars, and Bouchard withdrew on his own to richer waters in Central America.

Santa Barbara, like its neighbors Santa Inés and La Purisima, was dramatically touched by the ill-fated Chumash revolt of 1824. While most of the fighting took place at Santa Inés, where the trouble started, and La Purisima, where it ended, Santa Barbara—since it was collocated with the nearest *presidio*—became very involved in the battles. When soldiers from the *presidio* set up defensive positions at Santa Barbara, the mission neophytes became uneasy, particularly when Father Ripoll's suggested that they should surrender themselves to the *presidio* guardhouse. They launched a pre-emptive strike against the *presidio* guards, and then fled to the central valley. When Father Ripoll was asked to accompany the soldiers in pursuit of the fugitives, he refused to join the chase for his "beloved children." In the initial pursuit several Indians were killed, but the troop returned to Santa Barbara without the bulk of those who had fled. Finally, Father Ripoll agreed to accompany the troops with the promise from the military that the Indians would not be harmed, simply returned to the mission. On this expedition, apparently reassured by Ripoll's presence with the soldiers, almost all of the fugitives surrendered and were returned to the mission. When all was said and done, the governor of California pardoned those who returned with Ripoll and the soldiers.

When secularization came to the missions, Santa Barbara was the headquarters of the father president of the missions, Father Narciso Duran. The Franciscans as individuals had mixed reactions to secularization. Father José Sanchez from San Gabriel rejoiced, commenting that relief from duties he clearly found burdensome could not come soon enough. Father Juan Cabot from San Miguel expressed misgivings that it would actually result in any land being transferred to the natives. Father Jose Jiminez from Santa Cruz saw it as a practical solution to what was becoming an increasing burden for the Franciscans. But whatever disparate opinions the various missionaries may have had, there was really only one opinion that counted, and that was that of the father president.

Father President Duran was not necessarily opposed to any concept of secularization. He was, however, opposed to the specific plan produced by the government: the immediate removal of the Franciscans and the immediate transfer of all mission lands to the natives. Duran proposed an alternative plan for secularization that called for a trial secularization of eight missions, including his own, Santa Barbara. He proposed a gradual transfer, the timeline to be dictated by how well the Indians handled their own affairs and, significantly, how well the white population assisted them in obtaining true independence. This put him in direct conflict with the civilian rulers of California at a time when rumors of plots by the Franciscans and questions of loyalty were rife. The civilian authorities wanted an immediate dispossession of the Franciscans by *fiat*. Royalist sympathies was an easy charge to lay at the feet of the Spanish Franciscans, and Duran was one of those accused of working against the Mexican authorities and initially ordered deported. The basis for the charge was that Duran refused to conduct a religious ceremony in conjunction with the governor's celebration of the new constitution. He also refused to take an oath of loyalty to the Mexican Republic, and when in 1836 Juan Bautitsa Alvarado declared a short-lived California Republic, Duran refused to bless that flag. The highly-principled Duran would not take an oath of loyalty to any Mexican government until Spain itself formally acknowledged Mexico's independence in 1839, almost twenty years after Mexico had won its independence.

The end result of this was that while several missions can claim to have been central to military battles in the period from 1821 to 1846, Santa Barbara and the towering presence of Narciso Duran were central to a more significant battle of politics, words and ideas. Perhaps because of Duran's intransigence, Santa Barbara was the only one of the twenty-one missions that was never removed from the control of the Franciscans. It is today the only one of the missions that has been controlled and occupied by the Franciscans from its founding to the present day.

Santa Barbara's role as political center to the missions did not end with the question of secularization. All of the priests at all of the missions in California were from the College of San Fernando in Mexico City, and all of them had been born in Spain. The Mexican government decided to turn control of the missions over to a different group of Franciscans from a different college. The College of Our Lady of Guadalupe in Zacatecas had a student body and a faculty comprised almost entirely of native-born Mexicans.. All of the students, seminarians and priests at Zacatecas were Mexican, and thus more to be

177

trusted in matters such as independence and the new republic. In 1833, the first group of Zacatecans were sent to California and ordered to assume control of the seven northernmost missions: San Francisco de Solano, San Rafael, San Francisco de Assisi, San Jose, Santa Clara, Santa Cruz and Carmel. The remaining fourteen missions, from San Miguel south, remained, at least for the time, in the control of the Franciscans from San Fernando College. This change of control, while mandated by the Mexican government, was not much resisted by the established Franciscans from San Fernando. Likely their position was, "a Franciscan is a Franciscan," and it mattered not where he was born or where he had gotten his training. The transfer of control was amicable and collegial. It was in response to this change in structure that Father Narciso Duran transferred the locus of his presidency from Carmel to Santa Barbara. As part of that process, all of the Franciscan records—including a vast store of correspondence, legal papers and observations regarding civilian affairs—were moved to and stored at Santa Barbara, where they remain to this day. Father Garcia Diego y Moreno, the president of the Zacatecans and now responsible for the northernmost mission, established his headquarters at Santa Clara rather than taking up residence at Carmel.

These two presidents, Father Garcia and Father Duran, briefly lived together at Santa Barbara and collaborated on a joint recommendation to Mexico City, that California was now of sufficient size and importance to merit its own bishop. They also sent a report to Mexico City resisting the idea of secularization, their primary concern being a fear that none of the mission lands would ever be transferred to the Indians who had developed them.

Duran's concerns ensured that he remain a thorn in the side of the government. At least one attempt to arrest him was thwarted by the Indians, who went to the beach where the soldiers were planning to load him on a ship for return to Mexico and a trial. A cordon of women surrounded Duran and refused to let the soldiers through. Colonel Don Mariano Chico decided that discretion was the better part of valor, and withdrew without Father Duran. Duran remained at Santa Barbara until his death in 1843, and is buried there.

In 1853 there came to Santa Barbara one of its most famous residents. She was neither priest, soldier nor politician, but a simple Indian woman. Juana Maria, as she was named by the Franciscans, became known as the "Lone Woman of San Nicolas Island." Her story and her history cannot be thoroughly authenticated, but the basic facts are not in dispute, and are as follows.

San Nicolas is one of the smaller and most distant of all of the Channel Islands. The island had been populated for many years by several hundred Chumash Indians. Unfortunately, the surrounding waters were also richly populated by sea otters, much desired by the fur traders then working the California coast. In 1812, there was a bloody conflict between the fur traders and the natives on San Nicolas. The natives were slaughtered. Twenty years later, the native population stood at around twenty people. In1835, the decision was made to remove the few remaining natives from San Nicolas. A ship was sent from Monterey and for whatever reason, all were removed except one woman. Some say she left the group assembled on the beach because she had forgotten her child, some that she just ran away, and some that she was simply overlooked in the roundup. Perhaps she was off gathering food when the party was assembled. Whatever were the circumstances, she was left behind, and remained on the island, totally alone, for the next eighteen years. There were periodic sightings of her in her solitary existence for many years, but it wasn't until 1850 that specific expeditions were launched to find her. George Nidever, himself a fur trapper from Santa Barbara who was somewhat familiar with San Nicolas, made several trips to the island to find her. Finally in 1853, one of his men found footprints on the beach and some seal meat left to dry. They found the woman living in a crude shelter, clothed in a garment made from cormorant hides. Nidever and his men worked to convince the woman that it was in her best interest to give up her lonely existence and return with them to rejoin "her people" on the mainland. They could not speak her language, nor she theirs, so communication was totally in sign language. For several weeks, the men argued with the woman. Finally, she agreed to the idea. What evidence we have indicates that she left San Nicolas willingly and without resistance.

On her arrival at Santa Barbara the mystery only deepened, because none of the local natives, neither Chumash nor Tongva—who themselves had once lived on San Nicolas—nor any of the other native groups could understand her language or communicate with her. She was able to communicate with a crude sign language and gestures.

She also sang some sort of song, and danced in accompaniment to it. Although she had survived for so many years by herself on remote San Nicolas, her "rescue" to civilization was her undoing. A short seven weeks after arriving at Santa Barbara, Juana Maria died, likely from dysentery acquired from her well-meaning benefactors. She was buried in an unmarked grave at Mission Santa Barbara, perhaps in the Nidever family plot. She had brought from San Nicolas some basketwork, tools and clothing that on her death were sent to the California Academy of Science in San Francisco. They were unfortunately destroyed in the fire following San Francisco's 1906 earthquake. Juana Maria's life was immortalized in Scott O'Dell's still-popular children's book, *Island of The Blue Dolphins.*

An earthquake in 1925 extensively damaged the town of Santa Barbara and the mission. Both of the towers were virtually destroyed and the wooden statues of *Hope* and *Charity* were toppled. (*Faith* had inexplicably disappeared in the 1850s; her fate is still unknown.) These statues, the largest known examples of native carving, were crafted by Paciano Guilajahicet, a Chumash canoe builder and carpenter. On restoration of the mission, they were replaced with stone reproductions, but the originals were preserved and are now on display in the mission museum.

Mission Santa Barbara today:

Mission Santa Barbara is located at: 2201 Laguna St. (Los Olivos and Laguna Streets), Santa Barbara, CA, 93105; (805) 682-4713. http://www.sbmission.org
Nickname: The Queen of the Missions

The present church is the fourth church built on the site. The first three were simply replacements for each preceding it, as the population and congregation grew. The last of those three was destroyed by the earthquake in 1812. The present church was completed in 1820.

Another earthquake in 1925 caused serious damage to Mission Santa Barbara, but thanks to the fervor of the pastor, Father Augustine Hobrecht, and to the generosity of Californians of every persuasion, the church was repaired and restored in just two years. As part of the rededication ceremony, a list of all of the individual donors and societies who were responsible for the restoration was sealed in the wall of the west tower. Many of the mission have interred in their walls priests and faithful, but Santa Barbara is the only one which has a casket with the names of its later benefactors.

In its overall affect, Santa Barbara is certainly one of the most pleasing of all of the missions. It is flanked by two identical towers, the only one of the missions with twin towers. The towers are as tall as the building is wide. If San Gabriel is often referred to as the "Muslim mission," Santa Barbara might be referred to as the "Roman mission." Father Ripoll, in charge of building the mission, borrowed liberally from *The Six Books of Architecture,* written in the first century by Vitruvius Polion. The Spanish edition that Father Ripoll used is still in the mission library. The most obvious element copied from this book is the central façade of the front of the mission. In the interior, the "winged lighting" decorations at the top of the light fixtures are also direct copies from Vitruvius's work. Santa Barbara is one of the few missions that employed a professional stonemason in its construction. José Antonio Ramirez directed the local natives who did all of the construction. Thus, we have in twenty-first century California a structure designed by eighteenth-century Spaniards and built by eighteenth-century Chumash, representing first-century Roman/Hellenistic culture.

In the center of the church's façade is a niche with a statue of Saint Barbara. The statutes above her represent Faith, Hope and Charity and are concrete reproductions of the originals, two of which are displayed in the mission museum.

The church interior contains perhaps the best example of period chandeliers, set off by the Vitruvius-inspired ceiling decorations, which ironically must be considered pagan ornamentations in a Christian church. Santa Barbara is the only mission that contains a tabernacle constructed by Native Americans. It is a stunning example of their art. It is decorated with abalone shells, much favored by the Chumash in their artwork. It is not on the main altar but has its own niche at the side of the church. Current church rules require that the tabernacle must be made of "solid and inviolable material that is not transparent, and be locked in such a way that the danger of profanation is prevented to the greatest extent possible." This tabernacle may not meet the liturgical definitions of such, but it certainly meets every definition of beautiful art. Two hundred years ago some simple Indian peasant wanted to do something of his own for the edifice being built, and so he lovingly crafted this item.

The two large paintings on the side walls, the *Crucifixion* on the right and the *Assumption of Mary* on the left, are the two largest paintings in all of the California missions. They are more than 200 years old. Another of the church's interesting paintings is the depiction of souls in purgatory. Significant in this painting is the fact that, of the two central figures in the fires of purgatory, one is wearing a bishop's miter and next to him is an unclad woman. This is likely the artist's comment on the well-known lamentable morals of many medieval bishops. A further interesting observation on this painting is the figure of an infant. In today's theology it is unimaginable what an infant could have done to deserve the punishments of purgatory, but in the seventeenth century, a failure to have been baptized, although such could not be the fault of the child, would have consigned him to purgatory, if not hell. It was this theology that prompted the Franciscans to their endeavors in the New World.

Santa Barbara has two paintings depicting a grouping of three figures. On the wall to the left of the sanctuary are the three archangels, Michael, Gabriel and Raphael. On the opposite wall are three Italian women saints, Saint Clare of Assisi, Saint Agnes, and Saint Margaret of Cortona. The placement of these paintings directly across from the archangels is not accidental; they were a reminder to the faithful that human beings can aspire to an eternity with the angels.

Notable figures buried at Santa Barbara include Governor José Figueroa; Juana Maria, "the lost woman of San Nicolas;" Father Antonio Paterna, one of the mission's two founders; Father Andres Dulanto, who died at the very early age of thirty-four; Father Narciso Duran, who moved the presidency of the California missions from Carmel to Santa Barbara; Father José Jimeno; Father Francisco Uria; Father Mariano Payeras, who is also reportedly buried at La Purisima; and the first bishop of California, Diego Francisco Garcia, who briefly maintained his headquarters at Santa Barbara.

Although not open to the general public, one of Santa Barbara's prime attractions to scholars and historians is the Santa Barbara Mission Archive and Library. When the order of secularization was a reality that was devastating all of the other missions, Father President

Narciso Duran transferred his headquarters, and virtually all of the Franciscans records of the seventy years of their presence in California, to Santa Barbara. These records had been scattered throughout the California missions, and as the only mission never subject to the control of any group other than the Franciscans, Santa Barbara was uniquely suited to become the repository for them. Originally housed in the mission monastery, in 1967 they were moved to the present building. There are thousands of documents and manuscripts in the archive. Many of the original books the Franciscans brought from Spain and Mexico are preserved here, as are tens of thousands of letters, official documents, periodicals and publications from different eras. They contain not just Franciscan history, but important original sources on the military, political, private, social and cultural life of California in its Spanish and Mexican eras.

Aside from the church's style, architecturally significant is the mission's water system. It was begun in 1803 and completed in 1806. The source of the mission's water for agriculture and domestic use is Pedragoso Creek, more than two miles away. The Franciscans directed the natives in building a dam, a stone aqueduct, and a series of laterals and canals to conduct the water to their fountains, gardens and *lavanderias*. Much of that system is still in place. A testimony to the craftsmanship employed is the fact that much of what was constructed two hundred years ago is today part of the city of Santa Barbara's water system.

The mission's beautiful gardens were originally the location of workshops, craft areas and living quarters for the neophytes.

Mission Santa Barbara - cemetery gate.

"Mary"

Endnotes

1   Tibesar , Antonine. *Writings of Junipero Serra.* Washington DC: Academy of American Franciscan History, 1955.

2   Palou, Francisco. *Life and Apostolic Labors of the Venerable Father Junipero Serra, Founder of the Franciscan Mission of California.* Translated by C. Scott Williams. Pasadena: George Wharton James, 1913.

Chapter 14

LA PURISIMA CONCEPCION

The History of La Purísima Concepción

*L*a Mision de La Purísima Concepción de Santisima Virgen Maria* (the Mission of the Most Pure Conception of the the Holy Virgin Mary), the eleventh mission, was founded on December 8, 1787. December 8 is the feast of the Immaculate Conception. This feast, despite a popular belief to the contrary—even among many Catholics—has nothing to do with the conception of Jesus Christ. Rather, it is the belief that Mary herself, from the moment of her conception, was free from any trace of Adam and Eve's original sin. Mary, according to Catholic theology, is the only human being ever so blessed.

Father Fermin Lasuen, now serving as the president of the Franciscan missions, was the founder of La Purísima. He placed Father Mariano Payeras in charge; Father Payeras would serve the mission for the next nineteen years. Since the mission was founded at the beginning of coastal California's very wet winter, permanent construction had to wait until spring. Fairly crude, mostly mud-and-thatch buildings served the mission until 1802, when permanent adobe buildings with tile roofs were completed. La Purísima enjoyed a period of unusual prosperity, listing livestock of more than twenty thousand in 1810. All of this came to an end in 1812. On December 21 of that year, a series of earthquakes first damaged, then felled all of the buildings. Torrential rains followed the earthquake. Apparently the waters were concentrated in a vent caused by the earthquake in the nearby hillsides. A torrent of water and mud gushed forth, carrying the ruined buildings, the livestock, and all of the stores away. Faced with not only the complete destruction of their years of building efforts, as well as the need to shelter and care for the thousand Indians who had come to depend on the mission, the Franciscans, as they so often would, simply "girded their loins" and set about the task at hand.

A new site was picked for the rebuilding of the mission, on the other side of the river. The new mission was designed to be earthquake resistant. The walls were built more than four feet thick and buttressed with stone. The new mission was completed in 1818. La Purísima is unique among all of the California missions in that its buildings were not laid out in a rectangular or quadrangular form. Instead its church buildings, workshops and residences are fairly separate. It is often referred to as the "linear mission." Why, of all of the missions, this one was designed so differently has never been well explained. One theory suggests that because this was one of the later missions, the *padres* felt secure enough with the Indian population that they didn't see the need for the defensive quadrangle. (Certainly later events at this very mission would seem to disprove that theory.) Further, all of the ten missions built after La Purísima employed some form of the closed quadrangle in their design.

Another theory is that the Franciscans, after the earthquake of 1812, felt that a long linear design would allow greater chance of escape in the event of another earthquake. The problem with this theory is that while the earthquake of 1812 caused total destruction of the mission buildings, it was the occasion of no loss of life at Purísima. Most of the damage at Purísima was caused by an aftershock which opened a crevice and an apparently hidden spring in the hillsides to the south of the mission. The mission was destroyed by flood, not by the earthquake. La Purísima's one-of-a-kind design was likely just another example of the streak of independence that individual Franciscans were likely to demonstrate. Their vows of obedience applied only to their personal and religious life. There was no obligation to follow unthinkingly the norms of artistic nor architectural design.

Father Payeras, while he was the head of La Purísima was appointed to the presidency of the Franciscans in California, and so the mission served as the headquarters of the California mission system, from 1815 to 1819. Payeras was a reluctant but respected father president. He was probably one of the most forward-thinking of all of the Franciscans. While president, he constructed a thoughtful, honest and often grim report of the results of more than fifty years of missionary work in California. He notes that rather than the beautiful and flourishing church and thriving towns that had been anticipated at the inception of the California mission project, they found themselves ministering to an aging, sick and dying people. Payeras' letter, written in February of 1820, cast a very questioning eye on the Franciscan's efforts to bring the benefits of civilization to the people of California. Payeras does not just lament some obvious facts; he carefully studies what is taking place and comes to two clear conclusions. First, the magnitude of the situation is hidden in the annual reports, because while births, baptisms and deaths are all reported, the ages of the deaths and baptisms are not considered, and in many areas newly-converted adults are being added to the total. Payeras takes a more scientific approach to the numbers and concludes that by design or accident the annual reports, so faithfully filed, have only served to hide the tragedy unfolding. Perhaps the most important conclusion of Payeras' report is that the blame lies on the system itself. The mission system is destroying the people it was meant to save. Because of the facts he laid out and because of the obvious importance he gave to this matter, it is important to quote Payeras in full on this matter:

2 February 1820

To Reverend Father Guardian and Venerable *Discretorio* of Our Apostolic College of San Fernando de Mexico.
It is a goal of all missionaries to the heathen, based upon royal *cedulas* and the very essence of the Apostolic Institute of *Propaganda Fide* among Uncultured and Barbaric Nations, to draw them out of the sierras and ravines and gather them for catechism and polity on the plains, there forming towns (I recall here how many have argued against it) which have all religious and civil conveniences. That, my Fathers, has been the task of our predecessors and ourselves in Alta California, all of us being sons and dependents of that Holy College, from 1769 to the present time.

We have happily baptized all the heathens found in the chain of 220 leagues (I include here the ten leagues beyond the *Puerto de Nuestro Padre* [San Francisco] to San Rafael), and we can truthfully say that there is hardly one gentile from the coast to the interior of the sierra, a distance of 20 leagues.

Because we have given so many sons to religion and vassals to our King (may God keep him!), we ought to have received the greatest gratification and satisfaction, but on the contrary it pains and saddens our Christian hearts exceedingly because where we expected a beautiful and flourishing church and some beautiful towns which would be the joy of the sovereign majesties of heaven and earth, we find ourselves with missions or rather with a people miserable and sick, with rapid depopulation of *rancherias* which with profound horror fills the cemeteries.

Every thoughtful missionary has noted that while the gentiles procreate easily and are healthy and robust (though errant) in the wilds, in spite of hunger, nakedness, and living completely outdoors almost like beasts, as soon as they commit themselves to a sociable and Christian life, they become extremely feeble, lose weight, get sick, and die. This plague affects the women particularly, especially those who have recently become pregnant.

In the beginning of the conquest the friars, our predecessors, wisely believed that the change of home, climate, food, customs, and ideas contributed to this situation; and they used to console themselves with the idea that the sons of the mission or those born in it, having been raised in its rule and customs, would be different and would keep their normal health and constitution. However, the sad experience of 51 years has showed us all too well that we have erred in our calculation. Having already seen two generations in the missions, we sadly observe that the mission native dies equally, and perhaps more so than the Indian of the sierra, that they are consumed indiscriminately and are rapidly vanishing.

The notable lack of people and the horrible and unusual mortality among the Indians while those *de razon* remain healthy and seldom die; the fecundity of the latter's women and the sterility of the former, are scarcely evident in the annual reports. This is due to the fact that in many places in the province they are still baptizing gentiles, and by mixing one group with another, we still come out ahead in the total. But this decline can not be hidden in the places where the conquest has ended. Here is an example: In the mission of my actual residence, *La Purisima*, last year, 1819, out of 228 couples, the greater portion at the age of procreation, only 26 children were baptized from among them while 66 of its neophytes died of the 800 to 900 which it had. This means that in one year alone it had a decrease of 40 individuals. About the same thing happens, more or less, in the greater part of the missions so that this subject is for many Father Ministers the touchstone of their greatest despair and affliction. It also makes them uneasy (although they may wish to ignore it) among the Indians themselves whom they have redeemed and reared with so much sweat and labor.

Each missionary, according to his talent, energy, and the degree to which the resources of his mission have stretched, has endeavored to remedy and stop these evils. In general they are believed to result, not so much from the exchange of clothes and houses among them, but (where there are adobe *rancherias*) rather from the natural fermentation of the gathering so many people together into one place who scarcely know innate shame, or respect anything more than immediate consanguinity, and who do not value their health as they should but rather waste it and place it secondary to vile pleasures and whims. They are a people still preserving the bad habits of barbarism and heathenism, and their beliefs and ancient customs are all destructive to their natures and constitutions.

Nearly all the missions have built hospitals, bought med-
icines, have acquired medical knowledge from the sur-
geons of the province and from medical textbooks. In
short, since this country lacks licensed doctors, the Father
Ministers obtain the most expert *curanderos* and *curand-
eras*) from wherever they can (*gente de razón*) and they
insist in their curing these illnesses without sparing cost,
work, and effort. But despite all that I have said, they die.
I don't know if it can be said that they die as much as
before, but I believe there is no human recourse left to us,
and it only seems to me, according to my estimation, that
the Superior who sees the entire picture, must inform his
College as I am now doing with this clear report which
shows the Venerable Discretorio what is happening in
these missions in our care, which continue to follow the
methods established by our former and present friars and
have been generally adopted in all of our establishments.
This truth of this situation did not escape the sharp notice
of the present Lord Governor [Sola]. From the [records
of] births and deaths in a period of five years he made a
frightful calculation of this rate of decline. At a gathering
of the most serious of the religious, His Lordship threw it
in our face. He attempted to excite our religious zeal and
energy so that thinking about the question, we should try
to stop the progress of this evil which without any known
pestilence or epidemic is rapidly sweeping away our Indians.

I do not believe that any single missionary is authorized to
change or innovate [anything] in the fundamental administration of his mission. Therefore no one whosoever can
be blamed in particular for the situation. But I do think
that their Superior has the duty to explain to his immediate superior body what is happening to us. For a better
explanation, here is another example.

When the one who is reporting, having been assigned as
Minister of the Mission of San Carlos while he was at

that of Our Father San Francisco, arrived at his destination in July [17]96, he found 835 individuals residing at that mission. Despite the number of gentiles subsequently baptized there and regular births among its neophytes (proportionately equal to those of other missions), in the year [1]818 the Father Ministers of that mission informed us of 390 Indian inhabitants. I could say more about the Mission of *Nuestro Padre, Santa Cruz* and others; but in order to do it with greater personal knowledge, I shall add the example of my Soledad, which in this regard outdoes them all.

At the beginning of last year my office required me to establish my residence for a second time at La Soledad, 16 years after, having left it out of obedience to orders. On viewing its people and inspecting its census records, I discovered a skeleton of a mission with an unbalanced society made up of a group of 200 (or close to it) of either widowers or single men without one woman to whom to marry them, nor even the hope of doing it. Why? Because the women (though they had been in equal proportion) had been consumed and exhausted in a few years. There being no births or areas to conquer, except the disappointing one of the *Tulares,* three, four, or five days travel away, there is no other place for these involuntary single men and celibates to seek their so greatly desired *adjutorium simile sibi.**

Being forewarned by the judgment of foreigners who have little love for the Apostolic Institute on this point, I hasten then, my Fathers, to place before Your Reverence's eyes these developments which, after having been observed and meditated upon for many years and also perhaps communicated to my Superiors, it has finally seemed necessary for me to communicate formally to you, humbly and simply, with all due respect, at the same

---

*   Literally, "a help like himself," a reference to the description of Eve found in the Book of Genesis.

time at which I forward to Your Reverences the annual reports from this Presidency. May you meditate with your customary reflection and maturity on the fact that if from the aforementioned date of [1]796 until now the inhabitants of these missions have suffered such significant losses, with but two epidemics in 24 years (that of *dolor de costado* in [1]801 and of measles in [1]806); and despite the great number of gentiles who have come from a long distance to occupy and fill the void in the original native population here, what does the next equal amount of time promise, since there are no longer any live [Indians] in many missions to fill or occupy the place of the dead? It is horrible to go through the missions now, especially those of the north and ask after the many robust and young neophytes who lived there 20 years ago. Seldom have the Father Ministers answered me that there are one or two living whom I remember.

I fear that a few years hence on seeing Alta California deserted and depopulated of Indians within a century of its discovery and conquest by the Spaniards, it will be asked where is the numerous heathendom that used to populate it? And even the most pious and kindly of us will answer: The missionary priest baptized them, administered the sacraments to them, and buried them. It is necessary, my Fathers, to confess, whether we want to or not, that where we have not yet penetrated, as is the case of the frontier of the *tulares* and on the adjacent islands before conquest, all of that area is fully populated, while the field or vineyard where we labor is depopulated.

In truth, I have dedicated myself these days to reading somewhat thoughtfully about the various foundings of reductions or missions which the Reverend Father [Juan Domingo] Arricivita has so wisely treated in his *Crónica del Colegio de Santa Cruz*. It reminds me of all I have heard about this subject from missionaries from Guatemala, Panama, and Querétaro. I have not forgotten either what is happening in Antigua California, and although it is a common saying that the trouble of many is the consolation of all, it does not seem to me, my Fathers, that I can fulfilling my duty or be completely satisfied if I do not let Your Reverences know in detail what is happening to us here.

As a result, the Venerable *Discretorio,* having been informed in time about what is going on here, might wish to notify our Most Reverend Father or His Excellency the Lord Viceroy, about it immediately, or take some other measures which would free us for all time from undeserved reproach (I have heard that some of this is contained in the new history of the voyages of the Count of La Pérouse, the remarkable Frenchman who was here, I don't know in what year, at San Carlos) and censures, and would shelter us from slander and sarcasm.

I must confess to Your Reverences, my Fathers, that although I had these thoughts some days ago, I put them away endeavoring to forget the intention of this memorial; but my conscience argued daily that it was proper to forward it when completed to Your Reverences, and I am thus so doing in fulfillment of my duty, for the good of humanity, and for the proper information of that Holy College and its Venerable and worthy *Discretorio.*

If my Reverend Fathers *Discretos*, approve of this report, which was written solely for the greater glory of God, the good of these Indians, and the honor of our Institute of Propaganda, I shall give thanks to God a thousand times for it; but should see in it a lack of clarity and of the knowledge necessary for this poor, miserable, ignorant person to speak to such a respectable body, your least brother and useless subject confessing such truth without fear and prostrated in all humility before all Your Reverences' feet, requests pardon and indulgence..."[1]

With this letter, Payeras was well ahead of almost all of his contemporaries. Two hundred years later, we fully recognize that disease and crowded living conditions, both brought to California by the Spanish, were a tragedy for the native Californians. Payeras recognized it as it was happening and tried to bring it to the attention of his superiors. His pleas, unfortunately, apparently fell on deaf ears. Probably the political turmoil sweeping the territory—1820 was the tenth year of Mexico's rebellion against Spain—led to his report being shunted aside and buried, while issues more immediate to those in power were considered.

In 1823 Father Payeras died. His tomb is beneath the floor of the church marked with a plaque.* The loss of the leadership he had so long provided, along with the events shortly to come, brought great ruin to La Purísima.

In 1824, Mission La Purísima became the site of the most serious challenge ever to Mexican rule and to the mission system. Mistreatment of the Indians finally reached a flash point, and a full-scale revolt erupted. For more than two years, since Mexico won her independencein 1821, the soldiers stationed at La Purísima had not been paid. They compensated by making liberal use of the local Indians, forcing them to work for them, feed them and provide upkeep on their quarters. Finally, prompted by the flogging of an Indian by a Mexican soldier, the Indians rebelled, and did so in a spectacular fashion. They enlisted in their rebellion natives from Santa Barbara and Santa Inés. For some of the natives, rebellion was simply a flight to the Central Valley and away, they hoped, from the influence of the priests and soldiers. For some, though, their revolt took a more defiant turn. They seized the mission compound and declared themselves free of any control by the Mexicans, and threatened to kill all of the priests and soldiers.

Since the Indians built the mission, they were very familiar with its construction, its strong points and its weak points. They cut holes

---

*   Inexplicably, Father Payeras seems to be buried at two missions. He passed away April 28, 1823, and was buried at La Purísima. As late as 1936, the remains of that tomb were identified as indeed being those of Father Payeras. However, another tomb at Santa Barbara is also identified as Father Payeras' burial place. There are some records documenting that Father Francisco Sanchez, who served at Mission Santa Barbara from 1840 until 1880, removed at least some of Father Payeras' remains to Santa Barbara.

in the walls and mounted cannons to repel an invasion. They allowed the Mexican soldiers to leave, but Father Antonio Rodriquez, who was now running the mission, elected to stay with the Indians, realizing their defeat was inevitable but hoping to negotiate a just truce for them. Almost a month of their occupancy went by before soldiers from Monterey arrived to end the rebellion. The Indians were outmatched, not just in numbers and weaponry but in the training needed to fight an artillery battle. They could not accurately employ the cannons they had. The Mexican army, on the other hand, very accurately used its artillery, and in a matter of hours, reduced the walls of the church to ruins. As the hopelessness of their position became obvious, some of the Indians tried to escape, only to find their retreat cut off by Mexican cavalry. One interesting story comes out of this final desperate battle:

> When everyone, confused by fear of the soldiers and the havoc wrought by the cannon, was running from one end of the mission compound to another looking for a place to hide, this Indian entered the church. He remained there with his gaze fixed on a Christ figure about a foot in length. When he finished contemplating that image of the crucified he said, as if addressing him directly, "Now I will know if you are God almighty as the father says. Carrying you completely hidden so that no one will see you, I am going alone to fight against all the soldiers. If they don't kill me or shoot me I will serve you well until I die." He immediately took down the figure, hung it around his neck and covered it with his blanket so that it would not get in his way. He approached to within arrow-shot range and stood fast against the soldiers. He continued fighting until he shot the last arrow in his quiver. Then he immediately turned around walked at a a normal pace towards the church. Many shots were fired at him but not one hit him. He fulfilled his promise and served as sacristan, living an exemplary life as a true Catholic until he died.[2]

With their defensive works obliterated, the natives had only two choices: fight to the end and be pulverized as their walls had been, or surrender. They chose the latter course. At the request of the Indians,

Father Rodriquez approached the soldiers under a flag of truce, and effected a surrender with a promise of lenient treatment except for those who would be identified as leaders of the rebellion. Sixteen Indians had been killed in the siege. One Mexican soldier and three Mexican civilians were also killed. From among the captured Indians, seven were identified as ringleaders, sentenced to death and summarily executed. Eighteen others were imprisoned for indeterminate times. The most serious challenge ever, to either Spanish or Mexican control of California, was over.

The mission had been seriously damaged in the siege. It was rebuilt under the direction of Father Blas Ordaz, but La Purísima never really recovered from the siege nor, perhaps, from Father Ordaz's tenure. Father Ordaz was another Franciscan who had a very shabby reputation regarding his standard of morality, particularly in his relationships with women. At least three other Franciscans alluded to his "incontinence," and none other than the first bishop of San Francisco, Joseph Allemany, claimed that Ordaz had fathered three children. After leaving La Purísima, he was charged with murder, but never convicted.

The mission was secularized in 1835 and sold in 1845 for around $1,000. It remained nothing but crumbling ruins, a ready source of building material for its neighbors for almost 100 years. In the 1850s, the decay of the mission reached its nadir when the ruins proved to be convenient hideouts for Salomon Pico, a California outlaw and distant cousin of Governor Pio Pico. Salomon was a highwayman who was only too happy to relieve Californians of their gold as they traveled from San Luis Obispo to Santa Barbara. He boasted that he had a "rosary" of ears he had taken from his victim.

Throughout the 1850s and 1860s, the mission was owned by a variety of families and served as not just secular residences but as various mercantile establishments, stables and barns. Several houses in nearby Santa Barbara were roofed with purloined mission tiles. The mission itself degenerated into ruins.

In 1934, the mission was chosen as a worksite by the Civilian Conservation Corps. Rather than a willy-nilly make-work project, La Purísima became a major attraction to historians, architects, archeologists and engineers, and was carefully and meticulously restored. Not only did the plans follow the originals but, whenever possible, original tools and methods were used. It must be realized, though, that there is almost nothing you see above ground at Purísima today that is a survivor from the original buildings.

Mission La Purisima today:

Mission La Purísima is located at: La Purisima Mission State Historic Park, 2295 Purísima Road, Lompoc, CA 93436; (805) 733-1303.
Nickname: The Linear Mission

Mission La Purísima is part of California's state parks system. It is one of the most faithfully restored missions. The mission and its main buildings, including its workshops, tools and industries, are on display. There are exemplars of the hide-processing works, candle making, olive oil and tallow processing which made La Purísima, at its height, one of the most successful of all the missions. The mission and its grounds are open for a self-guided walking tour that will take you through all of the major working and living quarters of the mission. On certain holidays and feast days, the mission grounds are staffed with volunteer docents, in period dress, working at the tasks of the missions

One of the most striking features of the church at La Purísima is the lack of pews or seats in the church. This is actually a very accurate representation of the standard for Spanish and Mexican churches in the seventeenth and eighteenth centuries. At that time, there were no pews or kneelers. The congregation stood or knelt on the stone floor, not an accommodation any twenty-first century Catholics are likely to embrace. Look carefully at the floor tiles at La Purísima. In the center of the floor you will see a line of bricks laid not flat but on their sides. That demarcation was a line of separation between men and women. The congregation of all of the missions was separated, by convention for no known theological reason, with men on the left and women on the right.*

While the plaster and colors of the church have been reproduced from samples of the ruins, virtually all of the furniture and artwork in the church is of later design, having been brought from Mexico for the restoration. Many of the mission buildings appear to a visitor who have just visited the nearby "Queen of the Missions" at Santa Barbara to be rough and unfinished. This is a deliberate effect by the restorers. The original mission buildings were frontier establishments and would not have been exquisitely faced. La Purísima, in both its location in an oak-covered valley and in its architectural details, is one of the missions most likely to impart to the visitor a sense of stepping back in time to the eighteenth century.

Mission La Purisma - corridor.

* While there is no theological reason, this arrangement does suggest a disparate view of the two sexes. In the eighteenth century Catholic church, the left-hand side of the church (from the congregation's perspective) was the "Gospel" side. It was and still is the side from whence the Gospels, the story of the life of Christ, are read. It was considered superior to the "Epistle" side where the early history of the Church was read. Thus the men stood on the superior side. In today's Church, both the Gospel and the Epistles are read from the left hand side. The congregation, of course, places itself wherever it chooses regardless of sex.

Carpenter shop.

Floor tiles denoting separation between men and women.

Endnotes
1   Cutter, Donald, trans. and ed. *Writings of Mariano Payeras.* Santa Barbara: Bellerophon Books, 1995.

2   Osio, Antonio Maria. *The History of Alta California – A Memoir of Mexican California.* Translated by Rose Marie Beebe and Robert M. Senkewicz. Madison : University of Wisconsin Press, 1996.

LANDS NEVER TRODDEN

Chapter 15

SANTA CRUZ

The History of Santa Cruz

L *a Mision de la Exaltacion de la Santa Cruz* (The Mission of the Exaltation of the Holy Cross), the twelfth mission, was founded on August 28, 1791, by Father Lasuen. *Santa Cruz* which means Holy Cross, is the only mission named, not after a person or an event, but after a physical object: the cross on which Jesus was crucified.

Fathers Alonzo Salazar and Baldomero Lopez were put in charge of this mission. As was so often the case, the *padres* were attracted by the proximity of a river in building their church. What they did not consider was that a California river in August becomes something entirely different in winter. That very first winter, the San Lorenzo River overflowed its banks and destroyed the church. Two years later in December of 1793, the mission was attacked and partially burned by natives who inhabited the coastal mountains. Because of that attack, and because of the flooding, the mission was moved further up the hill to the site where the church is today. It was hoped that its location atop the hill would give it protection from both the river and the unfriendly natives. Santa Cruz, when it was completed, was a combination of stone and adobe.

This mission, founded just three years after the founding of La Purísima, was laid out in the classical quadrangle, which adds to the mystery of why La Purísima was not. In its early years, Santa Cruz enjoyed some success in producing grain and livestock, but overall it was always one of the least successful of all of the missions, both in terms of converted neophytes and agricultural endeavors.

Part of its poor showing was due to the fact that Santa Cruz had more than its share of challenges from civil authorities. In 1797, a decision was made by governor Diego Borica to establish a *pueblo* just across the river from the mission. Borica had ambitions for what might have been the first planned community in California. He envisioned, and actually created on paper, a community of houses arranged around a square, with a huge communal farming area with specific plots to be allotted to particular families. Borica's plan called for the population of this town by committed colonists who would receive an annual payment for the first three years, until they had their farming and other ventures up and running. Then they would be self-sufficient. Every other house was to be occupied by a native family, specifically to encourage intermarriage, and thus the stabilization of the frontier.

Borica's utopia never came to fruition for a variety of reasons. First of all was the fact that Spanish law mandated that no *pueblos* would be located within a league of any mission. Borica's plans ignored that small detail, and thus he incurred not just the anger, but the active resistance of the Franciscans. That issue, though, might have been amicably resolved had the colonists who were sent been the hardworking, upstanding citizens Borica envisioned. Instead, sent to populate Branciforte—such was the name of Borica's village—were the dregs of the Spanish penal system. Criminals and derelicts are not the stuff of which stable communities were built.

The town soon became a home and refuge to an unsavory lot of gamblers and criminals. The first public work the citizens of Branciforte undertook was not to parcel out the communal farming land but to build a racetrack. What work their endeavors required they transferred to the natives, thus drawing from the mission its own labor force. The wages available at Branciforte may not have been much ,and were often paid "in kind" with liquor, but they were better than the wages at the mission, which were non existent. For the natives, life at the mission was one of almost unremitting physical labor and the demanding religious and moral strictures of the Franciscans. Life in Branciforte, on the other hand, offered the inducements of gambling, drinking, and a decidedly more forgiving moral code.

The Franciscans protested to the governor, but since the settlement had been his idea to begin with, he was disinclined to get involved. The conflict between the town and mission never abated, and is a significant part of Santa Cruz's history. The attractions which proved so irresistable to the natives apparently had an allure for at least one Franciscan as well. Father Gil y Taboada, while serving at Santa Cruz, was accused by his superiors of gambling and other improprieties. Father Taboada raised the innovative defense that he frequented the gambling halls solely for the purpose of detecting cheating. More astonishing yet is that this defense was apparently accepted by his superiors.

As more and more of their neophytes were drawn to the pleasures of Branciforte, the Franciscans responded with increasingly harsh punishments. Father Andres Quintana was a cruel disciplinarian. He ordered beatings of children as young as eight years old. Indians who left the mission for the town were forcibly returned and severely punished. In 1812, Father Quintana ordered two runaway natives beaten with a new invention of his, a wire-tipped whip.

It is likely that it was for such zeal in inflicting punishments on the natives that Father Quintana was killed. The story of his death is a very confused and conflicting one. Some accounts hold that he died a natural death, some that he was poisoned or strangled; some report that his body was found in his bed, and some that it was found in the orchard.

The essential fact is that on October 12, 1812, Father Quintana was found dead in his bed. The door to his room was locked and Father Quintana had been in very poor health; so originally it was seen as a natural death. Shortly after the burial of Father Quintana, the governor of California, Pablo Sola received some information that suggested to him that the death may not have been from natural causes. Sola directed that the body be disinterred and examined. A surgeon, Manuel Quijano, performed the examination within a week and decided that the death was from natural causes.* It is unfortunate, given subsequent events that Surgeon Quijano did not made any observation about the condition of Father Quintana's nether regions.

Two years after Quinta's death, some of the natives began to boastfully take credit it. They claimed they had finally done for the good *padre,* not just because of his cruel punishments, but because of his

---

* This is the autopsy that Mission Santa Cruz often claims as California's first, when in fact we know that in 1801 one Surgeon Morales at least attempted an autopsy on Father Pujol at San Antonio.

predilection for the native women. One of the natives, who may have been the husband of one of the violated women, boasted that because of the priest's crimes of the flesh, he had, as part of the murder, cut off Quintana's testicles. According to the testimony of one Lorenzo Asisara* the natives used the opportunity of the priest's death to unlock the women's quarters and to have a night-long orgy with the young women of the mission. While Father Quintana may have been lying dead in his bed, Fathers José Viader and Narciso Duran were both on the premises at the time, and that a bacchanalia such as Asisara describes could have gone undetected is questionable to say the least. Whatever the events after Quintana's death it was decided—based entirely on their own boasts—that four of the natives were guilty. They were sentenced to 200 lashes each and then life imprisonment.

The circumstances surrounding Quintana's death continue to be a mystery 200 years later. Maynard Geiger in his recitation of this event makes much of the fact that Governor Pablo Sola conducted an extensive investigation of the case and found no fault with Quintana or his methods. In fact, Sola went to great lengths to praise not just Father Quintana, whom he had never met, but all of the Franciscans serving in California. What Geiger does not mention is the fact that Sola, who was not appointed governor until three years after Quintana's death, had a brother who was a Franciscan priest. Father Faustino Sola served in California from 1786 until 1790. He remained a Franciscan until his death in 1820.

The citizens of Branciforte showed their true colors in 1818 when Hippolyte Bouchard sacked and burned Monterey. Monterey Bay is a little more than a narrow depression on the California coast, with Monterey on the southern shore and Santa Cruz on the northern, and each town easily visible from the other. As Bouchard was raising havoc in Monterey, across the bay his ships would have been visible in Santa Cruz. Further, smoke from the burning buildings would have caught the eye of anyone across the bay. Father Ramon Olbes at Santa Cruz and his _confreres_ were ordered to leave the mission and flee to

* Asisara's account, which can be found in *Californio Voices: The Oral Memoirs of José María Amador and Lorenzo Asisara* **By José María Amador, Lorenzo Asisara, Thomas Savage** has to be read with a very questioning eye. Asisara was not born until seven years after the events took place. Sixty-five years after those events, he is telling a story that he heard from his father.

safety. They left the mission abandoned and unguarded. As they did, their neighbors from Branciforte decided that what Bouchard had threatened they would carry out. The church at Santa Cruz and all of its property were broken into and ransacked by the townspeople. Everything of value was taken, and what could not be taken was vandalized. Father Olbes, on his return, found the mission so damaged that he requested of his superiors that Santa Cruz be abandoned.

"The friars charges were sweeping, including the theft of every movable article, the wanton destruction of all that was unmovable or useless to the thieves, and the most shocking desecration of the church and holy images -- in fact, nothing but the bare walls of the buildings remained to show for all of the toil of the missionaries, and Olbes declared that the establishment must be abandoned, for he would not go back to submit longer to the outrages of the people of Branciforte." [1] What floods and cruel priests had been unable to accomplish had, in Father Olbes' view, been accomplished by the citizens of the town.

It is no surprise, given their dogged insistence on confronting adversity, that his superiors refused his suggestion and ordered him to continue his duties at Santa Cruz. Olbes himself, despite his contentions to the contrary, remained at the mission for three more years and fulfilled his full ten-year commitment to the California missions.

The mission never really recovered. With the declining population of local neophytes, attempts were made in the early 1800s to forcibly recruit new natives from the Central Valley. Given that they had not been successful in keeping the local Awaswas and Ohlones under mission rule, it is puzzling that the Franciscans thought they would be more successful in making the Yokuts, from one hundred miles away, happy participants in their endeavors. Father Manuel Fernandez persisted in having the Spanish soldiers violate Spanish law, kidnap natives and bring them as unwilling recruits to Santa Cruz. As fast as they were brought to the mission, they left, and the mission never again enjoyed the success it had in its early years.

As the nineteenth century progressed, Santa Cruz, along with all the missions, was swept up in the tide of political change. The Mexican revolution was waged from 1810 until 1821, and all during that time, support for the missions from the "mother" country became virtually non-existent. When Mexico won independence from Spain in 1821, the new republic had more pressing issues to address than the needs of the Franciscans. Not the least of these issues was the one of exactly what and who the new government would be. From independence in 1821 to surrender to the United States in 1846, California had a total of eleven governors. They ranged in persuasion from faithful royalist, to defenders of the Mexican Republic, to advocates of an independent California. One author has referred to what took place in California in those twenty- five years as "derangement and vertigo."[2] It is little wonder that the missions were shunted aside by the Mexican bureaucracy.

It is interesting to note that the Franciscans, who had begun their work under the authority of the Spanish Crown, never gave any thought to abandoning that work when the crown, for all practical purposes, ceased to the exist. The issue of loyalty to the Mexican Republic, though, was a delicate one for priests born in Spain. It divided the priests at Santa Cruz one from the other, as it did in all of the missions. At independence, when all was said and done, of the thirty-eight Franciscans in California, two left of their own accord to return to Spain; one was exiled by the new government; three took the new oath of loyalty; and the rest were left pretty much undisturbed until time, death and subsequent history resolved the issue.

Santa Cruz was one of the first missions to be secularized in 1834. As was typical of the process, little of the mission holdings went to the natives. A smallpox epidemic of 1838 reduced the already-declining native population by two-thirds.

In 1840, the first of a series of earthquakes did significant damage to the mission, and a second earthquake in 1857 caused the roof to fall in. The interior of the ruined church was sketched by a local artist the day after it collapsed. That sketch served as the model for the mission replica we have today.

The mission was abandoned, and as was so often the case, what nature hadn't destroyed, the local population did, carrying off stones, beams and roof tiles to use in private construction. In 1889, what few ruins remained were razed to clear a site for the new Holy Cross Church that replaced Mission Santa Cruz. Finally, in 1931 a local citizen funded the construction of a replica of the destroyed church based on the sketch of 1857.

Mission Santa Cruz today:

Mission Santa Cruz is located at: 130 Emmett St., Santa Cruz, CA, 95060. (831) 426-5686.
holycrosssantacruz.com
Nickname: The Hard Luck Mission

At Santa Cruz you are visiting not a restoration but a replica, built in 1931 on a smaller scale than the original mission, and funded by a private citizen, Mrs. Gladys Sullivan Doyle. Mrs. Doyle was a very religious person who suffered a childhood injury to her leg that resisted the best medical efforts toward a cure. After a visit to the shrine of Our Lady of Lourdes in France, she was able to walk without a crutch, for the first time since the injury. The daughter of a wealthy and prominent family, she used her own money to reconstruct the reduced-scale model of the lost mission. Only a year after the dedication of "her" church, Mrs. Doyle died, and is buried in a vault in the baptistery. Her son, who died after her, is also buried in the church. This makes Santa Cruz the only one of the California missions that has two laypersons, and no priests, buried in it.

The words on the arch in front of the altar are Latin and translated, they say *"We adore you, Christ and we bless you, because by your holy cross you have redeemed the world."* This phrase is one used repeatedly in the Good Friday devotionals in Catholic churches throughout the world. The tabernacle and candlesticks on the altar are all from the original church. They were recovered from other missions they were dispersed to when Santa Cruz fell into ruin.

The painting of Our Lady of Guadalupe was done in Mexico in 1791, and is documented as coming to Mission Santa Cruz in 1797. The three statues on the altar, Our Lady of Sorrows, Saint Joseph, and Saint Michael, were likewise originally in the old church. The statue of Our Lady of Sorrows is interesting in that it has movable arms and legs. Since it is a statute representing Mary as grieving after the death of Jesus, it would be placed in a position of recumbent grief during Lent.

Other interesting artwork(s) in the mission include: On the left side of the altar, Our Lady of Refuge; on the right side of the altar, the Assumption of Mary; to the middle left, Saint Catherine of Alexandria;* to the middle right, Saint Anthony of Padua, an earlier Franciscan; and the baptismal font at the front of the church.

At the museum adjacent to the mission, you can see many of the fixtures, vestments and appurtenances which came from the original church.

Holy Cross Church, across the street from the mission replica, was built on the site and over the ruins of the original Mission Santa Cruz and its graveyard. Behind the church you can see a small portion of a crumbled adobe wall that is all that remains of the original Mission Santa Cruz.

The only surviving mission building, a dormitory for the neophytes, is at the Santa Cruz Mission State Historic Park, which is one block north of the church. It is worth going to see while you are at Santa Cruz. It has been very well restored to its original appearance. The adobe building was once housing for the California Indian residents of the mission. A museum is attached to this building as well, and it gives a perspective on the life of the mission which is too often missing, that of the Native Americans who were displaced by the arrival of the Spanish.

Endnotes

1   Bancroft, Hubert Howe. *History of California Vol. II 1801-1824*. San Francisco: The History Company Publishers, 1886.

2   Richman, Irving Berdine. *California Under Spain and Mexico.* New York: Cooper Square Publishers, 1965.

---

*   Because she refused to give her virginity to her persecutors she was condemned to die by being broken on a wheel. Thus Catherine is the patron saint of unmarried women, and potters (the wheel.) In the mission era she would have been seen as the protectoress of the young girls in the mission compound.

Chapter 16

MISSION SOLEDAD

The History of *Nuestra Senora de la Soledad*

*L**a Mision de Maria Santisima Nuestra Senora Doloroisima del La Soledad (*the Mission of Mary our Lady Most Holy of the Lonely Sorrows), the thirteenth mission, was founded on October 9, 1791, less than two months after Santa Cruz. Our Lady of Solitude is one of the titles given to the Virgin Mary. It commemorates her vigil on Holy Saturday as she awaits, with faith, the resurrection of Christ. The feast of Our Lady of Solitude is celebrated on December 19, and is particularly observed in Mexico. Soledad is a very popular female name in Mexico.

We are told that Soledad may be the only mission actually named by a native Californian. Father Crespi, accompanying Gaspar de Portola on his meandering search for Monterey in 1769, heard one of the natives they encountered in this area use the Spanish word *"soledad"* (loneliness.) Two years later, Father Serra, visiting the same site, was surprised to hear an Indian woman give her name as "Soledad." Given its bleak location and these two instances of a familiar word in a foreign land, the mission of Our Lady of Solitude was named. Two of Mary's titles in the Catholic church are Our Lady of Solitude and Our Lady of Sorrows. These titles are often used interchangeably, although they refer to two different events in the life of Mary. Our Lady of Solitude, honors Mary grieving alone on Holy Saturday after the death of Jesus. Our Lady of Sorrows refers to the prophesy Simeon made when

Mary presented at the temple with the Christ child, for her ritual puri-fication under Jewish law.*

At its founding a temporary church was built, and in 1797, that structure was replaced by a thatch-roofed adobe structure. This leap in time from founding in 1791 to the first permanent structure six years later illustrates an important point often forgotten when tour-ing the California missions. When we see the missions today, we are seeing examples of them at the height of their prosperity with tile-roofed structures constructed of adobe and stone, filled with furniture which, while crude by today's standards, was very comfortable in the eighteenth century. There were books to peruse, more than adequate kitchen and dining facilities. Meals were prepared and served by In-dian servants. Every priest had his own cell; fireplaces kept the damp weather at bay. Wine and other alcoholic beverages were readily (in some instances, too readily) available. In most of the missions, mu-sic, albeit coming from crude homemade instruments, was part of the lifestyle.

But we need to keep constantly in mind that at Soledad and at ev-ery mission, what we are viewing is the finished product. To arrive there the Franciscans spent years of living in the most abject of condi-tions. Even in the relatively pleasant climate of California, six years of sleeping under a brushwood shelter, or in a hole dug into a hillside could not be any person's ideal. There were no sanitary facilities, and no way to wash with any efficacy either one's person, or one's meager clothes. Being a Franciscan in California two centuries ago was not for the faint of heart.

The California coastal valleys are known for their cold fogs and rainy winters. Soledad was unfortunately aptly named: it was a lonely and bleak site. The rooms were always damp, cold and gloomy, and ill health plagued the friars assigned to it. In its forty-year existence, almost thirty different priests were assigned to it, a record no other mission comes close to matching.

Two of the earliest priests at Soledad were an oddly-matched set, Fathers Bartolome Gili and Mariano Rubi. Gili and Rubi—sounds

---

*   " And Simeon blessed them and said to Mary his mother: Behold, this child is destined for the fall and for the rise of many in Israel, and for a sign that shall be contradicted. And thine own soul a sword shall pierce that the thoughts of many hearts may be revealed." (Luke 2:34-35)

rather like a team of acrobats—did engage in some unseemly hijinks, and brought the mission and its administrators nothing but trouble. They had been together at the College of San Fernando, and each had a reputation for mischief, laziness and troublemaking. How or why these two young men, much given to complaining and outright thievery, were ever considered for service in the California missions, much less in one of the most remote and primitive missions, is beyond comprehension. However, they both ended up at Soledad, Rubi shortly after it was founded, and Gili a year later. They performed no better here than they had at San Fernando. Their complaints and malingering continued. Rubi carried a sidearm as part of his accouterments, and once became so threating to his superior, Father Diego Garcia, that the latter felt compelled to call the corporal of the guard for protection. After less than two years, Father Lasuen had enough of them, and both were removed to Mexico, ostensibly because of health problems. The record is clear that whatever emotional problems either of them may have had, Father Rubi was infected with syphilis.

In 1802, Soledad was visited by what would prove to be the first of a series of epidemics that devastated the native population. Five or six natives a day died from an as-yet still undiagnosed respiratory illness. The president of the missions, Fermin de Lasuen himself, referred to the effects of the diseases as "horrible," having such an effect that they could not bury the bodies fast enough. The disease ultimately led to large-scale defections of the natives from the mission. They were convinced by one of their own that the disease was visited on them as punishment for having accepted the ways of the interlopers. Ironically, what we know today is that those who began those rumors were in fact correct. The diseases they were dying of were diseases brought to them by the Spanish, and they were greatly exacerbated by the crowed and unsanitary conditions of life in the mission compounds.

It was epidemics such as this, introduced by the Spanish themselves, which led to yet another of the practices, probably practical at the time but seen as completely insensitive today: that is, the burial of large numbers of the neophytes in mass, unmarked graves. When epidemics struck it was a common practice in the seventeenth and eighteenth centuries to bury the victims quickly, and the most expeditious way of doing that was in a mass grave.* As for the graves being unmarked, quite likely that was actually in deference to the wishes of the natives themselves. Most of the Native Californians followed a practice of burying their dead in unmarked graves. It was considered an insult to ever speak the name of a person who had died. The natives did not want their dead recalled by any of the living, and they would have objected strongly to the practice of memorializing the dead with their name on a marker as a reminder to all who saw it.

Surviving pestilence was no guarantee of a long life at Soledad. The same year that the epidemic struck, three of the mission's neophytes were murdered by other Indians, probably as a protest of their acceptance of the Spanish colonization. The natives must have been seriously demoralized by all of these events. Seemingly, if they accepted the ways of the newcomers they were accepting death, either death from diseases unknown until those newcomers arrived, or death from their neighbors who viewed them as traitors. On the other hand, their old way of life was clearly on the wane.

As if pestilence and death were not sufficient challenges for the mission to face, Soledad found itself embroiled in a property dispute with Mission San Carlos. Such disputes between the missions and other land holders in the area were not unheard of. In fact several of them were long-standing and historical. San Jose, Santa Cruz and San Gabriel stand out. A quarrel between two missions over who owns what calls into question the idea that all of the Franciscan missions were but offshoots of one big, happy family. Such a dispute was virtually unheard of until the *padres* at San Carlos petitioned the father president of the missions to have those of Soledad withdraw from some disputed property. Father Payeras at Soledad wrote a spirited refutation of San Carlos' claims. In so doing, he turned the question into a three-way battle by claiming that Mission San Antonio was encroaching on another portion of Soledad's land. It is ironic that in this argument over control of land, in his letter to Father Lasuen Payeras uses frequent sarcasm and even contempt for the claims made by San Carlos, but then closes with a wish that the "beautiful link of peace between missions" would be maintained. Lasuen, with his hands full dealing with eighteen missions and their troubles with civilian authorities, could

---

*   In 1791, the same year that La Purísima was founded, Wolfgang Amadeus Mozart was buried in a mass grave in Austria.

not be bothered with this internecine squabbling. He dismissed San Carlo's complaint and ignored the problems, if in fact there were any, with San Antonio.

In 1803, Father Florencio Ibanez came to Soledad. Father Ibanez was the complete opposite of his predecessors Gili and Rubi. He was dedicated to the mission and to his responsibilities. Despite very ill health of his own, he stayed at the mission for more than fifteen years. In 1805 he began enlarging the church, and replaced the thatched roof with tiles. Ibanez was a cultured and accomplished man. He wrote several pieces of music and plays. His richly-illustrated choir books are still preserved in the Franciscan archives. He had many friends in the Spanish political establishment, and in 1814 Governor José de Arrillaga, the interim governor of California, in poor health and likely preparing to die, came to Mission Soledad. Father Ibanez composed a program of music and songs to welcome him. Arrillaga did die while visiting the mission and was buried there by his friend Father Ibanez. Four years after burying the governor, Father Ibanez himself died and was buried in the same graveyard.

From 1810 until approximately 1833, the history of Mission Soledad, as with all the missions, was more the history of Mexico than of Spain; that is, a long, bloody war for independence followed by a series of civil disputes, the birth pangs of a new republic.

In a taste of things to come, there was a decided split between northern California and southern California, as well as divergences between the republic and the monarchy and liberal and conservative agendas. There were proclamations, pronouncements and battles culminating in a skirmish outside of Los Angeles with three dead, several wounded and, for the time being, the firm establishment of rule over California from Mexico City.

All of these events had an impact on all of the missions. Soledad, perhaps because of its isolated location, found itself serving a key role in these events. Soledad ended up being the unlikely refuge for one of the most outspoken of the resistors of the new government, Father Francisco Sarria, who arrived at Soledad in 1828. The issue was the loyalty oath crisis that embroiled all of Spain's Franciscan sons, with its underlying quesion loyalty and trustworthiness. Father Sarria was the president of the missions at the time, and the Franciscans were, almost without exception, privileged members of the upper strata of

213

royalist Spain. They had been sent to the New World and to California with specific authority and privileges from the Crown. There can be no serious suggestion now that the Franciscans could have or would have agitated for the overturning of the new Mexican government, but the fears were real in 1825. That fear, coupled with the fact that they were, for all purposes, in sole possession of the most valuable and extensive holdings in California, made their undoing inevitable. The Franciscans came under a series of interdictions and restrictions. Almost all were ordered deported, although few actually were. At least two of their number decided on their own to leave the ungrateful new government. A few were held under arrest, and ultimately they were dispossessed of all of their holdings.

Finally, Governor Louis Arguello ordered all public and clerical officials to take an oath to the new republic. Father Sarria refused to take the oath. "My Venerable Sir and Master," he wrote, "After reflecting on the oath we are ordered to take to the federal constitution of the United Mexican States...I have decided that I cannot do it without violating what I owe to anterior obligations of justice and fidelity..." The term of the oath which Sarria found repugnant to his role as a Franciscan was one that required the deponent to "take up arms, or use their influence in favor of taking up arms for differences of political opinion." Father Sarria found that phrase incompatible with his vows as a Franciscan priest. Sarria left it to the individual conscience of the priests serving under him to decide whether they took the oath or not, and few of them did.

Sarria's position of authority and the genuine respect he enjoyed, not just within his order but among the secular authorities, made his intransigence unacceptable to the Mexican government. President Guadalupe Victoria ordered Governor Arguello to arrest Sarria and deport him to Mexico. Sarria apparently *was* placed under arrest, but never returned to Mexico. He was held under house arrest at San Carlos, very much under the eye of the authorities in Monterey, until 1828, when he was allowed to take up residence at Soledad, apparently with no objection,where he remained until his death in 1835.

Soledad was, interestingly, one of the few missions where there is documentation that not only the Franciscans, but also the neophytes, signed an oath of loyalty to the new republic. Four years later an Indian from Soledad was elected to represent the area in a legislative meeting

214

called by the Mexican officials in Monterey. Soledad, it would seem, was one of the more politically stable of the missions.

Politics and nature were the two forces the Franciscans in California never got under control. They generally managed to deal with politics, but the forces of nature were an entirely different matter. Whatever other talents the Franciscans had, a recognition of natural flood plains does not seem to be one of them. Thirty years and eighteen missions after their first mission, and having seen several of their efforts swept away by rising rivers, they were still enthralled with the idea of nearby water as a prerequisite to a successful mission. Soledad was no exception. In 1824, the Salinas River overflowed its banks and destroyed the mission, its outbuildings and its cemetery, obliterating Governor Arriallga's grave.* While the mission was being rebuilt, yet another flood swept over it; and when it was finally finished in 1832, the mission was flooded once again. A temporary chapel was established in what had been a warehouse. Each time the mission was rebuilt by the indefatigable Franciscans. Unlike other missions, for some reason there was never any serious attempt to move the mission to someplace above the flood plain. Even today the Salinas River is within sight of the mission and while thanks to modern flood control efforts the mission is no longer threatened, the damage has been done.

It was at Soledad that the first ever medical treatise in California was written. In 1830, Father Sarria, while serving at Mission Soledad in his position as the vice prefect for the Franciscans, sent a circular to all of the priests, entitled *Descripcion de la operacion Cesaria.* Father Sarria had no medical training but, like most of the Franciscans, being the only educated person in the community, he was often faced with the necessity of serving as an attendant at a difficult birth. He read all that he could on the subject of Cesarean delivery and then shared his findings with his brothers. Father Sarria's treatise dealt primarily with the theological problems attendant when a woman died in childbirth, with a presumably viable child in her womb. He described the procedures necessary to extract the child at the death of the mother so that it might be properly baptized, and thus saved from eternal damnation. Whether anyone ever put Sarria's advice to a practical test is not

---

*   Arriallgas's grave was only rediscovered in a restoration in 1954.

known, but his treatise stands as the first document written in California discussing a medical procedure.

Ultimately, what nature and the Salinas River couldn't accomplish, secularization did. Soledad was one of the first missions to be secularized in 1834. Father Sarria remained at the mission, where he died in 1835. So grim were the circumstances at Soledad at his death that the neophytes carried his body more than twenty miles to Mission San Antonio for burial.

After Sarria's death, Soledad was abandoned as an active church. Its records and its removable artwork were transferred to Mission San Antonio. In 1846, the lands were sold for $800 by Governor Pio Pico, and the church was used as a residence, a store and finally a stable. It was finally abandoned even to that use. In 1859 the ruins were returned to the Catholic church by the United States government. Nothing was done with them; they remained deserted and continued to deteriorate until 1954, when the Native Daughters of the Golden West took Soledad under their wing and began a slow but conscientious restoration effort that continues to this day.

By then, between the ravages of time, weather and the river, nothing remained but crumbling piles of adobe. Hired to assist in the reconstruction was Harry Downie, most known for his work at Mission Carmel. Downie gets less credit for his work at Soledad than he does at Carmel. His approach seems to have been to bulldoze what was left and start over. That may have been the only practical answer for a mission in such a sorry state of repair, but his failure to conduct careful archeological examinations first and to document what was there is much lamented by today's experts.

Mission Soledad today:

Mission Soledad is located three miles south of Soledad, one mile west of Highway 101, at 36641 Fort Romie Road (P.O. Box 515), Soledad, CA; (831) 678-2586.
Nickname: The Lonely Mission

When restoration finally began in 1954, all that could be saved from the original structure was the left front corner. Because Mission Soledad, fifty years after restoration began, is still in the very early stages of this process, its primary attraction is its location in a beautiful coastal valley with the Coast Range Mountains looming over it. The church has been rebuilt and work is in progress on the reconstruction of the cemetery. In the cemetery along with dozens of unidentified neophytes are Governor Arrillaga, Father Florencio Ibanez (who died in 1818), and a particularly intriguing grave of an as-yet unidentified native woman. This grave is very near what was the entrance to the original church. Such a prominent burial place for a native woman is unusual. Hope and a present-day myth persist that this unmarked grave is the final resting place of Soledad the mysterious Salinan woman who gave her name to the "lonely mission."

In the chapel, the eerie statue of Our Lady of Sorrows surmounting the altar is like something out of a Fellini movie. The statue is dressed entirely in black. The face is a contrasting ghostly white. Sad eyes peer down at the church pews in an almost accusatory manner. It is a grim reminder of how faith in the eighteenth century was a powerful and emotive presence in everyday life. Since almost all of the missions are active churches, it is not unusual to find devotees praying in them. To come across a *mantilla*-draped Hispanic woman with head bowed before this statue at Mission Soledad is a faith-enriching experience in itself. The statue, the painting of Our Lady of Sorrows, and the stations of the cross all came come from the original church. Many of Soledad's other artifacts and artwork are in safekeeping at other missions, and hopefully someday, when the mission is fully restored, they will be returned.

Mission Soledad - Our Lady of Solitude.

Chapter 17

MISSION SAN JOSE

The History of San Jose

*M*ssion del Gloriosisimo Patriarca Senor San Jose* (Mission of the Glorious Patriarch Lord Saint Joseph), the fourteenth mission, was founded June 11, 1797. It is named after Saint Joseph, the earthly father of Jesus. Joseph is the patron of fathers, workers and the universal Church. Saint Joseph's feast day is March 19.

The founding of Mission San Jose might be seen as the beginning of phase two of the Franciscans' ambitious project. They now had thirteen missions covering the western edge of California, from San Diego to San Francisco. It had been almost seven years since the last mission, Soledad, was built. All of these missions had been located at strategic points along El Camino Real. Now came the time to "fill in the gaps." One of those gaps was the eastern side of San Francisco Bay.

San Francisco Bay is a huge indentation in the California coast line. The *presidio* and Mission Dolores discouraged explorers from the Pacific Ocean. As history would demonstrate, however, the Spanish dominance of California would be threatened not by Russian fur trappers or British traders arriving by sea, but rather by American explorers trekking overland. The Spanish anticipated this threat and built Missions Santa Clara and San Jose to address it. Their efforts to stop American encroachment would ultimately prove futile, but the two missions built twenty years and twenty miles apart would each play a significant role in the settling of California and the development of the Bay Area.

These plans to build mission San Jose and five other missions in particular locations were part of a plan that mission president, Father Fermin de Lasuen arrived at after a careful consideration of the direction California was moving and of his view of the role the missions should and would play in that. Father Lasuen had succeeded to the presidency of the California missions on the death of Junipero Serra.*

Father Lasuen is perhaps one of the best examples to be found of the faith, total commitment, and dedication of the early missionaries. As the man who would equal Serra's record of number of missions founded, his history deserves a somewhat expanded examination.

Lasuen's history in California is an interesting one, composed of equal parts dedication, despair and intrigue. He found missionary life distasteful and more than once tried to use personal connections to escape it, repeatedly asking to be returned to the College of San Fernando in Mexico, once imploring, "I am already an old man[†] and completely grey; and although it is the toll of years, the pace has been accelerated by the heavy burden of this office which I hold and especially by the five years which I am completing as superior at San Diego. This land is for apostles only…" [1] Nonetheless, despite lamenting his fate in being assigned to California, he performed all of his duties admirably, remaining faithful to his vow of obedience and never shirking his responsibilities. Indeed, less than a year after the tale of woe above, he wrote a report on his work at San Diego in which he listed the completion of the church, a granary, a storehouse, separate housing for women and men, sheds for wood and oxen, two houses for the priests assigned, a larder, a kitchen and a guest room. There was also a fountain, and two corrals for sheep and one for cows. Lasuen stayed at San Diego for eight years.

Somewhere in those eight years Lasuen had developed a close friendship with Fernando de Rivera, the military commandant of Alta California. He eventually became Rivera's spiritual advisor. The friendship developed despite the fact that Junipero Serra and Rivera

---

*   Junipero Serra died in 1784 and very briefly Father Francisco Palou was appointed to succeed him on a temporary basis. On February 6, 1785 father Lasuen was appointed to the post and he served in that position until he died in 1803.

†   Average life expectancy in the eighteenth century was only about forty-five years of age; when he wrote this letter, Lasuen was forty-five.

had, a very contentious relationship. Lasuen walked a very fine line between obedience and loyalty to Father Serra, his superior, with his personal friendship with Rivera. Lasuen was present at a meeting between Serra and Rivera in 1775 when a very heated exchange occurred between them regarding the provision of soldiers to support the founding of more missions. Lasuen prepared his own report of that meeting, directed to the guardian at San Fernando. In that report he tended towards Rivera's side, rather than Serra's.

Another complicated feature of this friendship was the matter of the "excommunication" of Rivera for violating the law of sanctuary at San Diego, and Serra's refusal to lift the interdict. Although the excommunication was imposed by Father Fuster, it was Father Lasuen who in effect "seconded" the excommunication the next day by ordering Rivera's men to leave mass. As Rivera's spiritual advisor, it is hard to believe he didn't know of the ongoing efforts Rivera had made to have Serra lift the order. There is speculation that Lasuen himself unofficially lifted the order, by explaining to Rivera that a priest really had no authority to excommunicate, and that was the beginning of the friendship.

We do know that when Rivera left San Diego after the incident in March of 1776, he invited Lasuen to accompany him back to Monterey and offered him the position of chaplain at the *presidio*. Lasuen very much desired the post, and duty at the Monterey *presidio* seemed much more to his liking than missionary life. He dutifully applied for permission to accompany Rivera to Monterey. Serra would not grant permission because it did not appear to be authorized by either the military or the College of San Fernando, to which all of the California Franciscans reported. Lasuen, citing his vow of obedience, accepted the decision, but Rivera, who had no such moral constraints, made a personal appeal to Mexico City, requesting that Lasuen accompany him. Permission was granted, and Serra felt that Lasuen had made an "end run" around his authority. It took a year for the issues to sort themselves out, but Serra and Lasuen certainly held a deep respect for each other.

In 1797, both Serra and Rivera were dead. Lasuen had been the father president of the Franciscans for twelve years. A new era began for the missions, that would see a doubling of the number of missions. Lasuen would match Serra's accomplishments in founding nine missions. He would continue as the president of the missions for eighteen years, three years longer than Serra and far longer than any of the other nine men who served in that post. Lasuen administered the missions during their period of most vibrant growth.

Lasuen maintained his headquarters at San Carlos, and oversaw the construction of the "great stone church" which Serra had envisioned. His lasting legacy would be his ambitious expansion of the missions during the years 1797-1798. In that one-year period, he had five new missions underway.

Father Lasuen set about convincing the Crown that if five more missions were built it would actually save the government money. In January of 1796, Lasuen sent a report to the civilian authorities suggesting the founding of these next five missions from north of San Francisco to south of San Juan Capistrano. Lasuen's argument was that if those missions were built, more Indians would be converted and pacified, and thus Spanish troops could be freed up from policing the frontier. Governor Borica accepted the idea and convinced Mexico City that more than $15,000 a year could be saved if those five missions were established.

While it is doubtful that there was ever any savings realized, Lasuen's ambitious plans went ahead full bore. From June of 1797 until June of 1798, five more missions—San Jose, San Juan Bautista, San Miguel, San Fernando Rey and San Luis Rey—were begun, several within scant weeks of the previous one. Again we have to marvel at the temerity of these priests in undertaking these projects. From San Jose to San Luis Rey is a distance of almost 400 miles, of primitive trails and undeveloped terrain. At each site two priests were essentially dropped off and told, "Build a mission." Somehow through difficulties that would have discouraged a battalion of professional builders, they did just as they were asked.

In 1803, Father Fermin de Lasuen died, twenty years and nine missions after he had held himself as "unfit for the job God had given him." At the time of his death, Lasuen was sixty-seven years old, and it may be an indication of the toll that life on the California frontier took on him that, ten years earlier, George Vancouver had described Lasuen as "about seventy-two years of age."

The site chosen for Mission San Jose, the first mission planned in Lasuen's "surge," had a long history of significance to the Native

Americans. The site was on the opposite side of the bay from San Francisco, in a well-favored valley with plenty of water. It had long been a gathering and resting spot for the natives on their semi-annual treks to California's Central Valley. It now filled that same purpose for fugitives from Missions Dolores and Santa Clara. It was just south of Altamont Pass, a natural path through the coastal mountains to the central valley. Through this pass, the escaping neophytes would flee, and at its approaches, the Spanish would wait in ambush to return them to the missions. Once in the Central Valley, the natives were, for all practical purposes, beyond the reach of the soldiers. The Spanish had no presence there and the natives occupying the valley were much less docile than their coastal cousins. Many of them were of Apache and Comanche familial groups and they would fiercely defend not just themselves but any of their kin who made it to their land. None of these inland tribes were cowed by the Spanish troops, and they certainly had no warm feelings towards the Franciscans. All of these facts would lead to repeated armed conflict in the environs of Mission San Jose.

All of the missions were primarily agrarian ventures and Mission San Jose was no exception. What may set Mission San Jose apart is that it likely was the mission that introduced cannabis to California: "…the authorities in Mexico sent Joaquin Sanchez, sergeant of marines and an expert in the cultivation of hemp and flax…(H)e arrived on the *Concepcion* in the middle of 1801 bringing with him the necessary tools and proceeded to San Jose, the only place where hemp had as yet been planted."[2] By 1804, hemp was being sown at not just San Jose, but at San Luis Obispo, Purísima, and Santa Ines. Several years later Sergeant Sanchez had the occasion to testify that while he did not think flax would be a successful crop in California, "hemp bade fair to succeed in California."[3] A very perceptive young man was Sergeant Sanchez.

The *padres* started an adobe church in 1805. The initial design for San Jose was copied from San Juan Bautista.* While the church at San Jose was still under construction, a series of earthquakes struck the area. These disturbances led to the decision to build San Jose with

---

* While San Juan Bautista was founded after San Jose, its permanent church building was started before.

a much-diminished bell tower than was originally planned, a decision that would be validated sixty years later.

San Jose seems to have suffered from an unusual run of bad luck in the missionaries who were assigned to it in its early years. Initially assigned to the newly-founded mission were Fathers Isidro Barcenilla and Augustine Merino. Neither was in good health, and shortly after his arrival at San Jose, Father Merino was brought to Monterey in a condition described by the fathers who received him there as "being completely deranged." He was returned to Mexico. His companion, Father Barcenilla, had problems at the other extreme, a hemorrhoid condition so debilitating that he could not effectively function. He described himself as of "a bad disposition, a lack of sociability with other missionaries and an impatience with the Indians."[4] One of his fellow missionaries, Father Jose Uria, apparently agreed with this dim assessment, requesting of Father Lasuen that Barcenilla be replaced as soon as possible. The unfortunate priest, however, had to stay at Mission San Jose for almost a full year until a replacement could be found.

Next was one Father Pedro de la Cueva, who came to San Jose in 1806. Father Pedro was apparently an alcoholic of the worst sort. In his checkered career there are documented episodes of his drinking and of his violent tendencies when in his cups. Those who shared quarters with him from time to time would lock themselves in their rooms to avoid his attacks. More than once, he pulled a knife on his companions; at least once he began smashing and breaking furniture; and once he attempted suicide. De la Cueva was finally disaffiliated and returned to Spain in 1809.

Finally, in 1806 Father Narciso Duran brought some stability to Mission San Jose. Father Duran, who would serve twenty-seven years at San Jose, was an accomplished musician, although with no formal training. He organized a choir and an orchestra, and built many of the instruments which he then taught the natives to play. A significant accomplishment was his composition of musical scores for the Indians, to perform. The natives had no written language, and thus no reading skills. Father Duran simplified many of the superfluities of conventional musical notation, with a series of symbols and colors that the natives could understand. This simplification of musical scoring apparently caused no degradation of the quality of the music. For forty years people came from miles around to hear concerts at Mission San

Jose. Padre Duran's choir book is preserved at the Bancroft Library at the University of California. Duran, late in his career at San Jose, became the father president of the California Missions, so from 1824 to 1827 Mission San Jose was the headquarters of the Franciscan missions in California.

San Jose was another of the missions graced with the presence of Jedediah Smith, who was apparently no more well-received there than he had been at San Gabriel a year earlier. Smith stopped at San Jose in 1827 after he had left San Gabriel under orders to quit California altogether. Franciscan hospitality did not extend to those whom the government had decided were enemies of the state. Father Duran, on Smith's arrival, notified Governor Echeandia that the American was still—or again—in the territory. Echeandia ordered Smith arrested. Duran complied and had soldiers hold him at the mission. Ultimately another American, a Captain Cooper, posted bond and Smith this time did in fact leave California, never to return to what he now decided was an inhospitable area.

From 1828 through 1829, Mission San Jose was caught up in a serious outbreak of native unrest. One of the leaders of the revolt—perhaps *the* leader—was an Indian named Estanislao Cucunuchi. Estanislao was a member of the Yokut people from the Central Valley. At the age of twenty-eight, he attached himself to Mission San Jose apparently of his own volition. He became a personal favorite of Father Duran, and was appointed as *alcade.* The *alcades,* or "mayors," were appointed by the Franciscans to be the direct supervisors of the neophyte population at the missions. This honor notwithstanding, in 1827 Estanislao left the mission to return to his former lifestyle, and to add insult to injury, he took about four hundred of the neophytes with him. They escaped to the ever-beckoning Central Valley and set up a community of their own on the river, which now bears the Anglicized version of his name, Stanislaus.

The proud Mexican military initially treated Estanislao's force with disdain, and paid the price. Two expeditions against him ended in failure and great loss of Mexican life. Estanislao was an enterprising and obviously very charismatic man. At one time he had a force estimated at one thousand men at his disposal, this at a time when the Mexican military presence in California was numbered at the most 300. From his years at the mission and his familiarity with the Spanish and Mexican military, he had gained a thorough knowledge of military tactics and the manner in which the Mexican army fought. He impressed on his people that because of the leather armor the soldiers wore, arrows aimed at the torso would have little effect. From time immemorial, even to the present day, conventional military wisdom is to "aim for the center of mass." Estanislao deviated from that wisdom and did so very effectively. Despite the obvious danger attached to such a tactic, he had his fighters conceal themselves until the soldiers were only six or eight feet away, and then fire their arrows at their faces and heads. The wounds inflicted by this strategy were not only disabling, but demoralizing to the Mexican soldiers.

Finally, in 1829 the Mexican troops under Mariano Vallejo defeated Estanislao, following up the military victory with a punitive one and indiscriminately slaughtering native men, women and children. Father Duran lodged charges of atrocities with the governor. The priest went one step further and interceded on behalf of Estanislao, who had escaped the massacre. In this he was successful, but Estanislao, rather than return to the mission fold, returned to the Central Valley to lead his people, or at least those who had survived the slaughter by the Mexican army, in their new life. In 1831, he was approached by another Indian leader, Yoscolo from Santa Clara, who wanted to continue the armed struggle. Estanislao, likely realizing the futility of such a venture based on his own experiences, declined, and in fact decided to return to Mission San Jose, where he stayed until his death from smallpox in 1838.

Father Duran stayed at San Jose until 1833 when, as part of the restructuring of the missions, the Franciscans from Zacatecas replaced those from San Fernando at all of the missions north of San Miguel. Again, as evidence of the amicability of this transition, Duran and his replacement Father Jose Maria de Jesus Gonzalez Rubio shared quarters at San Jose for several months, Duran as president of the southern missions, Rubio as president of the northern ones. There is no record of any conflict between the two presidents.

Rubio made several "cosmetic" changes to Mission San Jose, but the basic elements of the mission remained. One of his most important decisions was to hire the noted artist Agustin Davila, who had decorated Santa Clara, to embellish the interior of San Jose with intricate designs. Unfortunately Davila's artwork at San Jose was lost forever to a devastating earthquake in 1868, and unlike Santa Clara, there was no photographic record to aid in reconstruction.

In 1836, Mission San Jose was one of the last missions to be secularized. A lay administrator, José de Jesus Vallejo, was appointed. In 1840, Vallejo resigned under pressure related to charges that he was dissipating the mission assets and leaving the natives impoverished. In 1846, Governor Pico sold the mission to his brother and Juan Alvarado for $12,000. The United States Lands Commission, in 1856, declared Pico's sale to be fraudulent and returned the church and its immediate lands to the Catholic church.

The church continued with various priests making various changes according to the fashions of the time until 1868, when another earthquake tumbled it into ruins. A wooden, gothic-style church was constructed on the site in 1869, and it served under the now-Anglicized name of Saint Joseph until the early 1980s. In 1982, the wooden clapboard church was removed and a careful reconstruction of the original Mission San Jose was begun. That project was completed in 1985.

Mission San Jose today:

Mission San Jose is located at 43300 Mission Blvd. (P.O Box 3314), Fremont, CA, 94539; (510) 657-1797.

As has been pointed out, Mission San Jose is a reconstruction, not a preservation, of the original building. In the reconstruction undertaking, though, painstaking attention was paid to the features and defects of the original building. Given this, the careful observer will note walls that seem to be slightly out of plumb, and interior fittings that are less than perfect. Look up under the overhanging eaves of the church and you will note that the sub-roofing beneath the mission's tiles is constructed of thousands of closely-bound willow branches, as it would have been in the eighteenth century.

Three of the statues in the church are originals from the destroyed mission. The statue *Ecce Homo* ("Behold the Man") represents Christ, as Pontius Pilate presented him to the people after he had been scourged and crowned with thorns. This statue is on a side altar to the left near the rear of the church. On either side of altar at the front of the church are statues of Saint Bonaventure, an early Franciscan; and Saint Joachim, the father of Mary. Both of these are carved wood. Saint Joachim, while he is revered in the Catholic church, is very seldom presented in church art. It is interesting that in the museum at San Jose there is another statue of Anna, the mother of Mary, with Mary as a pre-teen girl. Obviously, this family had a very special place in the heart of one of the mission's founders.

Above the main altar there is a unique display representing the Holy Trinity. At the top is a patriarchal depiction of God the Father, with golden rays emanating from his figure. In the middle is a white dove representing God the Holy Spirit. Below that is a depiction of Jesus Christ, God the Son.

The hammered copper baptismal font at San Jose is, as far as is known, the only original work of the artist Agustin Davila existing today. Davila had richly decorated the interior of both Mission San Jose and Mission Santa Clara. Earthquakes and fire destroyed all of his original decoration, although at Santa Clara, photographs had been taken which allowed its reproduction. No such record existed for San Jose. Finally, the "*sanctus* wheel" used at the elevation of the host during the mass is the original one used in the old mission. The purpose of these wheels, on display at several of the missions, was to call the attention of the congregation to the fact that what seconds before had been a wafer of unleavened bread was now miraculously the Body of Christ. In the eighteenth century, the congregation stood or knelt on the floor itself. The priest on the altar was not much elevated from the crowd attending. Further, he had his back to the congregation. Except for those in the very front of the church, it was not obvious to those attending mass what was taking place. Thus the bells, which would call attention to this miraculous event.

Visitors to Mission San Jose today should realize that an interesting perspective of the development of the San Francisco Bay Area over the past three hundred years can be gained from the front steps of the church. San Jose is founded on the opposite side of the bay in a line with Mission Dolores in San Francisco. The site for Mission San Jose was chosen among other reasons because from it, one could see Mission Dolores. Given the development in the Bay Area, and the degradation of the air quality, that is an absolute impossibility today.

On the side of the church opposite the cemetery, you will note a series of squares and rectangles laid out with dark stones. These mark the outlines of the foundations for various rooms that were attached to the church before the 1868 earthquake. Those foundations were uncovered during an archeological examination done in preparation for the reconstruction in the 1980s. After careful examination, they were meticulously covered to protect them from the elements, and their outlines marked for our benefit.

Endnotes

1   Finbar, Kenneally. *Writings of Fermin Francisco de Lasuen. Vol I.* Washington D.C.: Academy of American Franciscan History, 1965.

2   Bancroft , Hubert Howe. *History of California, Vol II.* San Francisco: The History Company Publishers, 1886.

3   Ibid., p.179

4   Geiger, Maynard. *Franciscan Missionaries in Hispanic California: A Biographical Dictionary.* San Marino: The Huntington Library, 1969.

Chapter 18

SAN JUAN BAUTISTA

The History of San Juan Bautista

*L*a Mision de San Juan Bautista, Precursor de Jesucristo *(*the Mission of St. John the Baptist, Precursor of Jesus Christ), the fifteenth mission and the second in Father Lasuen's summer of fevered activity, was founded on June 24, 1797, the feast day of Saint John the Baptist. In Catholic tradition, John the Baptist was the cousin of Jesus Christ, and actually proclaimed Christ's divinity before the birth of either of them.*

Originally assigned to the mission were Fathers Adriano Martinez and Joseph de Martiarena. They constructed a mud chapel covered with thatch. This church served until 1803, when the present church was begun. San Juan Bautista is the largest of the California missions, and if it had been built as planned, it would have been even larger. When the permanent church was started, it was planned to have three aisles that would have had a capacity of over a thousand worshipers. Wiser heads prevailed, and out of a concern that a roof arching such a huge expanse would not withstand what had already been demonstrated as a propensity for earthquakes, the church was scaled down to one aisle. Although probably not based on much science, that was likely one of the wisest decisions the *padres* ever made. We know now what they did not; that San Juan Bautista is built literally on top of the

---

* Mary, after the Annunciation from the angel Gabriel, went to visit her cousin Elizabeth, who was also pregnant. When Elizabeth heard Mary's greeting, "she gave a loud cry and said, 'Why should I be honored with a visit from the mother of my Lord. For lo, the moment your greeting reached my ears, the child in my womb leapt for joy.'" (Luke 1:42)

infamous San Andreas fault. A series of earthquakes lasting almost the entire month of October in 1800 reduced the priests to sleeping outdoors for fear of falling walls.

In 1801, Mariano Castro occupied some of the mission lands, supposedly with authority from Mexico City. The priests protested his presence and the matter went all the way to the viceroy in Mexico City. Predictably, the Franciscans won the suit and Señor Castro had to relocate his planned estate elsewhere.

The site chosen for San Juan Bautista was not only tectonically unstable; it was also apparently very politically unstable among the local residents. It was in an area of somewhat fluid and overlapping boundaries between the Salinan, Mutsunes, Eselen, Coastanoan, and Yokut people. While they were free to roam about the land these distinctions were generally not important to the natives. Once the Franciscans began establishing boundaries and attempts were made to confine people to specific *ranchieras,* problems arose. Almost as soon as the mission compound was laid out, the natives took to surrounding it at night, chanting and shouting to intimidate those within. These inhabitants were constantly harassed and threatened by their former neighbors. The attacks continued, several times leading to the death of the mission neophytes, until the early 1800s.

Arriving at San Juan Bautista in 1808 was Father Felipe Arroyo de la Cuesta, who would serve San Juan Bautista for the next fifteen years. His first task was to get the church building finished, which he accomplished in 1812. Much of the credit for the interior decorations of the church goes to an American sailor, Thomas Doak. Doak worked for room and board after the previous artist demanded the outrageous sum of seventy-five cents a day. While his artistic talents were not of the highest, Doak, likely because of his nautical background, clearly had a knowledge of paint and pigments. His craftsmanship is as bright and sharp two hundred years later as it was the day he applied it.

Father Arroyo was an accomplished linguist. He spoke at least seven different Indian dialects and wrote a phrase book of the Mutsun language that was published by the Smithsonian Institute twelve years after his death. In addition, he wrote moral treatises and confessional guides in the native tongue. He was an accomplished musician as well, and given these two talents it was inevitable that he would translate several hymns and chorales to the Mutsun language.

The musical history of San Juan Bautista is not limited to Father Arroyo's work, now preserved in the Franciscan archives at Santa Barbara. Its famous barrel organ has been the subject of a huge amount of speculation and theory. The barrel organ is essentially a giant music box that has various tunes punched into tin cylinders. When turned with a huge hand crank, the "organ" plays various tunes.

The history of this organ is one of those minor details that has fascinated historians for two hundred years. It has long been presumed that this organ is the same one that Captain George Vancouver gave to Father Fermin de Lasuen during a visit to San Diego in 1793. This is still the most popular explanation of the organ's origins. We know that Father Lasuen had the organ moved from San Diego to his headquarters at Mission Carmel, which is only about thirty miles from San Juan Bautista.

The organ is first mentioned in 1829 by Father Arroyo. Father Arroyo simply writes that he has received *"an organo de 3 cilindros."* Arroyo does not say from whence the organ came, but the presumption has been made that the fathers at Carmel grew tired of trying to maintain the ancient instrument and gave it to their less fortunate brothers at San Juan Bautista. The three cylinders referred to are tin cylinders with a series of tunes represented by pre-punched holes. Each of these three cylinders has ten separate tunes. When Vancouver gave his organ to Lasuen it was already fifty years old.

Was it Captain Vancouver's organ or another one that Father Arroyo received? The record is confusing and unclear. What we do know is that there is not now any such organ at Mission Carmel, thus buttressing the argument that Carmel gave Vancouver's organ to San Juan Bautista. On the other hand, it appears that at least some of the tunes on the organ at San Juan were not known in Vancouver's day, and certainly not fifty years earlier, thus buttressing the argument that San Juan Bautista acquired its own organ from some other source. None of the tunes on the organ are of a religious nature; for the most part, they are sailor's tunes and sea chanteys. Hearing "Popeye the Sailorman" played in the hallowed confines of San Juan Bautista would certainly give one pause.*

---

*   One of the tunes on the barrels is "The College Hornpipe," popularly known today as "Popeye the Sailorman."

There are two questions that remain. What happened to the organ at Mission Carmel? Surely an asset as large as that would not be disposed of without the meticulous record-keepers that the Franciscans were making a note of it. Where did the organ at San Juan actually come from?

In 1833, as part of the transfer of the northernmost missions from the San Fernando Franciscans to the Zacatecan Franciscans, Father Antonio de Anzar came to San Juan Batista.

San Juan Bautista was secularized in 1834. In 1839 it briefly served as the headquarters for Juan Bautista Alvarado and his *Californios,* as he led the fight against Governor Micheltorena representing direct rule from Mexico.

The mission was once again the site of a military confrontation in 1846, this time in the Mexican-American War, a war that provided the United States the perfect opportunity to gain a foothold in California.

In 1845, President John Tyler had managed, with some adept political maneuvering, to get Congress to pass a joint resolution calling for the annexation of Texas. Mexico's response to this resolution was to make it clear that any move toward the annexation of its northern territories would be considered an act of war. War with Mexico was a fine idea, not just with President Tyler, but also with his successor, James Polk. Polk and his advisers were demonstrably sure that the outcome of such a war would be the acquisition of not just Texas, but New Mexico and Alta California as well. Despite the best efforts of the United States, which launched a series of military provocations on both land and on sea, Mexico would not take the bait. Finally, President Polk decided on the ultimate provocation. He ordered General Zachary Taylor and his troops to move south of the Rio Grande. The border between the United States and Mexico had long been a bone of contention between the two countries, but there was not much dispute that anything south of the Rio Grande was Mexican territory. This maneuver proved too blatant for Mexico to ignore. American and Mexican troops clashed near the Nueces River on April 25, 1846. Sixteen American soldiers were killed. President Polk advised Congress that Mexican troops had invaded the United States and killed American troops on American soil. This patently false statement was challenged by none other than an upstart young Congressman from Illinois named Abraham Lincoln. The protestations of Congressman Lincoln and many other Americans not withstanding, Polk asked for and got a declaration of war on May 13, 1846.

Lurking on the edge of the machinations in Texas was Captain John C. Fremont, of the United States Army Topographical Corps in California. Fremont had been in and out of California at least since 1845. Fremont's purpose in California, and the orders he was operating under, have never been properly explained. John Fremont's father-in-law was Senator Thomas Hart Benton of Missouri. Benton was certainly one of the most vocal advocates of the doctrine of Manifest Destiny, and particularly of western expansion to fulfill that destiny. After an 1845 meeting with Benton, President Polk noted in his diary, "Some conversation occurred concerning Capt. Fremont's expedition and his intention to visit California before his return."[1] What that conversation was, and what Fremont's real intentions were, we have no way of knowing. Fremont's adventures in the western United States, at the time undisputed territory of the Mexican Republic, gave rise to what is perhaps the first and longest-lived conspiracy theory in the annals of American politics. For his activity in California, Fremont was initially convicted of mutiny by a court martial, and subsequently pardoned by President Polk.

What we do know is that from December of 1845, Fremont had been in California; and in February of 1846, he began traveling south from San Jose, raising the hackles of the Mexican government and Mexican colonists. Seemingly forgetting—or more likely ignoring—the fact that he was an officer of a foreign power in another country's sovereign territory, Fremont responded to one complaint about his activities with the imperious and haughty suggestion that he couldn't respond to the complaint of everyone who happened to stumble across his camp. Having thus rather summarily dismissed any objections of the Mexican government to foreign troops in their territory, Fremont took himself and approximately sixty armed and ready Americans to a camp within sight of San Juan Bautista. To add insult to injury, this camp was less than forty miles from the Mexican capitol of California,

Monterey. Ensconcing himself on Gavilan Peak, on March 8, 1846, Fremont, raised an American flag on Mexican territory.*

From the summit of Gavilan Peak, Fremont observed the formation of a military response from the Mexican authorities at San Juan Bautista, and despite rhetoric that he was prepared to die under the flag of the United States, decided to withdraw. John Fremont and his troops abandoned their encampment on Mount Gavilan three days after establishing it, and headed north for the more secure environs of Sutters Fort. Having avoided a decisive encounter with the Mexican army, Fremont and his ever-present aide, Kit Carson, decided to do battle with the unfortunate natives of the upper Sacramento Valley. In Carson's words, it was "a perfect butchery…" Fremont remained in northern California, and was at least a bit player in the short-lived "Bear Flag Republic."

Although Pio Pico sold the mission lands in 1846, the church itself remained in Franciscan hands, and Father Antonio de Anzar remained as pastor. The Anzar family ultimately acquired large tracts of land in the area, and the record is somewhat murky as to whether it was an avaricious, and obviously *not* mendicant Father Anzar or his brother who acquired these holdings. It is known that at one time the California legislature actually prepared charges against Father Anzar for misappropriation of mission lands, but there was never any final disposition of the charges. Anzar's successor at San Juan testified that Anzar lived at the ranch in question and rarely visited the mission that was supposedly in his care. Anzar had a reputation among his charges as a man of avarice and immorality. When California became an American territory in 1846, Anzar stayed on until 1854, at which time he returned to Mexico. The church passed into the hands of the Jesuits, and the *rancho* stayed in the Anzar family.

In 1859, President Buchanan returned a little more than fifty-four acres of the surrounding land to the Catholic church, and in 1861, San Juan Bautista's first school was established at the mission when Father

---

*   Unbeknownst to Captain Fremont, as well as to the disconcerted Mexican forces below him, this was the same date on which General Zachary Taylor, more than one thousand miles away, led his troops south of the Rio Grande and into Mexican territory. From this date forward Mexico and the United States were at war.

Antonio Ubach had the Sisters of Charity found an orphanage and school behind the sacristy.

The "great renovator," Father Cipriano Rubio, came to San Juan Bautista in 1865. Father Rubio decided the church needed a bell tower, and he had a completely incongruous New England-style tower added. Father Rubio was not only a man of questionable architectural talents; he was apparently an unbelievably frugal one. His living quarters were directly below the tower, and he had holes drilled and the bell's rope dropped down to his quarters, so that he might save the money that would be needed to pay a bell ringer.

San Juan Bautista suffered serious damage in the 1906 earthquake that so devastated San Francisco, but survived and continued as a parish church, largely due to donations and support from the Native Sons of California. In 1928, San Juan was transferred yet again to another clerical order, the Maryknoll Fathers. Finally, in 1949, Father Rubio's monstrosity was completely done away with and a faithful reconstruction of the mission was completed. Today it is a church of the diocese of Monterey.

Mission San Juan Bautista today:

Mission San Juan Bautista is located at 406 Second Street, (P.O. Box 400), San Juan Bautista, CA 95045-1164; (831) 623-4528.

Mission San Juan Bautista is co-located with San Juan Bautista State Historic Park. The mission and the park are two separate entities; the mission is a Catholic church belonging to the Diocese of Monterey, while the park is a historic site maintained by the state of California. The proximity of the two facilities gives a visitor the opportunity to get a good feel for life in California in the waning days of Mexican rule.

It was for this reason that Alfred Hitchcock chose San Juan Bautista as the site of some of the most memorable sequences for his classic 1958 film, *Vertigo*. The movie's two most dramatic scenes, when Madeline falls from the tower, take place at San Juan Bautista. The grounds and plaza are obvious in the film, and the dialogue mentions San Juan Bautista. But San Juan Bautista has only a *campanero*, and no bell tower such as was shown in the movie. There was no winding staircase for Kim Novak and James Stewart to clamber up. Clever film editing and splicing created a tower where none existed.

The bell tower at San Juan Bautista is a perfect exemplar of the ongoing battle to make the missions, accurate historic representations of the Spanish era. San Juan Bautista was originally built without a tower. As has been mentioned, a totally incongruous tower *was* added in 1865. That tower was replaced in 1929, with a more "mission-looking" tower. Finally, during a restoration in 1949, it was decided that since the mission was originally built without a tower, it should not have a tower at all, and the tower was removed to restore the mission to its original configuration with an attached *campanero.*

The statue of Saint John the Baptist in the front of the church is a recent addition. It was commissioned in 2000 by Father Edward Fitz-Henry. It is the work of Thomas Marsh, a local sculptor. The statue has several interesting points to examine. First, it is a beautiful piece of work. Second, it provides a stunning bridge between the last prophet of the old world, and the people of the new. The statue is mounted on a base, depicting on its four sides the symbols of the four evangelists. Traditionally, the evangelists are represented by a lion, an ox, an eagle and a man. Here they are here represented by a mountain lion, a bison, a golden eagle and a Native American. The placement of the statue was specifically planned to highlight another intriguing feature of the church.

San Juan Bautista is supposedly oriented so that at the winter solstice, the rising sun casts its light through the open church door to shine directly on the tabernacle where, in Catholic belief, the body of Christ reposes. The church, now a parish of the Diocese of Monterey, opens its doors early on December 21 for those who may want to observe this phenomenon. The statue of Saint John the Baptist was planned and placed to give new insight into this geo-astronomical event. The sun, as it rises over the hills to the east and illuminates the front of the church, seems to be held up by the hands of John the Baptist, who it was predicted would welcome to the world the time when " . . . the dawn from on high shall break upon us, to shine on those who dwell in darkness. . ." (Luke 1: 78-79).

Although it is a demonstrable fact that at the winter solstice the sun does strike the front of the church, and if the front door is open, the tabernacle itself, skeptics insist that it is an accident of nature and not part of the plan in the mission's construction. The cornerstone for the church was laid on June 13, 1803, so any orientation with the winter solstice six months later would be pure happenstance. There is no indication that the Franciscans, nor any other Catholic order, ever attached much significance to the solstices or equinoxes. If they did, it likely would have been only to scorn them as pagan observances.

The graveyard of the mission lies to the north of the church and at a slightly lower elevation, bordering one of the few remaining original stretches of *El Camino Real,* "The King's Highway," which was the main route of travel and commerce in Spanish California. In the graveyard, you can find the grave of Ascension Solorazan, the last pureblood Native American from San Juan Bautista, as well as the grave of Angel Ramirez, a defrocked Franciscan, adventurer, soldier of fortune and politician, who died in 1840. The fence line of the cemetery between the church and the graveyard marks the approximate location of the San Andreas fault. As you enter the buildings at San Juan Bautista, you will see prominent signs posted, warning that you are entering an un-reinforced masonry building, and that it may not be safe should the San Andreas fault decide to give one of its periodic shrugs.

Inside the church, you can still see the arches that were intended to connect the three aisles of Father de la Cuesta's ambitious original church design. Except at the nave, they have been converted to shallow alcoves. Even though the three full aisles were never completed, San Juan Bautista still claims the distinction as the largest of the California missions. As you wander around the church, glance occasionally at the floor tiles. You will periodically find animal foot prints embedded in them.* The tiles were left in the sun to dry, and animals, both domestic and wild, would walk over them, leaving their prints for us to admire 200 years later.

Take a close look at the decorated pulpit and the stairs leading up to it. This is some of the sailor Thomas Doak's work. The statues behind the main altar represent the following: Lower center, Saint John the Baptist, the mission's patron; to his right, Saint Pascal Sayon, an earlier Franciscan; to the left, Saint Isadore, the patron saint of farmers. Top center: Saint Dominic, the founder of the Dominicans, often associated with Saint Francis; to his right, Saint Francis of Assisi; the

---

*   Look particularly near the side entrance to the left of the altar.

founder of the Franciscans; and to Dominic's left, Saint Anthony of Padua, another earlier Franciscan. Be sure to note the mysterious barrel organ in the church.

Buried in the church at San Juan Bautista are Fathers Andre Dulato (1774-1808) and Estevan Tapis (1756-1825).

Mission San Juan Bautista - sits literally on top of the San Andreas fault.

Endnotes

1   Quaife, Milo Milton, ed. *The Diary of James K. Polk During His Presidency 1845-1849, Vol. I.* Chicago: A.C. McClurg and Company, 1910.

Chapter 19

SAN MIGUEL, ARCANGEL

The History of San Miguel Arcangel

L *a Mision del Gloriosismo Principe Arcangel, Senor San Miguel*
(the Mission of the Glorious Prince Arcangel Lord Saint Michael), the sixteenth mission, was founded July 25,1797, less
than one month after San Juan Bautista.

St. Michael is the warrior archangel and the defender of the faithful. Michael is the angel credited with leading the heavenly hosts in
their victorious battle against Satan and the rebelling angels. He is
mentioned by name and prowess in both the Old Testament (Daniel)
and the New Testament (Revelations). One of Michael's duties in early church teachings was to escort the redeemed faithful from purgatory to heaven. For this reason, it is common to find a chapel to Saint
Michael in medieval European cemeteries. The feast day of Michael
and of all the archangels is September 29.

San Miguel was the third mission founded in Father Lasuen's fre-
netic summer of 1797. Left in charge of the project were Fathers Bue-
naventure Sitjar and Antonio de la Concepcion Horra. Neither would
stay long. Father Sitjar was actually on loan from Mission San Antonio, and in a year, he left San Miguel and returned to San Antonio.

Father Horra's departure, in the same year he was assigned, was
somewhat less benign. Father Horra was clearly not missionary material. Early on in his assignment at San Miguel, he began exhibiting some bizarre behavior. He required the soldiers to fire "salutes"
acknowledging his presence and, even more incongruously, had the
Indians fire arrows in the same fashion. He developed a pathological
fear of ants. His fellow missionaries and the Spanish military both
expressed some concern and even fear of Father Horra. He was exam-

ined by a physician at the *presidio* in Monterey, and it was the physician's conclusion that the *padre* was insane. The decision was made to return Father Horra to Mexico, but if Lasuen thought he was ridding himself of a troublemaker by sending Father Horra back to Mexico, he was seriously mistaken.

It is with Father Horra's departure that we gain some insight into one of the most disturbing chapters in the history of the Franciscans with regard to the Native Americans. The California mission project and the Franciscans have garnered ample—and unfortunately well deserved—criticism for their treatment of the Indians. There is no dearth of evidence that the native Californians were considered by the missionaries as children at best, and slaves for all practical purposes. Punishments for an infraction no more serious than an attempt to return to their old lifestyle might be a flogging, imprisonment, or the stocks. Father Horra was a Franciscan who, despite whatever personal idiosyncrasies he might have had, became concerned about the treatment of the natives. He began a debate that was ultimately quashed during his lifetime but that continues to this day, that is, the treatment of the Native Americans by the Franciscans. This question is still an emotionally-charged subject with passionate advocates on all sides.* Charges against the Franciscans range from a lack of respect for the native lifestyle to cruelty to genocide.

The first was certainly true as a matter of course. The Spanish plan for settling the New World called for the complete subjugation of the natives. There was no room for tolerance nor understanding of the native ways. They were to be remade in a totally new form and everything of their former lifestyle; from clothing to social customs, habitations to language was to be eliminated, and it very effectively was. The Franciscans pursued this objective with rigor.

---

*　　　Junipero Serra was originally proposed for official sainthood in the Catholic church in 1934. There are three stages to this process: being pronounced "venerable," being pronounced "beatific" and finally canonization as a saint. Serra was pronounced a venerable in 1985, and beatified in 1987. Both of these pronouncements created a furor among Native Americans because of their view of him as the destroyer of their lifestyle. Advocates for his canonization fear that he will be denied the crown of sainthood because of such opposition.

As to the second, there is ample evidence that many of the Franciscans were cruel taskmasters and sadistic punishers. The standards of the day regarding corporal punishment were much less restrictive than current standards, but even those standards were repeatedly ignored. No serious student of mission history can deny that there were far too many charges and accusations of unduly harsh punishments, from far too many quarters over far too many years, for them to be written off as inaccuracies or falsehoods, a claim that was invariably the response of the superiors of the Franciscan order.

With regard to the third charge, those who propose genocide as an objective of the Franciscans are on such unsure footing that they do great harm to a serious consideration of the other two well-founded charges. To get an informed citizenry of the twenty-first century to accept well documented facts considering certain circumstances by trying to force feed them specious theories about entirely different circumstances is to invite not just skepticism but disdain. There is no doubt that an objective of the conquest of the New World was to eliminate the native lifestyle. That does not translate to an objective of eliminating the native people. In fact the Spanish plan specifically contemplated that the native people would become tax-paying subjects of the king.

In answering the charges of genocide in seventeenth-century California, we need only look at the grim tale of the twentieth-century for some clarity. The history of the twentieth-century has unfortunately necessitated a clear definition of genocide. "Acts committed with intent to destroy, in whole or in part, a national, ethnical, racial or religious group as such" (Article II Geneva Genocide Convention enacted by the United Nations December 9, 1948). Key in this definition is what has been called the "intentionality clause." There is nothing in the mission system that comes anywhere close to meeting that definition. The Native Americans were forced by the system to live in unsanitary conditions, they were subject to unremitting work requirements, their food was inadequate and their medical care nonexistent. Living conditions were terrible, to be sure, but in actuality, very much the same circumstances under which the Franciscans themselves lived, and certainly not conditions imposed with the intent of destroying the race.

Genocide was nowhere in Father Horra's mind when he returned to the College of San Fernando in Mexico. Correcting what he saw as inherent ills in California was. He filed a detailed report charging his *confreres* in California with a variety of offenses, including multiple baptisms of the same person to inflate their numbers; inhumane treatment of the natives; and, inexplicably, speaking to the natives in their own tongue rather than in Spanish. (What results Father Horra expected from speaking to a native population in a tongue they could not understand is not entirely clear. If not actually insane, Father Horra might have been just a little bit crazy.) Be that as it may, his charges of cruelty to the California natives gained traction with government officials in Mexico. The ensuing investigations involved the Franciscans, particularly Father Lasuen, and the military and political establishment of Alta California in a *contretemps* that would last almost four years. The viceroy took Horra's charges of mistreatment of the Indians very seriously. Despite every attempt of the Franciscan establishment to discount them, a detailed investigation, including on-site interviews, was conducted. The records of the investigative proceedings give us a record of an Indian population subject to a steady diet of physical punishment that certainly would not be accepted in today's world, and that skirted the edges of acceptability in eighteenth-century Spanish colonialism.

Lasuen wrote a "refutation of charges," 130 paragraphs that can only be read as self-serving. One would have to read this document in its entirety to get a full sense of how, at least in today's terms, Lasuen with his defense is in fact creating a record of damnation of the Franciscans. According to histories of the era, public flagellations of both priests and laity was a commonly-accepted religious practice; extreme corporal punishments of children would not merit the slightest criticism.

Lasuen goes to great lengths to charge the Spanish military and not the Franciscans with abuse of the natives. He feels the whole issue of the accusations is some sort of underhanded conspiracy on the part of the military, seemingly forgetting that the charges originated not with the military but with one of his own priests.

Lasuen refers to the fact that the only way the Indians can be converted is to "denaturalize them;" he complains that the Indian women are too solicitous of their children to the extent that it interferes with their work. He cites one of his missionaries as saying that "the only service the expectant mother accomplishes in the five years or so, from becoming pregnant to weaning a somewhat independent child is to add to the problems of the missionary..." Lasuen never disputes the claims that punishments are meted out for offenses as innocuous as leaving the compound without permission, not completing work, or not wearing the clothing provided them. He does not refute the use, "should the need arise, [of] the lash, the shackles and the stocks...hence for some months we have been making use of the stocks for men confined...In Santa Barbara Mission...the stocks [are] used for women." He admits that sometimes women "are ordered to be flogged if they deserve it," but rationalizes that horror by stating that the flogging is only "carried out by other women..." While repeatedly denying that any punishment ever inflicted has been beyond the pale, he also asserts that "a barbarous, fierce and ignorant country needs punishments and penalties that are different from one that is cultured and enlightened," and while he claims that in the case of flogging "they are never given even one stroke more than twenty-one," six paragraphs later he admits that, "sometimes a missionary violates it...is it to be wondered at if a missionary should sometimes fall victim to uncontrolled passion...?"[1]

Lasuen's defense casts the Franciscans in a very poor light in matters of dealing with the Indians. When added to this defense the testimony of two separate *presidio* commanders—that indeed Indians at times received as many as fifty lashes and that the Franciscans had developed their own unique form of a novena (twenty-five lashes on each of nine consecutive days)—there is little that can be acceptable as apologetics for the twenty-first century.

Father Horra's complaint about San Miguel was the first glimpse of the "dirty little secret" of the California mission system. It was pretty much the first crack in a wall of impenetrability that had existed for thirty years, and that would continue for another thirty.

In 1801, serious stomach ailments beset the priests at San Miguel. The rumor was soon spread that they had been poisoned by the Indians. Father Francisco Pujol, on his mission of mercy described in the chapter on San Antonio, died of the ailment. An autopsy was attempted, but was inconclusive. Father Pujol's intestines were described as completely black. The rumor took on a life of its own. Father Lasuen, in a letter dated March 30, 1801, states, "It is now public knowledge and there is no room for any doubt that the missionary died of poisoning."[2] Three Indians who supposedly had boasted of the fact that they had committed the deed were arrested. Unfortunately, six months later Father Lasuen indeed does express some doubts about his initial conclusions, and on September 30, he announces his plans to "instruct the missionaries that in regard to eating and drinking they should take the greatest precautions, in case the unfortunate occurrences at San Miguel had their origin in some infection from poisoning."[3] Finally, on November 25th he comes full circle and suggests to the father guardian of the College of San Fernando that the poisoning was undoubtedly due to the *padres'* habit of storing *mescal* in copper containers. Father Lasuen's chemical surmise was likely correct. The copper containers he referred to were lined with tin, and the *mescal* likely leached lead from the tin. A steady diet of *mescal* laced with lead would undoubtedly have caused stomach difficulty for even the most robust constitution. Father Lasuen, politician that he was, quickly pointed out that, "I have never expressed myself in terms that would imply that the Indians were responsible for what happened..."[4] That was technically true, but a disingenuous statement at best in light of the fact that three men had been imprisoned for the past nine months, and no one, including Lasuen, seemed at all concerned about the possibility of their innocence. Almost a year after the incident, he refers to the fact that the prisoners have been released after "a mild whipping" for their intemperate boasting.

San Miguel's first crude church had to be replaced with a larger building within a year. In 1806, a devastating fire destroyed many of the outbuildings and industrial works at San Miguel; the church, while damaged, was largely spared. The next several years were devoted to preparing thousands of adobe bricks for the repair of the destroyed buildings and the enlargement of the church. This church, the current one, was completed in 1818, this time with tile roofs.

After its initial promise, San Miguel began experiencing problems, sometimes in administration, sometimes due to the forces of nature, and sometimes due to the resistance of the natives to conversion. More than any other mission except perhaps Soledad, San Miguel had a problem with *padres* who could not seem to deal with the challenges of mission life. Neither Fathers Sitjar, Horra or Carnicer lasted much longer than a year. Finally, the mission was blessed with two long-term administrators. Father Juan Martin came in 1797 and stayed for twenty-seven years until his death. He is buried in the church he devoted so much of his life to. Father Juan Cabot served from 1807 until 1819.

In 1824, Father Martin decided to beautify the interior of the church, perhaps to compensate for its rather plain and unimpressive exterior. He arranged to have Esteban Munras, a professionally-trained artist, cover the walls and ceilings with fanciful artwork. Munras personally painted many of the scenes, and many others were done by the Indians under his direction. Olive oil, plant coloring and powdered bones used as a fixative have maintained their glorious colors for more than two hundred years, this despite a thirty-year history of neglect and abuse from 1842 to 1878.

In 1831, three years before the official act of secularization, Governor Echeandia used San Miguel as an experiment in the process. He sent José Castro to the mission to read a decree of voluntary emancipation for the Indians. The story goes that after reading the decree and having it translated for the natives, Castro asked those Indians wishing freedom to stand on his left, while those who wished to stay under the *padres'* patronage would stand on his right. All the Indians stayed to the right. Exactly what took place at this moment of high drama is lost to history, but we must remember these are the same people who, thirty years earlier, had told Lasuen that they much preferred the best of both worlds: the security and minimal comforts the mission offered, combined with the freedom to wander the mountains and seaside at will.

The records from San Miguel provide yet another example of the difficulty the Franciscans had in attempting to impose their moral standards on the natives. In 1833, one Juan Pedro was accused of adultery, which was not just a moral failure, but a crime. Juan Pedro readily confessed to having multiple relationships with multiple married women. In his defense, he offered the testimony that he had never done so on mission grounds. Juan Pedro clearly felt that while he might be constrained in his behavior on the mission grounds, once off the property the Franciscan mores did not apply. The court was not impressed and found him guilty of adultery.

In the same year that Juan Pedro was unsuccessfully defending his morals, Mission San Miguel became the dividing line between the northern and southern missions. San Miguel and the ten missions north of it were the missions that came under the jurisdiction of the College of Zacatecas. At least for the time being, the eleven missions south of San Miguel would remain under the jurisdiction of the San Fernando Franciscans. The decision was largely insignificant since the very next year the secularization of all of the missions began, and twelve years later Alta California became a United States territory.

San Miguel was secularized in 1836, and fared no better than the other missions, and worse than most, as a result of its secularization. Without the protection of the Franciscans, however heavy-handed it may have been, the Indians were victimized, their property taken and themselves driven away. Ten years after secularization, the-then president of the missions, Father Narciso Duran, lamented that "Mission San Miguel Archangel is today without livestock and the neophytes are demoralized and dispersed." At one point it was actually a tavern named, ignominiously, "San Miguel Mission."

In 1846, just before the United States Navy raised the American flag over Monterey, Governor Pico, the last Mexican governor of California, sold most of the mission's property to one William Reed. It was Reed who formed the tavern from the bones of San Miguel. Reed and his family moved into some of the abandoned mission buildings, and he rented other of the outbuildings to travelers. In December of 1848, a group of six men spent the night in some of the old buildings. When they paid for the rooms in gold, Reed injudiciously boasted that he had hidden on the grounds "more gold than you can lift." They left, but returned the next night and killed everyone there. Reed, his wife, their four-year-old son, a brother-in-law, a midwife, her fifteen-year-old daughter and grandson, a cook, a sheepherder and his grandchild— eleven victims in all, counting the unborn child of Mrs. Reed, who was near delivery of her second child. All of the victims were killed with knives and axes, and their bodies left in a heap on the kitchen floor while the marauders searched unsuccessfully for the gold. The next day, the bodies were discovered by a messenger coming to deliver mail. A posse was quickly formed and the murderers were apprehended on December 10 near Santa Barbara. Two of the criminals and a posse member were killed in the ensuing affray. The three survivors were sentenced to hang by a drumhead court. There was some question regarding the authority of the court, since California was at that time under the authority of the United States Army. A query was sent to Colonel Mason in Monterey. Colonel Mason did vacate the hanging order but sent Lieutenant Edward Ord and nine soldiers to act as a firing squad. The men were executed on December 28, 1848, in Santa Barbara. They are buried in the cemetery of Mission Santa Barbara.*

San Miguel was returned to the Catholic church by President Buchanan in 1859. Although without a resident priest for many years, it was served as a mission parish from nearby San Antonio. In 1878, Father Phillip Farrell took up residence at San Miguel as a priest of the Diocese of Los Angeles. The first serious attempt at restoration was begun in 1897. In 1928, the church was returned to the Franciscan order, which still maintains it today as a local parish, a retreat house, and a novitiate for their order.

An earthquake in 2003 so damaged the church that it had to be closed to the public for six years. One of the challenges in retrofitting the church was that of preserving the two-hundred-year-old paintings and decorations on the walls. The job was very well done, and today Mission San Miguel proudly holds itself out as the "un-retouched" mission.

Mission San Miguel today:

Mission San Miguel is located at 801 Mission St. (P.O. Box 69), San Miguel CA, 93451-0069; (805) 467-3256.
http://missionsanmiguel.org
Nicknames: "The Un-Retouched Mission," "The Haunted Mission"

The mission at San Miguel is the third building on the site. The first, a small adobe church, was replaced a year later with a larger one. That second church was damaged in a fire in 1806. It took twelve more years until the church we see today was completed. The San Simeon earthquake in 2003 caused extensive damage to Mission San Miguel.

---

*   The United States Army post in Monterey was subsequently named Fort Ord, not because of Lieutenant Ord's swift dispatch of justice, but for his service and wounds suffered in the Civil War twenty years later. Major General Ord was one of the officers responsible for cutting off Robert E. Lee's line of retreat at Appomattox courthouse and bringing an end to the Civil War.

Because of safety concerns, the church was closed to the public until 2009, when repairs and structural retrofitting could be completed.

One of the most notable features of Mission San Miguel is the "Memorial Bell Tower" that defines the north wall of the mission courtyard. Weathered and ancient looking, that tower is actually of very recent construction, and is a reminder that the missions and the Franciscans who staffed them continued to be a very important part of American history. The tower was built in 1947 to honor "Franciscan priests and brothers who served in World War II." In particular it honors Father Fidelis Wieland, a former pastor at San Miguel. Father Wieland, along with six army nurses, perished as a result of a kamikaze attack on April 29, 1945. They were all serving on a hospital ship, the U.S.S. Comfort, which was tending the wounded from the Okinawa invasion.

The exterior of San Miguel itself is generally unimpressive, a plain white façade with virtually no ornamentation or decoration. It is upon stepping inside that one is immediately struck a sense of awe. The church walls are a beautiful display of murals, painting and decorations. Damages by earthquake, neglect and nature notwithstanding, the decorations are still vibrant and beautiful. Esteban Munra's brilliant colors have managed to survive not just the ravages of time, neglect, and nature, but the restorer's efforts. Windows, balconies and archways are depicted on the walls. Columns and "draperies" have a three-dimensional look; and pulls and swags were added to make them more realistic. Particularly eye-catching is the "Eye of God" above the main altar. Although found in a few early churches in Mexico and Texas, this symbol appears nowhere else in the California missions. The scalloped design surrounding the precarious-looking pulpit is another feature unique to San Miguel. While the works were designed by a professional artist, they were applied by the local Salinan Indians, working under his direction; and the colors, stains and pigments came from local sources.

Certainly one of the mission's most impressive works is an eighteenth-century portrayal of Michael the Archangel at judgment day. Since Michael is the principal figure in the painting, Mission San Miguel may be an appropriate "home" for the painting, but it was originally sent to Mission San Antonio.

The altar and its *reredos* are original to the mission. The central statue is Saint Michael, the mission's patron saint. Michael, as the official escort of the faithful from purgatory to heaven, is depicted wearing the cap of a seventeenth-century Spanish judge, and carrying the scales of justice. The two statues below and to the side are Saint Francis and Saint Anthony another Franciscan (with the Christ child in his arms). In front of Saint Anthony's statue is a large upholstered chair. This is called the "wishing chair," from a local legend that if a child sat in it and made a wish, the wish would come true. There are side altars dedicated to the Blessed Virgin and to Saint Joseph. All of these statues, and the paintings of Saint Michael and Saint Anthony, are of eighteenth- century origin. The paintings hanging on the walls, although only one of them is signed, are believed to be the work of the Mexican artist José de Paez. They were originally sent to Mission San Antonio and at some point moved to San Miguel. The three to the left of the altar are the archangels Michael, Gabriel and Rafael. To the right of the altar, the paintings represent paradise, Saint Anthony, Mary as the Mother of Sorrow, and the Baptism of Christ by John the Baptist.

On the outside, the colonnade running down the mission's left side is unique in that the arches are not symmetrical, but are of different sizes and shapes. Hanging in one of the arches is a small Mexican bell with a hole in one side. Popular history claims this was an errant gunshot one night when the mission was suffering as the Mission San Miguel bar. Actually, the hole is a casting defect, and not the result of an alcohol-fueled bar fight.

The Reed family murder gives San Miguel a nickname that the current Franciscans try to downplay. Sam Miguel is sometimes referred to as the "haunted mission." Legend has it that on certain nights, a blood-covered Mrs. Reed can be seen walking the mission grounds, bewailing her murdered children. If strange thumps and bumps are heard in the old family quarters, it is the sound of the thieves looking for the gold. The treasure—if ever there was one—has never been uncovered. The victims are buried in the church cemetery, and the perpetrators in the cemetery at Mission Santa Barbara.

Buried in the church at San Miguel are Fathers Marcelino Cipres (1769-1810) and Juan Martin (1770 -1824.)

Mission San Miguel - gate to courtyard.

Franciscan coat of arms.

Memorial to the Franciscans killed in WWII.

252

San Miguel.

All-seeing eye of God.

San Miguel cemetery wall.

Endnotes

1   Kenneally, Finbar. *Writings of Fermin Francisco de Lasuen, Volume Two.* Washington D.C.: William Byrd Press, 1965.

2   Ibid., 186

3   Ibid., 249

4   Ibid., 254

Chapter 20

San Fernando Rey de Espana

The History of San Fernando Rey de Espana

*L*a *Mision del Senor Fernando, Rey de Espana* (the Mission of The Lord Fernando King of Spain), the seventeenth mission, was dedicated by Fermin de Lasuen on September 8, 1797. This was the last of the four missions built during the summer of 1797. The mission was named, not after the Ferdinand who sponsored Columbus's first voyage to America, but after one of his predecessors.

Ferdinand was king of Leon and Castile in the thirteenth century, and a third-order Franciscan. Third-order Franciscans are lay members of the Franciscan religious order. They do not take vows nor actually join a monastery or cloister. They make a personal commitment to the precepts of the Franciscan order, and commit themselves to living in the world guided by Franciscan principals and spirituality. Ferdinand devoted his life to freeing Spain from the Moors, and did succeed in removing them from almost all of Spain except Granada. Saint Ferdinand's feast day is May 30.

Mission San Fernando was intended to be halfway between San Buenaventura and San Gabriel. It is actually twice as far to San Gabriel from San Fernando as it is to San Buenaventura. San Fernando Rey was the only one of the missions to be established on land already occupied and claimed by a Spanish settler. It was also the only mission where the Franciscans were able to move into already-built quarters. Francisco de los Reyes, an *alcade* from Mission San Gabriel, had claimed the land as his own. This prior claim notwithstanding, Father Lasuen, on September 8, 1797, dedicated it as a mission and named it San Fernando Rey. Señor Reyes was dispossessed, and the Franciscans used his ranch house and the other buildings he had on the land for their first church and residences. Initially assigned to the mission were Fathers Francisco Dumetz and Javier Uria.

San Fernando Rey, almost from its founding, was a prosperous and successful mission. At one time it had housing for almost a thousand neophytes. Its vineyards had more than 30,000 vines and there were 1,500 fruit trees in its orchards. Over 12,000 head of cattle were tended by the mission vaqueros. The mission provided tallow, soap, hides, shoes and leather goods to all of Spanish California. In 1800, the first permanent church was built at San Fernando. It was replaced in 1806 with a bigger structure. *Padres'* quarters—the *convento*—were added in 1810. This long building, which runs to the right of the church itself for more than 240 feet, is still in use today, and is the largest adobe building in California. The earthquake of 1812 damaged San Fernando, but serious retrofitting was done, and many of the adobe walls and supports were replaced with fired brick. It is significant that this work, the first earthquake retrofitting in California, was undertaken by a group of Tongvans and withstood a long history of earthquakes for another 150 years.*

San Fernando Rey, and all of the missions built in the early 1800s, bore the brunt of the turmoil of the Mexican revolution. All during those ten years (1810-1821), and for several years thereafter, the missions suffered interruptions in shipments and supplies. Once independence was gained, forces were unleashed that would change completely the life and systems the Franciscans thought would endure forever. The problems created for the missions by the Mexican government were twofold. First, the struggling republic endured years of strife and civil unrest, particularly in California, from competing factions seeking control of Alta California. There was no time, money, nor patience available to support these previously heavily-subsidized ventures. On the other hand, the missions, with their well-developed farming and livestock operations, and their huge tracts of land, were very attractive to a government trying to buttress colonization of the area.

---

*   In 1971, the Sylmar earthquake so damaged the mission that it had to be demolished, and a replica built in its place. To the credit of the Tongvans who did the 1812 work, the same earthquake that undid their repairs of 150 years earlier also destroyed several modern freeway overpasses, as well as a hospital that had been completed just one month before the quake struck.

Mission San Fernando was the mission most known for its development of the visual arts among the native people. While all of the missions taught some of their neophytes carpentry, leatherwork and metal work, San Fernando seems to have emphasized more of the fine arts. The most famous example of this is of course the Way of the Cross now on display at Mission San Gabriel. These beautiful pieces, seen by some as the work of several artists, were done at Mission San Fernando. We do not know who the instructor was. The detail of this artwork and its complexity cries out for further elucidation on who instructed and supervised the natives who created these beautiful pieces. There are also carved statues, finely-wrought sacred vessels and vestments, distributed throughout the missions that we know originated at San Fernando.

In 1815, the Spanish military brought to Mission San Fernando a group of Russian sailors and seal-hunting Aleuts who had been captured near San Pedro. They were taken to the mission to be held as prisoners. They, like so many others, had the misfortune to be caught up in the savagery and confusion of the Mexican Revolution. Their story was first chronicled by one Simeon Yanovsky, who was not one of the group but who wrote a third-hand account which he had gotten from Boris Tarasov, who was one of the unfortunates captured. Yanovsky's report describes the attempts of "Spanish clerics" to get the Russians to repudiate their Orthodox religion and adopt Roman Catholicism. According to Yanovsky's report they were horribly tortured, fingers were cut off, and one man killed by disemboweling. Yanovsky's story has subsequently been thoroughly examined and analyzed by historians and generally deemed to be almost a complete fabrication. There is nothing in any contemporaneous record, anywhere that indicates that such practices were engaged in by the Spanish, and particularly not by the Franciscans. In their almost 300 year history in California, whatever other evils they may have perpetrated, the Franciscans have never been accused of "conversion by torture" by anyone other than Tarasov and Yanoskvy. In fact, all of the Franciscans in California in the seventeenth and eighteenth-centuries were highly educated men, particularly in matters of church doctrine and theology. They would have understood full well that a conversion must be a free act of will, and a conversion under duress would not be a conversion at all. One of the things that makes Tarasov's story most suspect is that, in addition to the torture, he complains that several of his crew took Indian wives and left the Russians to live under the Franciscans. It is hard to believe that someone who had been tortured or, at a minimum, seen his companions tortured would, even in an extreme romantic ardor, choose to live with the torturers.

When the mission was secularized in 1834, the resident pastor, Father Francisco de Ibarra Gonzalez, was so disconcerted that he deserted the premises and returned to Mexico without the approval or permission of his order. His understanding superior, Narciso Duran, sent him the papers necessary to effect a proper retirement. Ibarra eventually returned to California, served at several other missions, and died at the other "king" mission, San Luis Rey, around 1842.

In 1842, six years before John Sutter's mill changed the history of California, the United States, and indeed the world, gold was discovered on the grounds of Mission San Fernando. The story is that Francisco Lopez was preparing his birthday dinner and he wanted some onions. When he pulled them up from the garden of one of the mission's *rancherias*, he noticed gold flakes in the soil adhering to the bulbs. A brief "gold rush" ensued. While this initial find was a paltry $344, ultimately more than $100,000 was extracted from the nearby fields. The discovery of gold on mission property indirectly led to a rapid deterioration of Mission San Fernando when it was secularized and abandoned. For years, rumors of a horde of gold hidden in the buildings led treasure seekers to knock down walls and dig up floors. No golden treasure was ever found, but the treasure of historic buildings were seriously damaged.

Gold of a different sort, "black gold," was much in evidence in the area, but generally unrecognized for its value. The earliest of the Spanish explorers had noted the black pitch the natives used to waterproof their canoes and water storage implements. From time to time the Spaniards emulated the natives in using the material as a fire starter. The material was readily available in seeps occurring throughout the region. It wasn't until late in the nineteenth-century, though, that Standard Oil sank the first productive oil well in the area and shortly after that the iconic symbol of the southern California skyline was oil derricks, not palm trees.

All of the missions, located as they were very strategically along El Camino Real, and because they were the most imposing and well-built structures in California, often found themselves serving as military redoubts. San Fernando was no exception, it became the locus of several military campaigns.

In 1837, two of the Mexican factions struggling for control of California clashed at the mission. Troops under the control of Juan Bautista Alvarado, trying to establish an independent Californio republic, met soldiers of General José Castro, loyal to the central Mexican government, at Mission San Fernando. Threats and remonstrances were exchanged, and a mutual withdrawal left the mission, and ultimately California, under Alvarado's control—at least for the time being. In 1842, another nascent rebellion—although not as an independent republic, and ultimately not as a Mexican territory for very long—came to a head at San Fernando. This time it was Governor Manuel Micheltorena, trying to wrest the mission from a group of rebels under José Castro. The ideas of honor and chivalry were decidedly different in nineteenth-century California than they are today. Micheltorena, besides suffering the challenge to his authority, had to put up with the insult of being called an invalid because he rode to the battle in a carriage instead of on a rearing charger. In this battle, artillery fire was exchanged, with some accounts reporting that the rebels were reduced to firing stones from their cannons. Casualties were a horse on one side, and a mule on the other. Once again, a truce was arranged, leaving the mission and California under the control of the Mexican government.

Five years later, Mission San Fernando found itself once more as the locus of a military engagement. This time, the long-term consequences were more dramatic. In January of 1847, Colonel John C. Fremont of the United States Army occupied the mission as part of his campaign in the Mexican-American War. Mexican resistance to the Americans in California effectively ended when General Andres Pico withdrew and left the mission to Fremont. Although the Mexican American War continued for another several months Mission San Fernando, and all of California, shortly thereafter passed from Mexico to the United States.

Governor Pico did the same injustice to San Fernando as he did to several of the missions, selling it to speculators just days before the American conquest of California. The few neophytes who remained on the mission grounds were served by priests from Our Lady of Angels in Los Angeles. Ultimately, the courts returned the mission to the

Catholic church, but the damage done by years of neglect and vandalism was irrevocable. Tiles, beams, bells and even nails used in the building were taken by any and all for their own use. At one time, the enclosure around the *convento* was used as a hog farm.

While Charles Lummis began as early as 1896 to rescue Mission San Fernando from its ignominy as a pig farm, serious and ongoing efforts to preserve the church didn't begin until 1916. In August of that year, the local community held a "San Fernando Candle Day." Votive candles were sold for a dollar each, and then a candlelight procession proceeded throughout the mission ruins. Six thousand candles were sold at that first festival; a new roof was purchased to replace the missing one, and San Fernando began its path back from oblivion and ruin.

Several of the California missions have had their history and artifacts damaged by overzealous "restorers." San Fernando was no exception. In 1905, Father Le Bellegny, a French priest at San Fernando, decided to do something with the crumbling ruins. He took the baptismal font from the old church and had it installed in a new one. He removed tiles from the roof for use in other buildings, and most offensive of all, he exhumed and re-interred the bodies of the priests who had been buried in the church. When his efforts were greeted with horror by preservationists and historians he tried to return things to the way they were, but the damage had been done.

In 1971, the Sylmar earthquake almost consigned Mission San Fernando to oblivion. The quake so damaged the mission that it had to be demolished. It was reconstructed as an exact replica using material from the ruined church. The *convento* was also damaged, but not to the extent that it couldn't be repaired. Thus, the *convento* is the only original building at Mission San Fernando. It is the very long, imposing building running to the east of the mission church. It is the largest adobe building in California. This is the only one of the mission buildings known to be specifically devoted to housing guests. Any of the missions might have provided shelter to travelers, and all of them did at one time or another, but the *convento* at Mission San Fernando, constructed very late in the history of the missions and strategically located "half way between San Buenaventura and San Gabriel," seems to be the only one with rooms specifically designated for travelers.

Mission San Fernando today:

Mission San Fernando Rey de Espana is located at: 15151 San Fernando Mission Blvd., Mission Hills, CA, 93145-1109; (818) 361-0186.
Nickname: The Mission of the Valley

The first church was dedicated in 1797 and completed in 1799. No sooner was it completed than it was replaced by a second church. In 1806, a third church was dedicated. This third church was severely damaged by the 1812 earthquake, but continued to serve until 1971, when the Sylmar earthquake damaged it beyond repair. The ancient church was demolished and its material used to build the church you see today. It is an exact replica, rebuilt using material salvaged from the 1806 church. While the building is, of necessity, a replica, the furnishings and artwork are largely from the original church.

The most spectacular artwork in the mission, the altar and its surrounding reredos, are not original to the mission. In fact they are a very recent (1991) addition. Although they are new to the mission, they are actually older than the mission, probably dating from the late 1600s. They were originally designed for a church in Ezcaray, Spain.* They had been purchased by an art dealer in Los Angeles in the 1920s and had long languished in pieces in a warehouse. At some point they were donated to the Archdiocese of Los Angeles and were installed at San Luis Rey in the 1991 reconstruction after the Sylmar earthquake. The reassembly/reconstruction of the altar was headed up by Richard Menn, who was the curator at Mission San Carlos. Although the altar and reredos are not part of the original church, they have been so artfully restored and installed that they fit perfectly in San Fernando. Almost all visitors assume they are survivors from the original mission.

The long building at the front of the mission property is the largest adobe structure in California and is the only building on the site which is of original construction. This is perhaps the only building in the entire mission chain that might support the generally discredited theory that the missions were built as way stations for travelers. It is referred to as the *convento,* which was the term given to the priests' quarters. Clearly this building, almost 250 feet long, is far more than

---

*   The altar is commonly referred to as the "Ezcaray altar."

would be needed to accommodate the two priests who would have been assigned to the mission. Recent archeological examinations have revealed that not only were there several rooms for travelers, there was a specially-appointed room designated as the "governor's suite," which was reserved for distinguished guests.

The fountain in the east garden is a replica of one at the cathedral in Cordova, Spain. The Moorish influence in Spanish architecture is obvious in the star shape of this fountain, as well in the peaked arch over some of the doorways. The doors themselves are decorated with the carved "river of life" motif which can be found in several of the missions.

Several workshops have been recreated on the grounds. Carpentry, pottery, blacksmithing and leatherwork were all taught to the natives by the Franciscans. Many of the "graduates" of these programs went on to become highly sought-after artisans in southern California, and some of their creations are still in use today.

San Fernando Rey has an interesting historical museum where you can see a pictorial timeline of the mission as well as some early pottery and carved *santos*. There is also housed, interestingly in what was probably originally a jail, several hundred statues and depictions of the Blessed Mother. The room is now referred to as "The Madonna Room."

One of the most interesting artifacts at Mission San Fernando Rey is the "Russian Bell." This bell has an inscription on it stating that it was cast in 1796 on Kodiak Island. It was unearthed in one of the orchards at San Fernando in 1920. No one knows for sure how a bell, cast for an Orthodox church in Alaska, ended up at a Catholic mission in California. Perhaps it was captured along with the Russian fur traders in 1815. When the Russian sailors were captured, their ship and all of its furnishings would have been confiscated.

Probably of more interest to scholars and historians than to the general public is the Archival Center of the Diocese of Los Angeles. This library contains thousands of documents relating not just to the mission but to the history of southern California and the Catholic church there. The Archival Center is open to the public on a limited basis, but researchers are invited to make an appointment to use the facility.

Buried in the church at San Fernando Rey are Fathers José de Miguel (1761-1813) and Jose Antonio Urresti (1725-1812). Buried in the graveyard are Fathers Pedro Cabot (1777-1836) and Martin de Landaeta (1760-1809). Entombment in the church itself or in an adjacent graveyard is simply a question of a decision made by the officiating priest. It has nothing to with stature or hierarchy. In the case of San Fernando, earthquake damage to the church occasioned the removal of some graves from the church to the graveyard.

More famous than the church graveyard itself is the Bob Hope Memorial Garden, which was dedicated in 2005. Hope was married to a Catholic, and in later years he himself converted to Catholicism. Supposedly when his wife and he were discussing death and burial arrangements, she asked him where he wanted to be buried. "Surprise me," was the answer. She had him buried in the graveyard at Mission San Fernando, where his mother was buried. Two years later, the Bob Hope Memorial Garden was dedicated as a large expansion of the graveyard.

San Fernando might want to start calling itself: "The Mission of the Stars." In addition to Bob Hope, other Hollywood notables in this graveyard include Ritchie Valens, Chuck Connors, Walter Brennan and William Bendix.

Mission San Fernando Rey.

Chapter 21

SAN LUIS REY DE FRANCIA

The History of San Luis Rey

*L*a *Mision de San Luis, Rey de Francia* (the Mission of Saint Louis King of France), was founded June 13, 1798, the eighteenth of the California missions and the ninth founded by Fermin de Lasuen. Thus, the first two father presidents of the California missions, Junipero Serra and Fermin de Lasuen, between them founded eighteen of the twenty-one missions. Only three more missions would be established by all of their ten successors. San Luis Rey was the last of five missions Lasuen founded in 1797-1798.

Louis IX was named a saint because of his exemplary life, and his support for the crusades. He died on a crusade in Tunis in 1270. He is the only French king ever canonized by the Catholic church. St. Louis has another distinction to claim: he is the only saint with his likeness in the United States Supreme Court. He is depicted in a frieze showing significant law-makers throughout history. Louis is honored as the first ruler to recognize the right of appeal of a verdict. He established the first Court of Appeals. His feast day is August 25.

San Luis Rey was the second of the "king" missions in California. It was at one time the most successful of the Spanish missions, in terms of agricultural output, in either North or South America. For these reasons it is sometimes referred to as "The King of the Missions."

In charge of the mission from its founding until its secularization was one man—Father Antonio Peyri. This is a singular accomplishment in the history of the California missions. No other Franciscan was ever present, from the birth to the death, of a single mission. It is interesting to observe, at the founding of Mission San Luis Rey, some of the practicalities the Franciscans adopted since their first mission. When the first two missions were founded, those natives who expressed an interest in becoming Christian would embark on a program of months—if not years—of instruction in the articles of the faith, before they were baptized. At San Luis Rey and indeed at most of the later missions, the records are clear that more than twenty natives were baptized within two weeks of its founding. There is nothing to suggest that this shortened time between contact and baptism was an increasing enthusiasm or understanding of Church doctrine on the part of the natives. Rather it probably reflects a growing urgency on the part of the Franciscans, as secularization loomed ever larger, to inflate the numbers of persons under their control, and a diminishing of lifestyle choices for the natives. While the mission lifestyle may not have been the optimal choice for the natives, increasingly it was the only choice.

The mission was established to close what was seen as an unmanageable gap between Mission San Diego and Mission San Juan Capistrano. The first church was completed in 1802. San Luis Rey is another example of the obstacles overcome by the early Franciscans, and the tremendous labor expended by the local natives. Father Peyri, when tasked with founding the mission, was completely unfamiliar with the local language. Despite this, within six weeks he had 8,000 adobe bricks prepared for building material. The natives cut and transported pine and fir logs for the buildings beams almost twenty miles to the site. The missions already established in the area, San Diego, San Gabriel and San Juan Capistrano, sent livestock and workers to assist in the endeavor. The present church was begun in 1811, and when finished in 1815, was 165 feet by twenty-seven feet. It was one of only two of the missions laid out in a cruciform shape, with a domed ceiling overhead, and it is the only onein this style surviving today.* It was also one of the few churches designed by a professional architect. Jose Antonio Ramirez, who also gets credit for Mission Santa Barbara and San Buenaventura, is identified on its cornerstone as "architect and director." Once the church was completed, building continued with barracks, workshops, *lavanderia* and agricultural compounds. By the 1830s, Mission San Luis Rey was the largest building complex in

---

* The other was San Juan Capistrano, and it was destroyed in the 1812 earthquake.

266

California. The church, quarters, workshops, *lavenderia* and outbuildings of San Luis Rey covered more than five acres.

Father Peyri, in addition to being an accomplished administrator and enlightened missionary, was very interested in the lifestyle of the natives. He sent detailed reports to the governor of the native beliefs, rituals and curing ceremonies. He described poultices they used for wounds, and treatments they had for poisonous bites. They had a belief in an afterlife, not far removed from those of Christianity.

In 1816, an *asistencia* to San Luis Rey was founded about twenty miles inland from the mission. This *asistencia,* San Antonio de Pala, is one of only two *assistencias* out of nine still in existence. The other is Our Lady of the Angels, in "Old Town" Los Angeles, that was originally built as an *asistencia* to Mission San Gabriel.* San Antonio de Pala survived longer than its mother mission, and it was at San Antonio that much of the art and artifacts from San Luis were preserved when the mission was abandoned. The *assistencia* of San Luis Rey at San Antonio de Pala is still an active parish today, with a mostly Indian population. Like the mission itself, the *assistencia* has suffered the vagaries of time and history, including an overzealous pastor who in 1903 whitewashed over Native American artwork on the walls.

San Luis Rey was destined to become one of the largest of the California missions, not just in physical size, but in agricultural output and convert population. More than 3,000 natives ultimately came to call San Luis home, and they herded over 50,000 head of livestock. Grapes, oranges, olives, wheat and corn were produced for the mission and sold to the surrounding communities. In 1830, the church was the largest building in California.

In 1842, Father Jose Maria Zalvidea was assigned to mission San Luis Rey. Father Zalvidea was a kindly and well-liked priest, but apparently a religious zealot of the most extreme type. He was oftentimes overheard engaging in loud conversations with Satan, invoking the "Prince of Darkness" to "get thee behind me" or "go away." He engaged in extreme practices of mortification, wearing a belt studded with spikes that pierced his body. He whipped and flailed himself mercilessly, and his house keeper, despite her best efforts to keep

---

*   Mission San Rafael north of San Francisco was originally planned as an *asistencia* to Mission San Francisco, but it became a full mission five years after its founding.

instruments of punishment away from him, often found his bedding covered with blood. Although he seemed to be a very capable priest and administrator, he was childlike in his own personal behavior. As he was dying, the women tending to him noted that he had long ago driven nails into his feet. Plans were made to take him to Mission San Juan Capistrano. Father Zalvidea protested, and those who had come to move him decided to wait until the next morning. Zalvidea died that night and was buried at San Luis Rey.

Unlike many of the missions, San Luis Rey never experienced any periods of great strife between the *padres* and the natives. This is undoubtedly because of Father Peyri. Peyri, who was only twenty-nine years old and had been just two years in California when he was given what would turn out to be his life's work, is viewed by all historians as an exemplary man, and one who always kept in mind his duties as a missionary and his role as teacher to the natives. Peyri made the decision to leave the native population largely undisturbed on their own lands; relocation to the mission grounds was not part of his administration. With this innovative approach to winning over the natives Peyri was flying in the face of Spanish law, which specifically called for the reduction of the indigenous peoples to a mission compound. Peyri's success was hard to argue with and it seems he never came under any official criticism for them.

While he allowed the natives to continue their lives in their own village. Father Peyri imposed specific standards regarding their villages. Water was brought by means of a ditch to separate bathing areas for men and women. The individual huts had to be built a minimum distance from each other. This facilitated the process of burning to the ground a hut that had been occupied by a sick family. Probably due to these rules, San Luis Rey never suffered the decimating diseases that brought so much suffering and death to the neophytes at the other missions. Perhaps, in the thirty years since the founding of their first mission, some important lessons had been learned by the Franciscans, or at least by Peyri. The disease and death rate at San Luis Rey was a fraction of what it was at any of the other missions. Peyri's enlightened administration may have had effects even to the present day. The *asistencia* of San Luis Rey, San Antonio de Pala, is still in existence and it is one of the few mission establishments that has always had an active and viable native congregation.

In 1827 San Luis Rey was one of the missions visited by the French explorer, Auguste Duhaut-Cilly. He was impressed by the gleaming white edifice and its grounds, fountains and gardens. He described a sumptuous dinner and an evening of dancing and other performances by the natives. He described olives as the "best grown in California" and kept for seven years a bottle of the wine he was given. Duhaut-Cilly was most impressed by the fact that San Luis Rey had separate infirmaries, one for men and one for women, and that they had been so constructed that they could be entered from the church without the need to go out into the weather. Thus the spiritual as well as the physical needs of the ill could be attended to. Duhaut-Cilly considered San Luis's natives the best-treated in any of the California missions.

While Peyri's time at San Luis Rey is essentially the history of San Luis Rey, Peyri's departure from San Luis Rey is one of the "mission mysteries" that remains to be solved. He had been at the mission since its founding under Spanish rule. He was one of a minority of Franciscans who had no issue with taking the oath of loyalty required by the Mexican government in 1826, but he was still a Spaniard, and when the Mexican government expelled all Spaniards in 1827, he asked to be included. He didn't leave for Spain until 1832, and when he left, he did so under cover of night. He took with him two Indian boys he was preparing for the priesthood. The popular story would have us believe that his night flight was due to the fact that he could not face his "beloved" Indians with his wrenching decision. The next day when the Indians discovered he had gone, they jumped on their horses and rode to San Diego in a last-ditch attempt to keep him from leaving. They arrived at the harbor just as the ship was sailing, and rode out into the surf to plead with him to stay.

As emotionally touching as this scene may be, it is suspect for several reason. One, as has been amply demonstrated, the Indians were by no means free to just up and leave the mission grounds whenever they felt like it. Peyri may have left, but Father José Anzar was still there and very much in charge. It is unimaginable that Father Anzar would have said to a large group of neophytes, "By all means, take off and see if you can convince Father Peyri to come back." Most suspect, though, is the idea of them riding horses for the chase. The mission neophytes had no horses (nor mules, nor cattle, nor much of anything else). In fact, it was against the law to provide the Indians with horses, or to teach them to ride.

As for the two young men who accompanied Peyri (at least one narrator says there were four, and Bancroft says "several"), their names are given as Pablo Tac and Agapito [or Agapitus] Amamix. We are told they did go on to Rome for their studies. We know that at least Pablo did, for while he was there, he wrote a very detailed account of life at San Luis Rey. His manuscript is written in Latin, which would have been the *"lingua franca"* of a seminary student in Rome. In the document Pablo describes in great detail the buildings of the mission compound, and its gardens, orchards and fields. He describes a game the natives played that is clearly a form of lacrosse or field hockey. He also talks about several of the dances the natives perform for various occasions. Pablo, himself destined to be a priest, gives an interesting view of the priest in charge of the mission. It is probably a very accurate description of the situation in any of the missions:

> In the mission of San Luis Rey de Francia the Fernandino Father is like a king. He has his pages, alcaldes, majordomos, musicians, soldiers, gardens, ranchos, livestock, horses by the thousand, cows, bulls, by the thousand, oxen, mules, asses, 12,000 lambs, 200 goats etc. The pages are for him and for the Spanish and Mexican, English and Anglo-American travelers. The alcaldes to help him govern all the people of the Mission of San Luis Rey de Francia. The majordomos are in the distant districts, almost all Spaniards. The musicians of the Mission for the holy days and all the Sundays and holidays of the year, with them the singers, all Indian neophytes. Soldiers so that nobody does injury to Spaniard or to Indian; there are ten of them and they go on horseback. There are five gardens that are for all, very large. The Fernandino Father drinks little, and as almost all the gardens produce wine, he who knows the customs of the neophytes well does not wish to give any wine to any of them, but sells it to the English, or Anglo-Americans, not for money but for clothing for the neophytes, linen for the church, hats, muskets, plates, coffee, tea, sugar and other things. The

products of the mission are butter, tallow, hides, chamois, leather, bear skins, wine, white wine, brandy, oil, maize, wheat, beans and also bull horns which the English take by the thousand to Boston.[1]

Pablo goes on for at least twenty pages, in great detail and very eloquently, about the food, the clothing, the work day, the surrounding lands. It is unfortunate that as detailed as his report is, he tells us nothing about himself. The listing of all neophytes at San Luis Rey tells us that he was baptized on January 15, 1822, shortly after his birth, so his birth year is presumed to be late 1821 or early 1822. How he came to be chosen for the priesthood and study in Rome, what his travels there were like and what his impressions of the "Eternal City" were, we have no idea. He never mentions his companion, who died several years before him. Pablo never made it back to California or to his people. He died in Rome in 1841, probably just short of his twentieth birthday. Virtually nothing else is known of either of the two who left California with Peyri. It would be a fascinating study to know more of the young men who had been born in the wilds of eighteenth-century California and died in the urbanity of Rome.

San Luis Rey was secularized in 1834. Captain Pablo de la Portillo was named administrator. There was the usual turmoil and discord regarding claims to the lands and properties. Pio Pico and his brother claimed a large portion of the mission lands as their own, and were displaced only when he was given Rancho Temecula in exchange. In 1843, Governor Micheltorena restored the Franciscans to control of San Luis Rey. Father José Zalvidea came to the mission and stayed until his death in 1846. At that time, San Luis Rey became a mission parish of San Juan Capistrano, and was largely unattended except for feast days or special celebrations. Many of the mission's furnishing, artifacts, and records disappeared at this time. Thirty years later, some of the records turned up in a bookstore in Barcelona, where a priest from Milpitas, California, purchased them for fifteen cents and returned them to San Luis Rey. In 1846, Pico, now governor, sold the mission for $2,000, and shortly after fled to Mexico.

After the American conquest and occupation of California, the United States Army transferred some members of its "Mormon Battalion" in San Diego to San Luis Rey. As long as it was occupied, the mission was generally protected from ruin. When the army left in 1852, San Luis Rey fell into rapid decline. Although President Lincoln returned the mission to the Catholic church in 1865, it continued to be largely neglected. In 1892, because of the increasing difficulty with the secular and anti-religious government in Mexico, a group of Zacatecan Franciscans sought refuge in the United States and were given Mission San Luis Rey as their residence. They embarked on an ambitious program of rebuilding and restoration under the direction of Father Joseph O'Keefe. Thus, one hundred years after being founded by Franciscans from Spain, San Luis Rey was saved by Franciscans from Mexico, under the direction of an Irish priest.

With the Franciscans reoccupying the "King of the Missions," many of its lost and strayed treasures were returned. The stations of the cross were returned from a local home where they had been taken for safekeeping. The original baptismal font and founding cross were returned. Long-covered murals were restored. Serious efforts at restoration were begun and continue to this day, for both San Luis Rey and its *assistencia* San Antonio at Pala.

Mission San Luis Rey today:

Mission San Luis Rey de Francia is located at 4070 Mission Ave., San Luis Rey, CA, 92068; (760) 757-3651.
http://www.sanluisrey.org
Nickname: "King of the Missions"

The myth persists that San Luis Rey is perhaps an unfinished mission, meant to have twin towers. An early drawing by the French artist Duflos de Mofras shows two towers, but de Mofras, who had visited several of the missions in 1839, was drawing from memory in 1841. A drawing of San Luis Rey done in 1827, while very similar to de Mofras's, shows only one tower. There is no evidence that a second tower was ever planned.

Extensive restoration continues at San Luis Rey today, and will for years. San Luis Rey shares the distinction of being the only cruciform, domed mission building in the California chain. San Juan Capistrano was built in the same fashion, but it was destroyed in the earthquake of 1812. San Luis Rey is another "Hollywood" mission. Its grounds were used for the filming of the original Zorro movies in the 1930s, and in fact the skull and crossbones adorning the cemetery gates, although common to cemetery gates in the mission era, were added by Disney artists for the movies. The stations of the cross along the mission walls were indeed painted for the original mission church in Mexico in the 1780s.

The mission grounds at San Luis Rey offer more than most of the missions. In addition to the oldest pepper tree in California, and the cemetery, there is the most extensive *lavendaria* of any of the missions. Then, as now, water was a precious commodity in southern California. The Franciscans used the San Luis Rey River as their source, and through a series of dams and aqueducts bought the water to the mission grounds. Once there, the water passed through the *lavenderia* in a series of hierarchical uses. First it came to fountains, through decorative, whimsical spouts and spigots, where it was used for drinking and cooking. Next, it flowed down to a broad, flat area used for bathing and laundry. Finally, the water ran out at the base of the area to irrigate nearby fields.

One of San Luis's unique features is the mortuary chapel to the right as you enter the main doors. This was a multi-level area where the deceased would lie below, in front of the altar, and the watchers would keep watch from above the night before the funeral. The funeral service would be performed the next day in this chapel, and the deceased taken out the side door directly to the cemetery.

The interior decoration of the church is dominated by pillars made of fired brick, but painted to look like marble. Wall paintings and murals are the original work of native artisans. The pulpit with its sounding board is an excellent example of the eighteenth-century approach to enhancing acoustics. The altar table, or *retablo,* is of the neo-classical style installed in the later missions. Careful study and restoration have been applied to most of the original murals and wall decorations done by Native American artisans.

Mission San Luis Rey

Lavenderia.

Endnotes

1   This remarkable document, the most detailed recitation of any of the Native Californians regarding the mission experience, can be read in *Ethnology of the California Indians II: Post Contact,* edited and with an introduction by Lowell John Bean and Sylvia Brakke Vane, Garland Publishing Inc. New York and London 1991. The document is titled *Indian Life and Customs at Mission San Luis Rey a Record of California Mission Life by Pablo Tac an Indian Neophyte Written about 1835, Edited and Translated with Historical Introduction by Minna and Gordon Hewes, Old Mission San Luis Rey, California 1958.*

274

Chapter 22

SANTA INES

The History of Santa Inés

*L**a Mision de Nuestra Santa Ines, Virgen y Martir* (the Mission
of our Saint Agnes Virgin and Martyr), was founded on September 17, 1804. It was the nineteenth mission founded, and
the first mission founded in the nineteenth century. The mission was
named for Saint Agnes ("Inés" in Spanish.) Tradition has it that Agnes was a singularly beautiful girl of thirteen. The emperor Semproni-
ous wanted her to marry his son. At her refusal, he condemned her to
death. Roman law did not permit the execution of a virgin, so Semp-
ronious had her dragged naked through the streets to a brothel. All of
the men who attempted to rape her were struck blind. She was tied to
a stake to be burned, but the wood would not ignite. Finally, the officer
of the guard stabbed her in the throat. Agnes is the patron of young
girls and, understandably, of rape victims. Her feast day is January 21.

Santa Ines was founded under the authority of Father Estevan Tapis. The mission was not located in an area with much of a native population, so many of tits neophytes were transfers from Santa Barbara
and La Purísima, a fact that would have a serious impact on those two
missions when things went awry twenty years later. In charge of the
building of the mission were Fathers José Calzada and Romualdo Gui-
terrrez. Father Guitierrez was only twenty-two when he was given this
challenging assignment, and it indeed proved too much for him. Less
than two years later, diagnosed as suffering *afectio hysterico,* he was
returned to the College of San Fernando in Mexico. Father Calzada
was apparently better suited to missionary life. He stayed at Santa Inés
for ten years, until he died in 1814. He supervised the neophytes in

the construction of a row of tile-roofed adobe buildings, as houses for those natives who had attached themselves to the mission.

Because Santa Inés was the mission that was newest in the chain when the Mexican Revolution raged (1810-1821), it was perhaps the one most impacted by the disruption in supplies from Mexico which that war occasioned. Bancroft minimizes these problems, noting, "The fact that Mexico was in trouble, and either could not or would not aid this distant province with money or supplies, was the sum and sub-stance of the rebellion so far as it had effect in California."[1] In fact the deprivation of money and supplies was a serious problem for all of the missions, and most acutely for one just being built. Even before deal-ing with these mundane but highly significant issues of money and supplies, the first question to be resolved was, again, that of personal loyalties. Now the Franciscans were serving in a territory that, at least indirectly, was in armed rebellion against their king. Bancroft, with his dismissive comment, is undoubtedly referring to the fact that there were no battles being fought in Alta California that pitted revolution-aries against the Spanish army. This was true, but there were certainly battles of ideology being waged, and the Franciscan priests were in the very forefront of these. Aside from obtuse questions about where loyalties lay were the practical matters of payment for the soldiers guarding the mission, and uniforms and clothing for them and their families. The missionaries not only had their stipends suspended, but they were now obliged to provide cloth, food and other necessities for the military from the stores they had saved for the neophytes.

Clerical and military animosities that had their origins as far back as Junipero Serra and Captain Rivera once more rose to the fore. The missionaries begrudged the soldiers any but the most meager part of their stores, and the soldiers saw the priests more concerned about "savages" than they were about the soldiers who were protecting them from those savages.

It is significant, and perhaps indicative of things to come, that in a report filed in 1814 the priests assigned to the mission described the population as some Indians, some soldiers assigned to the guard, and six families who "regard themselves as Americans." Fifty years before the United States took control of Alta California, those troublesome Americans were making themselves noticed.

With the normal routes of re-supply disrupted, the situation was perfect for the development of a black market and smuggling. The annals of the next several years are replete with expeditions against smugglers, capture of smugglers, and in some cases the death of smugglers. American and Russian ships were seized repeatedly and their crews taken prisoner until an exchange could be arranged.

As if political upheaval was not enough, Santa Ines, like all of the southern missions, was stricken by the earthquake of 1812. All of the building roofs were damaged and the corner of the church fell off. Despite these troubles, in 1814 they began laying a stone foundation for a new church, and dedicated it on July 4, 1817.

In 1822, one of Santa Inés's and California's most colorful characters enters the record. On November 5 of that year, "Pirate Joe" Chapman was married to Maria Guadalupe Ortega in the mission chapel. Actually, at his marriage his name was José Juan Chapman, and his story is an amazing blend of the fact and fantasy that gives such color to the history of the area. Joe Chapman was captured by Maria's father when Hippolyte Bouchard made one of his ineffective raids near Santa Barbara in 1818. It turns out that Chapman was not a willing member of Bouchard's crew, but had been captured by him in the Hawaiian Islands. At least that was Chapman's claim. His powers of persuasion must have been considerable, because despite the fact that he was captured, cutlass in hand as the pirates waded ashore, he was very soon placed on probation and put to work in Los Angeles. Eventually he received a full amnesty from Governor Sola. He was a skilled craftsman and built the first grist mill in California at Santa Inés.

He was baptized a Catholic in 1822, and that same year married the daughter of the man who had captured him. In 1831 he became a Mexican citizen. In 1834 the Chapman family is listed on the census records as Don José, his wife Guadalupe and five children. Don José died in 1848. The Chapman family descendants still live in the area.

In 1824, an incident at Santa Inés triggered a serious challenge by the natives to Mexican rule. A neophyte from La Purísima who happened to be at Santa Inés was flogged by a Mexican soldier, for what infraction, or how seriously, is not recorded. Some accounts say that the "flogee" was actually a member of the Mexican army, and the "flogger" was simply enforcing military discipline. Whatever the

circumstances, years of abuse and frustration with Mexican rule ex-
ploded into armed confrontation. Two Indians were killed and much
of the mission destroyed by fire. At La Purísima the revolt continued,
ultimately to the disadvantage of the Indians.*

Father Blas Ordaz came to Mission Santa Inés in March of 1824
and served there until 1833. Bancroft describes Ordaz as overly fond
of women. With that characterization he may have been more Christian than Ordaz's confreres, who accused him of outright immorality.
Visitors to the mission commented on the priest's flagrant violations
of his vow of chastity, and Joseph Alemany, the first bishop of San
Francisco, was quite sure that Ordaz had fathered not one, but three
illegitimate children. Two of the entries on the Santa Inez baptismal
register, in conjunction with the rumors spread, certainly give grounds
for suspicion.†

The secularization of Santa Inés was finally effected in 1836. Santa
Inés may have had its secularization hastened by Governor Mariano
Chico, because he felt he had not been accorded proper respect by the
friars at the mission. On June 10, 1836, Governor Chico arrived at the
mission for a visit. By his recitation, he had sent a messenger ahead
to notify the priests he was coming; by the accounting of the priests,
they had no idea he was on his way until his carriage clattered to a
halt at the front door. An arrogant Chico felt that he should have been
received with some sort of welcoming ceremony. The apologies of
the Franciscans were to no avail, and Governor Chico turned around
and drove off in a high dudgeon. The matter was not helped when Father Duran, the president of the missions, responded to the governor's
complaint by telling him that the missions had no duty of hospitality
to visiting government officials. This reply should have put to rest
forever the idea that the missions were built "a day's journey apart for
travelers."

One version of this story is that Chico was indeed slighted by the
Franciscans and deliberately so, because the woman accompanying
him in the carriage was not Mrs. Chico, but one Señora Cruz. Señora

---

*   This conflict is treated in some detail in the chapter on La Purísima.
†   Entry number 1,311 lists the child being baptized as that of "Maria
Soledad Ortega and an unknown father," and entry 1,326 describes another
child as that of "Maria Soledad and an unknown father."

Chico was still in Mexico. The highly moral Franciscans were not about to give a warm welcome to such scandalous conduct.

Whatever the facts, less than two weeks later, Chico appointed José Covarrubias as secular administrator of Mission Santa Inés. At the transfer to Covarrubias, the value of the mission and all of its holdings was noted as approximately $51,000. Covarrubias was married to a niece of soon-to-be appointed Governor Pio Pico. Pico, as has been seen, was most infamous for despoiling the missions by using them to settle his own personal debts. With Covarrubias as administrator, disputes between the priests and politicians reached the depths of pettiness, and resulted in the "father's wall" that divided the mission courtyard at Santa Inés down the middle: one side for the administrator to pen his horse, one side for the priests to graze their cows.

After secularizing the missions, the Mexican government later found itself somewhat unsure of what to do with them. Hence, in 1843 Governor Micheltorena signed a decree returning certain of the missions to the Franciscans. Santa Inés was one of the favored few that was able to recover from the damage done by the order of secularization ten years earlier. While Micheltorena's decision was a happy one in the Franciscan's eyes, it was not well received by the civilian population in California. They had, even before the original decree, been looking with greedy eyes at the missions. Micheltorena's order and other aspects of his tenure caused the *Californios* to rise up in revolt, and he was forced to flee to Mexico.

The College of our Lady of Guadalupe was established at Santa Inés in 1844. Although it was primarily a seminary for the training of priests, the college was open to lay students as well, and so Santa Inés may offer a challenge to Santa Clara's claim as the first institution of higher education in California. A major difference between the two is that the University of Santa Clara has operated uninterrupted since the day it was founded, and the College of Our Lady of Guadalupe ceased to function in 1883.

Micheltorena's decree and Santa Inés's good fortune was very short-lived. Micheltorena's successor was Pio Pico, who lost no time in voiding the earlier order and, on June 15, 1846, the mission was formally sold to José Covarrubias and Joaquin Carillo for $7,000. This for the mission that, ten years earlier, had been valued at $56,000. The land the church occupied, the church and the College of Our Lady of

Guadalupe, one-and-a-half miles from the mission proper, were not included in the sale. Three weeks later on July 7, 1846, the United States flag was raised over Monterey, and all Mexican claims to land in California came under scrutiny from the American legal system. In 1862, President Abraham Lincoln signed an order returning title to Mission Santa Inés to the Catholic church.

In 1865 Santa Inés found itself as the locus of a series of murders and revenge killings. These killings might give some insight into the dynamics of race and ethnicity in nineteenth-century California. The Indians from the former missions were essentially derelicts on their own lands. The increasing numbers of white settlers had no compunctions about exploiting their labor by supplying them with alcoholic beverages as payment. The attraction of readily available alcohol drew other Indians from the Central Valley. One of the visitors from the valley, Cayetano* by name, got into a fight with a mission Indian identified only as José. Cayetano not only killed José, he managed to stab another José (Cordona) who came to his friend's aid. The wounded man made it back to the mission. Before he died, he told the priest what had happened. Cayetano was arrested in Santa Barbara but released three months later for good behavior. It is likely that the authorities in Santa Barbara did not attach much importance to Indians killing Indians. Cayetano returned to Santa Inés. On Easter Sunday he himself was killed by a Mexican named Garcia who was apparently avenging José Cordona. What punishment, Garcia received is not part of the record.

The mission church and the college were maintained by various priests and orders until 1881 when, due to declining enrollment, the college was closed. The mission continued as an active Catholic church, which it is today. In 1904, Father Alfred Buckler arrived, planning to stay only a few weeks. He ended up staying more than twenty years, and deserves great credit for rescuing Santa Inés from an inevitable slide into ruin. When Father Buckner arrived, the mission had been taken over by squatters who maintained chickens in the *sala* and a blacksmith shop in the living quarters. Father Buckner reclaimed the ruins and slowly and patiently restored Mission Santa Inés, if not

---

*   It is interesting to note, and perhaps indicative of the circumstances of the argument, that Cayetano is a Christian name, and that Saint Cayetano is the patron saint of gamblers.

to its former glory, at least to a point where future generations could finish what he had begun. He would often put tramps up in the mission quarters in return for their labor in repairing the mission. It has been estimated that in his twenty-plus years at Santa Inés, Father Buckner gave shelter and food to more than three thousand itinerants, from whom he got both skilled and unskilled labor in his restoration project.

Father Buckner's accomplishments at Santa Inés were truly heroic, but much of the credit for the mission's salvation goes not to Buckner, but to his amazing twenty-three-year-old niece. Mamie Goulet-Abbot arrived shortly after her uncle did in 1904 to serve as his housekeeper. Her first view of the mission, and her description of it, puts into perspective the amazing courage and fortitude of this young woman. She saw only some crumbled adobe ruins which she thought were the remains of a long-abandoned fort. She was aghast to discover that these ruins were the mission, and her home. She had left a comfortable home in Minnesota and made the long trip to California for this? Her first night was a torment of fleas, to such an extent that she resolved to tell her uncle she could not stay the very next day. She did stay, living in the most primitive and harsh conditions, and dealing not just with fleas but with snakes, spiders and some of the more unsavory tramps for twenty years. Ms. Goulet-Abbot did more than just endure the rigors of this primitive existence. She personally began repairing much of the mission's most serious damage. She took it upon herself to learn the rudiments of carpentry, plastering and even art restoration to undo years of neglect. Art historians recoil in horror when she describes scrubbing with soap and water a painting of San Rafael, which she describes as a "very crude painting." Ms. Goulet-Abbot's naïve efforts notwithstanding, the painting of San Rafael at Santa Inés is today recognized as perhaps the single most significant piece of Native American art in all of the California missions. She recovered long-lost implements and vestments, and gets credit for rescuing and restoring what is today considered one of the best collections in existence of sixteenth- and seventeenth-century church vestments in the Americas.

Her description of the winter of 1910-1911 is particularly fascinating. More than forty inches of rain fell that year. Throughout February and March, Ms. Goulet-Abbott, her visiting brother, and Father Buckner stood by helplessly while the one-hundred-year old adobe gave way to the relentless rain. The damage culminated on the night of February 26, when seven inches fell in that one night. She describes the night in harrowing terms of crumbling adobe and collapsing walls, until finally the bell tower itself fell to the ground. Through it all, Ms. Goulet-Abbott literally took her life in her hands to rescue the tabernacle, altar cloths and candlesticks from the disintegrating building. The following year, the bishop of Los Angeles made the money available to repair most of the damage caused by that storm.

In November of 1924 Father Buckner, in declining health, resigned his position at Santa Inés and joined his niece in purchasing a home in Santa Barbara. Father Buckner died the following March. Ms. Abbott-Goulet published a book of her experiences in 1951.* She died in 1957.

Mission Santa Inés today:

Mission Santa Inés is located at 1760 Mission Drive (off Highway 246), Solvang, CA 93463; 805-688-4815
www.missionsantaines.org

San Inés is a mission better known for its art than its architecture. Perhaps the most famous of all the Native American paintings, the archangel Rafael as a Chumash Indian, is in the museum at Santa Inés. The archangel Raphael is famous from the Old Testament book of Tobit. In the biblical account, Tobit is blind and Raphael appears to his son Tobias, and tells him that he can cure his father's blindness with the oil from a fish. The oil is applied and Tobit recovers his sight. The Chumash were accomplished fishermen and this story of the fish's miraculous power obviously resonated with a talented member of their tribe. Although Raphael is much depicted in European art with a fish suspended from a line, the depiction at Santa Inés is with the fish held close to the body, and the fish itself seems to be one of the Santa Barbara channels rockfish groups. These elements suggest that the painter, working with oil on canvas, was not simply copying a religious picture, but developing his own theme from the story.

---

*   *Santa Ines Hermosa, The Journal of the Padre's Niece.* Goulet-Abbot, Mamie.

The museum at Santa Inés also houses the most extensive collection of sixteenth-, seventeenth-, and eighteenth-century liturgical vestments in the United States.

Santa Inés is one of the few missions that does not have an elaborate pulpit extending out over the first few rows of pews. The mission did have a pulpit and it was much in use, until a somewhat portly Father Juan Basso, on Rosary Sunday, in 1870, mounted it to deliver his sermon. The aging pulpit and the startled Father Basso crashed to the floor. Father Basso was not seriously injured, but the pulpit was destroyed and never replaced.

The stations of the cross were imported from Mexico in 1818, and have been restored. The wall dados and scrollwork are faithful reproductions of original Indian artwork, as is the work on the *reredos,* and the murals surrounding the altar. Other period artwork in the nave has unfortunately been painted over. The chandeliers at Santa Inés are some of the best examples true mission-period lighting in existence. There are two statues of Saint Agnes, one above the altar and one on the side. The one above the altar was carved by one of the Chumash tribe, based on an illustration in a book. Several of the carved wooden candlesticks are also the work of skilled Chumash artisans.

As you enter the Madonna Chapel from the museum, glance down at the floor. There is one tile outlined in white, just inside the door. If you look carefully you can discern the footprint of a small child. Two hundred years ago, an errant child walked across some tiles drying in the sun, and today we can see the result of that trespass.

There are several Franciscans buried in the church at Santa Inés: Father José Abello (1764-1842); Father Arroyo de la Cuesta (1780-1840); Father José Antonio Calzada (1760-1814); Father Marcus Antonio de Victoria y Orriozola de Victoria Saizar (1760-1836); and Father Juan Morena (1799-1845).

Mission Santa Ines - Stations of the Cross.

Endnotes
1   Bancroft, Hubert Howe. *History of California Vol. II 1801-1824.* San Francisco: The History Company Publishers, 1886.

Chapter 23

SAN RAFAEL ARCÁNGEL

The History of San Rafael Arcángel

*L**a Mision del Gloriosisimo Principe San Rafael Arcangel* (the Mission of the Glorious Prince Saint Rafael Arcangel), the twentieth mission, was founded on December 14, 1817. It is the third mission named after one of the archangels. Rafael is the healing archangel who appears in the book of Tobit as a traveling companion to the younger Tobias. After he cures Tobias's father of his blindness, he reveals himself as "the angel Rafael, one of the seven who stands before the Lord" (Tobit 12:15). He is the patron saint of healing, and his feast day is celebrated on September 29 along with Michael and Gabriel, the other two archangels. San Rafael would be the last mission built in California under Spanish rule.

San Rafael began as an *asistencia* to San Francisco, and was the only one of the *asistencia*s to ever gain full mission status. The father president at its founding was Father Vincent Sarria. The hope was that building an *asistencia* just across the Golden Gate from San Francisco would prove a more salubrious site for the health of the Indians at San Francisco who, between their enforced living in cramped quarters, San Francisco's damp fog, and their exposure to the diseases of the Spanish, were suffering a terrible morbidity and mortality rate. Aside from any humanitarian or religious objectives, San Rafael was built with military and political considerations at least as important as religious ones. San Rafael would serve as a barrier to further expansion by the Russians who had the temerity to build a fort near Bodega Bay.

Russian fur traders had been sailing the west coast of the North American continent since the early sixteenth century. The Russians were not dissuaded at all by Spanish claims to the west coast of

North America. Those claims were based primarily on the Treaty of Tordesillas, which had been emplaced in 1494 by Pope Alexander VI. The treaty was meant to settle a dispute between Spain and Portugal regarding their claims in the New World. Orthodox Russia was not about to give much weight to a treaty emplaced by a Catholic pope between two Catholic countries. By the time the Russians established their first—and, as it turns out, their only—fort in California near Bodega Bay in 1812, all but two of the Spanish missions had been completed. The Russians had come to the game much too late, with much too little. They could not hope to match the colonizing efforts of the Spanish, nor the fervor of the Franciscans.

The Spanish took nothing for granted, even though they had nineteen missions along the California coast. When the Russians actually built a stockade north of San Francisco Bay, the Spanish government began to take seriously the Franciscan's pleas for an *asistencia* at San Raphael. This would be the first mission built north of what would come to be called the "Golden Gate." There were plans to build other missions at Petaluma and Suisun, but they never came to fruition.*

Assigned to this new endeavor was Father Gil y Taboada. Father Gil was a Franciscan of some experience in California. He had served at several missions and most significantly at San Francisco in two separate tours from 1801 to 1806. Since San Rafael was founded as an *asistencia,* and primarily as a hospital for the ailing Indians at San Francisco, Father Gil volunteered to serve them in the new location. He had no delusions about what he was founding. This mission, which was not originally meant to be a mission, was very simply constructed. Father Gil initially built a long, low building which housed a chapel, the priests quarters and some storage. In 1818 Father Gil had to return to Mexico because of ill health.

He was replaced by Father Juan Amoros. Father Amoros added a shorter building at right angles to the original one. He moved the chapel into this area. When completed the two structures comprised one L shaped building with the chapel occupying the shorter arm of the L and the longer side containing a rooms for the sick, storage, and the

---

*   Fort Ross remained the sole Russian outpost in Spanish California until 1841, when the Russians sold it to John Sutter, who was at that time a Mexican citizen.

padres' quarters. At its founding San Raphael had no aspiration to become a full mission. Thus, it was very simply constructed and never had rich artwork or adornment. It never aspired to the conventional quadrangle of the other missions, and it never had a bell tower nor even a decent *campanero.* The bells were hung on a simple wooden frame at the front of the church. The building originally was roofed with reeds.

The neophytes attached to the mission lived in small adobe huts scattered about the grounds of the mission. There were orchards and gardens. Since the mission was founded at the end of the Mexican Revolution, it found itself from its beginning highly dependent on its own resources and native population. San Rafael often had only one priest assigned to it, and soldiers to enforce discipline were very few. The neophytes at San Raphael were assigned positions of responsibility at the mission much more readily than their brothers at the other mission.

It is a fact that in a very short time of living in a somewhat warmer climate, the Indians did improve and thrive remarkably. Father Amoros managed the *assistencia* and expanded it in both buildings and neophyte population, such that in 1823 it was granted full mission status. Amoros's tenure was not entirely free of conflict, though none of the troubles can be properly laid at Father Amoros's doorstep. The mission livestock, which roamed the hills north of the bay, were subject to frequent depravations by the local Indians. Leaders of these raids were a chief, Marin, and his ally Quentin.* When the Mexican army finally decided to put an end to their cattle rustling it was not a simple task. Mariano Vallejo, the Mexican general in charge of this campaign, paid his foe the compliment of referring to him as "The great Indian chief Marin." The campaign lasted over two months, with Marin using his knowledge of the terrain and the sympathy of the local clans to his best advantage. Marin and the majority of his force retreated to a small island in San Raphael Bay. As the army prepared to embark in small boats to confront them, Lieutenant Ignacio Martinez realized that Quentin and a smaller group had remained on the mainland. It became obvious to the lieutenant that the Indians' strategy was to allow the soldiers to get into the water between the mainland and the island,

---

*   San Quentin Prison and Marin County take their names from these two men.

and then attack them from both sides. It would have been a disaster for the army. Martinez turned back from his pursuit of the main body, and instead attacked Quentin and his smaller force. Quentin was captured and imprisoned at the *presidio* in San Francisco, apparently in order to be executed. The priests at Mission Dolores interceded on his behalf, since he was a baptized Catholic. He was released to their custody and within two years was working as a ferryman and boater on the bay.

Meanwhile, Marin had escaped, like so many of the California Indians, to the Central Valley. It was another year before the Mexican army caught up with him. He was captured as he made a return visit to Bodega Bay. Marin was held prisoner at the *presidio* in San Francisco, but allowed to wander about the grounds with his feet shackled. The freedom-loving Marin escaped once again.

This time his freedom lasted almost ten years. Ultimately, Marin once more found himself surrounded by the Mexican army. Chief Marin was apparently not just a skilled tactician and resolutely brave man but a wily judge of human nature and politics. He demanded that he be allowed to surrender, not to the Mexican Army but to the Franciscans at San Rafael. Glad to have this thorn in their side in any sort of custody, the soldiers agreed. Marin was accepted by the Franciscan, baptized, and lived his final days at Mission San Rafael. He died in 1834.

Amoros was not just a mission administrator of great wisdom, but a man who involved himself in the political and social issues of the day. He tried to interact amicably with his Russian neighbors. He argued with the governor who had imposed excessive import taxes on foreign ships. Very early on, he saw the importance San Francisco Bay could have for foreign trade, and he tried to get the authorities to encourage its development as a trading center. He would not take the oath of loyalty to the Mexican government, but declared that he would obey any government under which he lived. Father Amoros served at San Raphael until he died in 1832.

At his death, San Rafael, which had been blessed with two patient and wise pastors for its first years, ran out of luck. Two Zacatecans were assigned to San Rafael in 1833 and 1834. These were Father Rafael de Jesus Moreno and Father Jesus Maria del Mercado Vasquez. Both were rash and intemperate men. Neither one of them had the slightest tolerance for the Spanish soldiery; at a minimum they were dismissive of them and disdainful. Their contempt for the military would come back to haunt them, and their compassion for their native parishioners was apparently no better than their tolerance for the soldiers.

Father Vasquez in particular, who was only twenty-five when assigned to San Rafael, had no patience for any failings of the natives. He never hesitated to flog the Indians, despite the fact that Governor Echeandia had, in a decree in 1826, forbidden the flogging of adult Indians.*

His treatment of the Indians was such that in at least one instance the corporal of the guard not only refused to turn an Indian over to him for punishment, but he reported the *padre's* behavior to General Vallejo. Undoubtedly the lack of respect the priests had shown the soldiers was motivation for the corporal's report. The controversy might have remained just another of the many conflicts between priests and politicians that define the history of the California missions, but ensuing events brought matters to a head.

In November of 1833, a group of natives from one of the outlying *rancherias* came to San Rafael. They asked to speak with the *padre*. They were put off until the next day. During the night, some property was stolen from the mission. Father Vasquez was sure it was the work of the visiting Indians, and presumably believing in the theory of "collective guilt," had the whole lot arrested and sent to San Francisco for imprisonment at the *presidio*. Three days later, another group of natives was seen approaching the mission, undoubtedly looking for their missing friends. The paranoid Father Vasquez decided it was an attempt to free the prisoners, and responded, as was his wont, intemperately. He armed a group of the mission neophytes and sent them out on a preemptive strike against the interlopers. Twenty-one of the visiting Indians died, and another twenty, mostly women and children, were "captured." The clueless Father Vasquez not only coolly reported his triumph to Governor José Figueroa, but asked for reinforcements to quell what he saw as a full-blown revolt. Figueroa, who had made better relationships with the Indians a hallmark of his administration,

---

*   By its terms, the decree had no application to San Rafael or San Francisco de Solano. Whether constrained by law or not, though, had Vasquez been a more mature and patient man, he might have seen the handwriting on the wall. The days of treating the natives as obstinate children were over.

was outraged. He sent the matter to the prefect of the Zacatecan Franciscans at Santa Clara, and Vasquez was recalled for trial.

A year later, Father Vasquez was found innocent of the charges regarding the massacre of the visiting Indians, primarily because it could not be proved whether it was he or Father Moreno, both present during the incident, who had ordered the attack. Apparently neither of the two men would admit responsibility for the fateful order. Even today the historical record is fuzzy, some accounts blaming Moreno and others Vasquez. Obviously this is one of those unfortunate historical incidents where the sum is less than the total of the parts. It really doesn't matter who issued the order to attack the party of Indians. The order never should have been issued. Had there been two more judicious men assigned to San Rafael in 1833, the tragedy would never have occurred.

Subsequent examinations of each man's character might shed a little light on who should bear the responsibility for the matter. Father Moreno, in all of his assignments at six missions besides San Raphael, had never been charged with any misbehaviors, but rather was characterized as "a great advocate in favor of Indian civilization." Father Moreno died in 1834, and the priest who buried him noted in the burial register that Father Moreno had "suffered much because of the unfounded accusations" against him.

Father Vasquez, on the other hand, was characterized as a man always ready to argue with anyone who did not agree with him. Father José Maria Suarez del Real, who years earlier had replaced Vasquez at Santa Clara, complained because he found himself charged with the responsibility of caring for Vasquez's children by a woman of the town. Bancroft characterizes Father Vasquez as "a hard drinker, a gambler and a libertine, the father of many half-breed children at each of the missions where he served. . ."[1]

The mission has the singular distinction of being the first mission to be secularized, in 1834. The church remained in Franciscan hands, but Lieutenant Ignacio Martinez, he who had displayed such an eye for the tactics of the Indians at the "Battle of Quentin Point," was appointed administrator of the lands.

San Raphael was another of the missions that had the "honor" of serving as temporary headquarters to John C. Fremont in 1846, during the Mexican-American War. The mission, according to the reports of the soldiers who stayed there, was even then in a sad state of repair, but it provided enough shelter for the troops who otherwise would be sleeping in the open. One of San Rafael's more grim incidents occurred during this occupation. Three Mexican men stopped at the mission to see if they could acquire fresh horses. Kit Carson, one of Fremont's entourage, asked the colonel if they should be taken prisoner. Fremont's response was something along the lines of, "I can't be bothered with prisoners; do whatever you have to." Kit Carson decided that what he had to do was to kill the men. He marched them down to the nearby landing and shot them. It turns out that the three were a prominent rancher, and the twin sons of the *alcade* of Yerba Buena. Both Fremont and Carson tried to disavow any responsibility for this heinous act. These were the same two men who a month earlier had described their encounter with natives in the upper Sacramento Valley as "a perfect butchery."

In 1869, the last remains of the original mission were torn down, and many of the materials hauled away for use in other building projects. In 1919, a large, vaguely Spanish but not mission-style church, Saint Raphael's, was built on the site. This church burned down in 1919, and was rebuilt at the same location. In 1949, a reproduction of the mission was built to the right of the parish church. This is the building we consider Mission San Rafael today.

Mission San Rafael today:

Mission San Rafael is located at 1104 5ᵗʰ Ave. (5ᵗʰ Ave. and A Street), San Rafael, CA, 94901-2916; (415) 456-3016.
http://saintraphael.com
Nickname: Mission of Healing

San Rafael, like its neighbor across the Golden Gate, is today dwarfed by its more recent iteration. The parish church of San Raphael covers all of the ground once occupied by the mission, and towers over the insignificant building to its right, which is a reproduction of the actual mission that once stood there.

It is important that we keep in mind that at San Raphael, as at Santa Cruz, what we are visiting is a replica, built in 1949, and not a restoration. Even as a replica it is suspect, since there were no surviving drawings of the original mission except for a sketch done from memory, forty years after it was abandoned. And San Raphael is even less of a reproduction than Santa Cruz. At Santa Cruz, while the building is a modern reproduction, many of the furnishings and artifacts are originals. At San Raphael, the statues, altar, and furnishings are all contemporary. The scroll painting of the archangel Rafael, and three bells, are all that are original to San Rafael. If it serves no other purpose, San Rafael can remind us of how close we came to losing these priceless monuments.

At the side of the church is a stone tribute to Chief Marin, the native leader who gave the Mexican army such trouble. San Rafael is in Marin County, and the county is named after him. California's infamous San Quentin prison was built on what had been called "Quentin Point," for it was on this spit of land that that Quentin and Marin almost trapped the Mexican army. When the Americans took control of the territory in 1846, they mistakenly attached the beatific "San" to this point. Thus, in one of those ironical twists of history, Quentin, the Indian warrior who challenged Mexican rule of his land, has become "Saint Quentin."

Endnotes

1   Bancroft , Hubert Howe. History of California, Vol IV San Francisco: The History Company, Publishers, 1886.

Chapter 24

SAN FRANCISCO DE SOLANO

The History of San Francisco de Solano

*L*a *Mision de San Francisco Solano* (the Mission of Saint Francis Solanus, was the twenty-first of the California missions, founded July 4, 1823, by Father José Altimira. As with several of the missions, the founding date and the date when actual construction began are not the same. Immediately after the founding ceremonies, Father Altimira returned to San Francisco, and it wasn't until late August or early September that he returned and began the actual work of building a mission. San Francisco Solano is named for Saint Francis of Solanus, a Spanish Franciscan who, like his brothers who came after him, dedicated his life to missionary work in the New World. Francis Solanus was born in 1549 in Cordoba, Spain, and died in 1610 in Lima, Peru. His feast day is July 24.* San Francisco de Solano was the last of the California missions to be built, and the only one built under Mexican rule.

Father José Altimira, whom we met briefly in the chapter on San Francisco de Assisi, was not the usual docile, obedient priest. He had been assigned to Mission San Francisco de Assisi in San Francisco, but he found it not at all to his liking. He wanted to move across the Golden Gate, and while there was a mission at San Rafael, that apparently was not far enough away for Father Altimira. As was narrated in the chapter on Mission Dolores, Father Altimira began pushing for the permanent closure of San Francisco and San Rafael and the removal of those enterprises further north, into present-day Sonoma County.

---

*   It was Saint Francis of Solano that Junipero Serra was imitating when he flogged himself with a chain during his sermon in Mexico City.

Father Altimira is undoubtedly the only Franciscan in history who tried to close not one but two Franciscan churches.

Father Altimira did approach the superiors of his order with his plans, but he apparently found their response too slow. He went to Governor Don Luis Arguello, who had concerns about the Russians expanding their presence in California from their enclave at Fort Ross. In his letter to the governor, Father Altimira not only complained about the obstructionist ways of his superiors, he threatened to resign and return to Spain if his plans were not given immediate sanction. The idea of a mission at Sonoma as a buffer to Russian expansion appealed to the governor. In March 1823, Arguello put before the Territorial Assembly a proposal, very likely drafted by Father Altimira, to build a mission in Sonoma and staff it by closing the existing missions at San Francisco and San Rafael.

Even in 1823, it didn't take long for news of this attempted usurpation to reach the president of the Franciscan missions, Father José Senan. Father Senan was at this time very ill, likely on his deathbed, and he had already designated as his successor Father Vincente Sarria. When Father Senan got word of Altimira's plot, he dictated three missives. The first was a rebuke to Altimira, reminding him of his lowly standing in the Franciscan hierarchy and of his lack of authority to make any decisions of the sort he had been making. Next was a letter to the successor he had chosen, Father Sarria, essentially telling him to not allow this outrage to take place. Finally, he wrote a memorandum to his superiors in Mexico City and to the civil authorities in Monterey, pointing out that the civil legislature had no authority to authorize anything with regard to any of the missions, much less the closure of two of them and the construction of another one.

Father Sarria followed through on his predecessor's concerns and, on becoming interim president, sent Father Altimira a "cease and desist" order, just as he was beginning his building. Work that had already begun on Mission San Francisco de Solano came to a screeching halt. Father Altimira ceased, but he did not desist. He continued to use his friendship with Governor Arguello and other civilian legislatures to lobby for the mission in Sonoma, once threatening to quit California and return to Spain if he was not allowed to proceed. This from a priest who had been in California less than three years, but who seemed to have no problem asserting that he should be the sole judge of the future course for the mission system that had been in place for half a century.

Lengthy, three-way negotiations now commenced between Father Sarria, Governor Arguello, and Father Altimira. Ultimately, the decision was made to let Father Altimira proceed with his mission, but Mission Dolores and Mission San Rafael were not to be interfered with. On April 4,1824, Father Altimira presided at the dedication of the church, a whitewashed wooden structure. He had founded it without authority nine months earlier, but now his endeavor had been legitimized. Many of the furnishings, altar clothes, candles and linens were provided by the despised Russians at Fort Ross. Father Sarria, who had so vigorously resisted the establishment of this mission, had been replaced as president of the missions just two days earlier by Father Francisco Duran.

Father Altimira's triumph was not complete, though, for while he was appointed as the first pastor of Mission San Francisco de Solano, it was also made clear that he was an associate of Mission San Rafael. True to his character, one of his first acts as the head of Mission San Francisco de Solano was to write a letter to the governor and complain that the new president of the missions, by appointing him subordinate to Mission San Rafael, was not giving him the authority he needed, and that the other missions were not supporting him. He mentioned Mission San Jose and Father Narciso Duran by name. For a Franciscan priest to vent his feelings on these kinds of internal issues to the civilian authorities was unheard of. Had Father Serra or Father Lasuen still been in charge of the missions, Altimira's rebuke would undoubtedly have been immediate and scathing. Alas, a new era was dawning in the Franciscan's rule in California. There is no record of any sort of censure of Father Altimira.

It is interesting that in the same letter, Altimira complained to the governor that the Indians were always running away from the mission, and that a show of military force might help him restrict their liberties. Apparently not only his superiors, but also his charges found Father Altimira insufferable. Although he got his mission built and operating, he so incensed the natives with his cruel and oppressive management that just two years later they rose up in arms, stormed the mission, burned a good portion of the buildings and forced Father Altimira to flee. He briefly resurfaced at Mission San Buenaventura, but two years later Father Altimira probably did everyone a big favor, left California under very strange circumstances, and returned to Spain.*

San Francisco de Solano sat empty for a while after the attack, until into the breach stepped Father Buenaventura Fortuny. Father Fortuny was able to establish amicable relations with the natives. He expanded on Father Altimira's work and built a larger church of adobe in 1827. The tide of history, however, was running out on all of the missions. Less than eight years after Father Fortuny's arrival, the missions were all secularized. San Francisco de Solano had the shortest life span of any of the missions, barely more than ten years from its founding in 1823 to its secularization in 1834. Fortuny had just completed his construction in 1832.

At secularization, the mission came under the control of General Mariano Vallejo. Vallejo was only twenty-seven years old, and was actually a lieutenant in the Mexican Army when independence came. He was a responsible and conscientious soldier, but even that would not explain his promotion from lieutenant to general. The fact that his cousin Juan Bautista Alvarado was the governor of Alta California is more likely the reason.

Even before secularization, in 1833 General Vallejo laid out the town plaza for Sonoma in the area adjacent to the mission. When San Francisco de Solano was secularized in 1834, Vallejo's town plaza became the central point of activity between Mexico, California and America for the next several years. General Vallejo converted some of the mission buildings to homes for settlers, but actually contributed his own money to keeping the church in repair, making fairly extensive renovations. He added a bell tower where none had existed, and donated the bells for the mission, some of which are still on display today. Eventually the mission fell victim to the same fate of so many of the missions. It proved to be more valuable as a source of building material for other structures than as actual habitation. In the late 1830s the original adobe church crumbled into ruins. Again, Vallejo came to the rescue and ordered a small adobe chapel to be built as a replacement. Vallejo's church served as a parish church for the increasingly American population of Sonoma.

---

*   Father Altimira does get credit for the area's romantic nickname. It was apparently Father Altimira who first used the phrase "Valley of the Moon" to describe the Sonoma Valley.

On June 14, 1846, John Fremont was present, as he always seemed to be at political hot spots, when a motley group of American settlers in the square in front of the mission raised the Bear Flag of the "California Republic."* The American government quickly recognized this new republic. Before the startled Mexicans could truly react to this affront, on July 9, Commander William Sloat raised the United States flag over Monterey. The United States and Mexico were at war, and the "California Republic" was one of the first casualties of the war, now becoming the territory of California as part of the United States of America. As a measure of how far California had drifted from the sphere of Mexican influence, when Commander Sloat wanted to formalize the American conquest of Monterey, he had to wait until a Mexican flag could be located, raised to the top of the flagstaff and then immediately lowered, whence a United States flag was raised, accompanied by the appropriate twenty-one gun salute.

The western expansion of the United States had for some time come up against the interests of other nations. What is now the largest part of the continental United States was at various times claimed by the French, the English, the Spanish, the Mexican and even the Russian governments. It was Mexico, though, that had the lion's share of the region at the time when the United States had a seemingly insatiable appetite for land in the west. As Porifiro Diaz would later lament, "Poor Mexico, so far from God and so close to the United States."

In 1881, the church sold the property and used the proceeds to construct a new parish church a few blocks away. The former mission holdings went through several iterations, ranging from wine-making to hay storage to a blacksmith shop. In 1903, the Landmarks League purchased the property with an eye toward restoring it, but restoration did not begin until 1911. In the interim, the 1906 earthquake further reduced the remains to rubble. In 1926, the Landmarks League deeded the site to the state which made it a State Historic Park, a status San Francisco de Solano enjoys to this day.

San Francisco de Solano, as the last mission and the one with the shortest history, is the appropriate one to launch a discussion of some

---

* The original "Bear Flag" probably seemed more like a "pig flag." The animal depicted had a more porcine than ursus outline. The flag for years was stored at the California Museum of Arts and Sciences in San Francisco. It was unfortunately lost in the fire that followed the 1906 earthquake.

overall historic impacts of the system. The first question is, why were the missions not more successful in effecting the long-term conversion of the Native Californians. Catholicism is not, by any stretch, the preferred religion of the majority of the people today who are in some degree descended from the indigenous tribes of the seventeeth- and eighteenth-centuries. Why, with the wide range of works the Franciscans emplaced, were not more native Californians brought to the fold of Catholicism? Some part of the answer to that question is obvious. They were brought into the system without real choice; they were treated very poorly while under mission control; and they were kept there by duress and fear. They were never converted in large numbers, and clearly never committed themselves to Catholicism. Those who did convert quite often did so as a matter of necessity and indifference, and as quickly as the Franciscan influence waned, so did the religious beliefs they had taught.

Consider, in the matter of conversion, the difference between Mexico and California. Just a little more than one hundred years before the settlement of Alta California, Hernandan Cortes, with methods admittedly not very Christian nor even very civilized, brought the entire Aztec empire and ultimately the entire country of Mexico to Catholicism. That conversion experience of the Mexican people, while accomplished by the sword and terror, has lasted more than four hundred years through persecution, neglect and overt attacks. Mexico is today a decidedly Catholic country. The conversion experience of the native Californians on the other hand, by all credible evidence, lasted only as long as the missions and the Franciscans held them to it. Cross the border between Alta (United States) and Baja (Mexican) California, and one today can hardly find any evidence among the natives of the former of the religion the Franciscans toiled for nearly seventy years to impose. There are several possibilities for this.

First, the native people of Mexico proper, at least in the central and southern regions, were a largely homogenous and well-structured culture under the rule of the Aztecs. They had a common language, Nahuatl, and held allegiance and paid tribute to the central rulers in Mexico City. The peoples of California were nomadic hunter-gatherers; they had no central authority and very little in the way of organized rule. There were at least twenty-one separate tribal identities between San Diego and San Francisco, and at least that many spoken languages. They had no common social or cultural norms.

Next, the Aztecs had a religious tradition that was formal and structured, albeit bloody. All religious traditions depend on some sort of central myth. Much of the Aztec myth was wisely appropriated by the Dominicans and Franciscans who followed Cortes, bringing the natives to the fold without asking them to totally abandon long-held beliefs. Our Lady of Guadalupe—the iconic representation of Mexican Catholicism—appeared to Juan Diego, an Indian, on Mount Tepeyac, a hill deemed sacred as a worship place for the Nahuatl mother goddess. The Lady speaks Nahuatl, and in her depiction is clearly Indian. The California Indians had no common formal religious tradition and no myth to transfer. To ask them to believe in God, a virgin mother, and an eternity far superior to this one was not the same as asking them to take a just-slightly different view of long-held beliefs.

Third, once the conquest of Mexico was complete, the country became a very important, very rich, very vibrant part of the Spanish empire. There was a constant inflow of power and prestige to Mexico City, and thus a constant reinforcement of the values and religious beliefs that were very much part of the Spanish court. In striking contrast, California was always viewed by both the Spanish, and the Mexicans after independence, as a frontier outpost, a hardship posting for military and civilian alike. Other than the Franciscans who were few and far between, there was generally no upper class to join.

Finally, because the California Indians as a whole had no real organized social structure, and lived a largely nomadic life, there were no central locations or villages the missionaries could visit to deliver their message. It was in Mexico City, the capitol of the Aztec empire, that Cortes proclaimed and enforced adherence to the new religion. No such forum was available in Alta California. The Indians of California were directly or indirectly forced into the mission compounds, and with very harsh measures made to stay there. If a religious message is imposed along with a state of captivity, it is not likely that it is going to be remembered with a fondness that calls for its preservation when the captive is ultimately given his freedom. For all of these reasons, once secularization came into full effect the mission system, and along with it Catholicism in California, began to disappear.*

If the missions failed in their primary task of conversion, did they succeed in any other respect? What did the missions bring to the history of the United States?

To answer that question consider this. When the westward expansion of the United States began in earnest in the 1840s, the jumping off point for those settling the west was generally St. Louis or one of the cities along the Mississippi. The erstwhile settlers left St. Louis and crossed a generally empty Missouri; empty Kansas and Colorado; more empty Utah, and absolutely empty Nevada to arrive in California. A California of roads, highways, cities and developed harbors. Churches, schools, industrial works, farming, agriculture and ranching were thriving. Their were skilled craftsmen and artisans. There was an established upper class as well as readily-available workers and laborers. The American settlers did not have to conquer the wilderness in California. The Franciscans had done that for them.

Mission San Francisco de Solano today:

Mission San Francisco de Solano is located at 114 East Spain St. (Spain and First Sts.), Sonoma, CA 95476; (707) 938-1519. http://napanet.net/~sshpa/mission.htm

San Franciso Solano is today one of two missions operated as a state park. Virtually all of the mission grounds and its interior are restorations. The bell hanging in front of the mission, however, is one of the mission's original bells.

San Francisco de Solano had the good fortune to be one of the earliest sites in California subjected to serious archeological investigations. The work, which has been carried out in several different iterations, today shows that what we consider Mission San Francisco

---

*   Interestingly, what the Franciscans couldn't accomplish in the seventeenth and eighteenth centuries, the inevitable tide of history has accomplished in the twenty-first. The Roman Catholic Diocese of Los Angeles can now make the claim that there are twice as many Catholics in Los Angeles as there are Episcopalians in the entire United States. Most of these are immigrants from Mexico and Central America.

300

de Solano is but a very small representation of what was once there. Workshops and guest quarters were contained in a second row of rooms behind the existing ones, which today serves as a museum for several exhibits. There are also foundations of buildings to the east of the chapel and to the north. For many years San Francisco de Solano was presumed to be just a simple chapel and a few storerooms. It now appears as if there may have been at least the beginnings of the quadrangle compound so common to the missions

San Francisco de Solano, the very last of the missions, is the only one where there is memorialization, by name, of the natives who died there. Using the death registers from the mission, in 1999 a plaque was constructed listing the baptismal names of 837 neophytes buried in the mission cemetery. They are buried in unmarked graves, as at all the missions, but we do know their names. These names are engraved on the marker to the left of the mission building, actually three separate stones. The central stone is inscribed, *"In this sacred ground lie buried, men, women and children of the local Coast Miwok, Patwin, Wappo and Pomo tribes. They built, labored and died at Mission San Francisco Solano."* This monument is hopefully just the beginning of recognizing and reconciling the sacrifices of the Native Americans with the triumphs of their Spanish conquerors.

SELECT BIBLIOGRAPHY

Books

Ahlstrom, Sydney E. *A Religious History of the American People.* New Haven: Yale University Press. 1972.

Bancroft, Hubert Howe. *History of California, Vol. I: 1542-1800.* San Francisco: A.L. Bancroft & Company. 1884.
_____. *History of California, Vol. II: 1801-1824,* and *History of California, Vol. III. 1825-1840.* San Francisco: The History Company. 1886.

Beebe, Rose Marie and Robert M. Senkewicz, eds. *Lands of Promise and Despair, Chronicles of Early California, 1535 -1846.* Berkeley: Heyday Books. 2001.
_____. *To Toil in the Vineyards of the Lord: Contemporary Scholarship on Junipero Serra.* Berkeley: Academy of American Franciscan History. 2010.

Casey, (Tid) Beatrice. *Padres and People of Old Mission San Antonio.* King City: Casey Printing Inc. 2006.

Chaffin, Tom. *Pathfinder: John Charles Fremont and the Course of American Empire.* New York: Hill and Wang. 2002.

Clary, D. A. *Eagles and Empire; the United States, Mexico and the Struggle for a Continent.* New York: Bantam Books. 2009.

Culleton, James. *Indians and Pioneers of Old Monterey.* Fresno: Academy of California Church History. 1950.

Cutter, Donald, trans. *Writings of Mariano Payeras.* Santa Barbara: Bellerophon Books. 1995.

De Nevi, Don and Noel F. Moholy, O.F.M. *Junipero Serra: The Illustrated Story of the Franciscan Founder of California's Missions.*

San Francisco: Harper and Row. 1985.

Denton, Sally. *Passion and Prinicple: John and Jessie Fremont, The Couple Whose Power, Politics and Love Shaped Nineteenth-Century America.* New York: Bloomsbury. 2007.

Duhaut-Cilly, Auguste.
"Duhuat-Cilly's Account of California in the Years 1827-28." *Wisconsin Historical Society Digital Library and Archives.* Document no. AJ 098. 1929. www.americanjourneys.org/aj-098/

Egan, F. *Fremont: Explorer for a Restless Nation.* Garden City: Doubleday and Company. 1977.

Englehardt, Rev. Zephyrin, O.F.M. *The Franciscans in California.* Harbor Springs: Holy Childhood Indian School. 1897.
Missions and Missionaries of California. San Francisco: The James H. Barry Co. 1908.
_____. *Missions and Missionaries of California, II.* San Francisco: The James H. Barry Co. 1911.
_____. *San Gabriel Mission and the Beginnings of Los Angeles.* Chicago: Franciscan Herald Press. 1927.
_____. *Mission Santa Ines Virgin y Martir and Its Ecclesiastical Seminary.* Santa Barbara: Martin and Loftin Publishers. 1986.

Geiger, Maynard J., O.F.M. *The Long Road: Padre Serra's March to Saintly Honors.* Santa Barbara: The Old Mission Santa Barbara. 1957.
_____. *The Life and Times of Fray Junipero Serra,* 2 vols. Washington, D.C.: Academy of American Franciscan History. 1959.
_____. *Franciscan Missionaries in Hispanic California 1769-1848: A Biographical Dictionary.* San Marino: The Huntington Library. 1969.

Goulet-Abbot, Mamie. *Santa Ines Hermosa: The Journal of the Padre's Niece.* Los Olivos: Olive Press Publications. 2002.

Guest, Francis F., O.F.M. *Fermin Francisco De Lasuen (1736-1803):*

A Biography. Washington, D.C.: Academy of American Franciscan History. 1973.

Hackel, Steven W. *Children of Coyote: Missionaries of Saint Francis: Indian-Spanish Relations in Colonial California 1769-1850.* Chapel Hill: University of North Carolina Press. 2005.

Hawthorne, Hildegarde. *California's Missions: Their Romance and Beauty.* New York: D. Appleton Century Company, Inc. 1942.

James, George Wharton. *In and Out of the Old Missions of California: An Historical and Pictorial Account of the Franciscan Missions.* Boston: Little, Brown and Company. 1905.

Kenneally, Finbar. O.F.M. *Writings of Fermin Francisco de Lausen. Vols. I and II.* Washington D.C.: Academy of American Franciscan History. 1965.

Kimbro, Edna E, Julia G. Costello, and Tevvy Ball. *The California Missions History, Art and Preservation.* Los Angeles: The Getty Conservation Institution. 2009.

Lightfoot, Kent G. *Indians, Missionaries, and Merchants; The Legacy of Colonial Encounters on the California Frontier.* Berkeley: University of California Press. 2005.

Maynard, Theodore. *The Long Road of Father Serra.* New York: Appleton Century Crofts. 1954.

McLaughlin, David J. and Ruben G. Mendoza. *The California Missions Source Book: Key Information, Dramatic Images, and Fascinating Anecdotes Covering All 21 Missions.* Scottsdale: Pentacle Press. 2009.

Miller, Bruce W. *The Gabrielino.* Los Osos: Sand River Press. 1991.

Monroy, Douglas. *Thrown Among Strangers: The Making of Mexican Culture in Frontier California.* Berkeley: University of California

Press. 1990.

Neurenberg, Norman. *Decoration of the California Missions.* Santa Barbara: Bellerophon Press. 1987.

Newell, Quincy D. *Constructing Lives at Mission San Francisco: Native Californians and Hispanic Colonists, 1776-1821.* Albuquerque: University of New Mexico Press. 2011.

Older, Mrs. Fremont. *California Missions and Their Romances.* New York: Coward-McCann Inc. 1938.

Osio, Antonio Maria. *The History of Alta California: A Memoir of Mexican California.* Translated by Rose Marie Beebe and Robert M. Senkewiczz. Madison: University of Wisconsin Press. 1996.

Padelsky, Londie Garcia. *California Missions.* Ketchum: Stoecklein Publishing. 2006.

Palou, Francisco, O. F. M. *Noticias de la Antigua y Nueva California, I-IV.* San Francisco. 1875.
Relación Histórica de la Vida del Ven. P. Fr. Junipero Serra (Mexico, 1787). Translated by C. Scott Williams. Pasadena: George Wharton James. 1913.

Pelzel Thomas O. "The San Gabriel Stations of the Cross From an Art-Historical Perspective." *The Journal of California Anthropology*: Vol. 3:1, 115-119. 1976.

Phillips ,George Hardwood. "Indian Paintings from Mission San Fernando: An Historical Interpretation." *The Journal of California Anthropology*: Vol. 3:1, Article 10. 1976.
_____. *Vineyards and Vaqueros: Indian Labor and the Economic Expansion of Southern California, 1771-1877.* Norman: University of Oklahoma Press. 2010.

Reyes, Barbara O. *Private Women, Public Life: Gender and the Missions of California.* Austin: Universtity of Texas Press. 2009.

Ruiz, Ramon Eduardo. *Triumphs and Tragedy: A History of the Mexican People.* New York: W.W. Norton & Company. 1999.

Russell, Craig H. *From Serra to Sancho; Music and Pageantry in the California Missions.* Oxford: Oxford University Press. 2009.

Sandos, James A. *Converting California: Indians and the Franciscans in the Missions.* New Haven: Yale University Press. 2004.

Shea, John Gilmore. *A History of the Catholic Church in the United States.* New York: D. H. McBride and Co. 1886.

Stone, Irving. *Men to Match My Mountains.* Edison: Castle Books. 2001.

Sunset Magazine. *The California Missions: A Pictorial History.* Menlo Park: Sunset Books Inc. 1979.

Thomas, David H., ed. *Columbian Consequences, vol.3: The Spanish Borderlands in Pan American Perspectives.* Washington, D.C.: Smithsonian Institution Press. 1991.

Tibesar, Antonine, O.F. M., ed. *Writings of Junipero Serra Vols. 1-4.* Washington, D.C.: Academy of American Franciscan History. 1955.

Internet Resources

A Virtual Tour of the California Missions:
http://missiontour.org

California Mission Studies Association:
http://californiamissionstudies.com

California Missions Foundation:
http://californiamissionsfoundation.org

California Mission Resource Center:
http://www.missionscalifornia.com

California Mission Trail and Maps:
http://www.mtycounty.com

Historical photos of the Missions:
http://www.ucr.edu

Library of Congress floor plans of the missions:
http://www.loc.gov/pictures/collection

Mission Resources:
http://www.californias-missions.org

Santa Barbara Mission Archives Library:
http://sbmal.org

Wisconsin Historical Society Digital Library and Archive:
http://www.wiconsinhistory.org

THE AUTHOR

John O'Hagan is an amateur historian and member of the California Mission Studies Association. Having grown up on the central California coast, he very early developed a lifelong love affair with these beautiful buildings. He has lectured extensively on the missions and led tours of them for visitors from throughout the United States.

For a free catalog of Caxton titles write to:

CAXTON PRESS
312 Main Street
Caldwell, ID 83605-3299

or

Visit our Internet website:

www.caxtonpress.com

Caxton Press is a division of The Caxton Printers, Ltd.